SAP R/3 System: A Client/Server Technology

SAP R/3 SYSTEM:
A CLIENT/SERVER
TECHNOLOGY

RÜDIGER BUCK-EMDEN
JÜRGEN GALIMOW

SAP Aktiengesellschaft
Translated by Audrey Weinland

Addison-Wesley

Harlow, England • Reading, Massachusetts • Menlo Park, California
New York • Don Mills, Ontario • Amsterdam • Bonn • Sydney • Singapore
Tokyo • Madrid • San Juan • Milan • Mexico City • Seoul • Taipei

© Addison Wesley Longman 1996

Addison Wesley Longman Limited
Edinburgh Gate
Harlow
Essex
CM20 2JE
England

and Associated Companies throughout the world.

Translated by Audrey Weinland.
Cover designed by op den Brouw Design and Illustration, Reading.
Illustrations by Margaret Macknelly Design, Tadley.
Typeset by Meridian Colour Repro Limited, Pangbourne.
Printed and bound in the United States of America.

First printed in 1996. Reprinted in 1996 and 1997.

ISBN 0-201-40350-1

British Library Cataloguing-in-Publication Data
A catalogue record for this book is available from the British Library.

Library of Congress Cataloging-in-Publication Data is available

Introduction
by Hasso Plattner, PhD

Client/Server Architectures Revolutionalized Business Data Processing

Introduction

Until a few years ago, the personal computer was considered an unsuitable resource for serious business data processing. Today, however, the tight integration of single-user and multi-user systems is a pronounced characteristic of modern business applications. The radical rethinking that this reflects was accompanied by the development of entirely new design principles and software architectures for business application solutions. The scope of this current change becomes clear in a brief overview of the development history.

A look at the history of business data processing

The classic batch processing of the 1960s and 70s practically excluded the end user from the processing procedure. The user simply gave a processing request to the computer center and received, after a certain waiting period, a list of results. Interaction between the user and the computer was not intended. This did not change until the introduction of terminals and online processing. From then on, online applications and traditional batch processing competed for the scarce resources of the central computer. The online users' demands for quick response times of less than one to two seconds was often in direct opposition to the efforts of computer center management to use the expensive computers to optimal capacity with as many parallel applications as possible. An additional problem was posed by the general practice of passing on the costs of the computer center services to the departments in proportion to usage. This practice regularly penalized intelligent use of computing power. As a result, developers for the most part had to refuse to include comfort functions in the design of online business applications. The emphasis was on minimizing resource use and runtime costs.

Not until the wide dissemination of PCs were the conditions set for an entirely new way of thinking. High-performance, inexpensive computers allowed application developers to begin following new paths in the design of applications. Comfortable use and learnability of the system moved into the foreground. Graphical user interfaces and interaction with the mouse added a new dimension to computer use.

At first, the personal computer was largely ignored by management in computer centers as a platform for business data processing. Then, for several years it was thought that the PC could perhaps serve as a graphical front-end for business applications, but that the applications themselves would continue to have to run on the central mainframe. But this approach was not radical enough to achieve real progress in the design of commercial applications. Not until the second half of the 1980s, with the market success of linked PC solutions, which were based on LANs (Local Area Networks), did a new approach win out: the client/server principle.

The client/server principle

Client/server systems divide the applications fundamentally into two or more components. The client portion uses the functions of the server. Typically, separate hardware systems are used for clients and servers. The distribution of the application load across several computers linked in a network keeps the individual units relatively favorable. For the first time in the history of data processing, extremely inexpensive computing power is available.

Not every client/server architecture is suited for implementing company-wide applications. This is true, for example, of architectures that can only separate the graphical user interface from the still-closely-linked application and database functions. It also applies when the functions of the graphical user interface are a fixed part of the applications and only the database functions can be installed on a separate computer. In the former case, the scalability of the system as a whole is extremely limited, since the monolithic system of application and database functions remains intact. In the latter case, the communication between the front-end and the database server can very quickly become a bottleneck. In addition, every end user of the database system is registered as a separate user. With a typical number of three to four windows per user, 1000 users translate into 3000 to 4000 database processes. Even if the database system can handle this large number of users, considerable performance problems are sure to emerge.

For these reasons, the three-layer client/server approach, with its distribution of presentation, applications and database functions on separate computers, has prevailed as a viable foundation for company-wide client/server solutions. In addition to processing the business programs, application servers can perform an n:m copy of user processes onto the corresponding processes in the database. In typical business applications, it is easy to reach copy ratios of between 5:1 and 10:1. This allows the scalability of the system as a whole to reach an entirely new dimension.

The three-layer client/server approach provides the foundation for a completely new generation of business applications. This generation is distinguished by sophisticated graphical user interfaces, interfaces to external applications, use of multimedia technology, functionality unimpaired by scarce resources, high performance and expansive scalability. The limit of the ability to develop such systems is reached only when reliable system management and stable operation of the system as a whole can no longer be guaranteed.

Suppliers of standard software become system integrators

The challenge currently faced by suppliers of standard client/server business solutions is to seamlessly incorporate external software, for example PC spreadsheet applications and word processors, or special business application modules. Individual software manufacturers can no longer develop all of the required application components themselves with all of the required functionality. Rather, the trend is toward special component suppliers who offer application modules for selected areas. Next to these are system integrators who develop some components themselves, but who in increasing numbers integrate external components into a comprehensive business solution. The challenge faced by the system integrator is to hide the complexity of the system as a whole from the end user and ensure the functionality of the linked systems. For the end user, this trend signifies another step in the direction of comprehensive application solutions. In most cases, users will no longer know if at a certain point in time they are using an application from Company X or an application from Company Y. The system integrator ensures standardized system operation and seamless data exchange between function modules from different manufacturers. Object-oriented procedures with asynchronous message exchange between the applications provide the infrastructure necessary for this. In any type of problem situation, the system integrator is available to the customer as a central contact.

Distributed application systems must be redefined

With the availability of powerful client/server architectures, redesign of business data processing should also be considered in companies that are spread across several locations and that strive to achieve integrated business processes spanning these locations. Various attempts have been made in the past to meet this requirement:

- implementation and maintenance of a multitude of interfaces for batch data exchange between heterogeneous systems;

- attempt to integrate decentralized applications using the capabilities of EDI (Electronic Data Interchange);

- attempt to achieve integration of distributed applications with the help of distributed database servers.

Upon closer examination, all three of these approaches prove to be insufficient or not realizable. However, a new quality of support for location-spanning business processes can be achieved by using object-oriented procedures. Business applications from one or from many manufacturers will in the future cooperate in a framework of integrated business processes. The foundation for this is the exchange of business objects based on message-oriented communication procedures. In this respect the Internet has a central role to play in creating consumer-to-business and business-to-business relationships.

Future outlook

The division of system functions and application functions according to the client/server principle, and rapid progress in the definition of exchange formats for business objects, make possible a software architecture whose functionality goes beyond that of the centralized systems used in the past. Already today, client/server systems have caught up with central mainframes in terms of pure performance. This is a breakthrough for this new technology, and it optimizes the use of commercial applications.

Hasso Plattner, PhD
Co-founder and Vice Chairman of the Board of SAP AG.
December 1994

Preface to the 3rd Edition

This is the English version of our German book, *Die Client/Server-Technologie des SAP-Systems R/3* which is now in its third edition. Our goal is to lay the foundation for a detailed discussion of client/server technology and to describe its implementation with SAP's R/3 System. With Release 3.x of the R/3 System, SAP provides standard business software that has undergone extensive expansion in terms of technology and functionality; we have tried to cover all the new technical features implemented in this release. The book covers:

- Component software with OLE, CORBA2, etc.
- Object orientation in the R/3 System
- Integration of online information services such as the WWW (World Wide Web), CompuServe, etc.
- Electronic commerce solutions using R/3
- SAP's Data Warehouse concept
- The new GUI (graphical user interface) of the R/3 System
- Multiple languages and code pages
- Automatic load distribution during dialog and background processing
- Memory management in the R/3 runtime environment
- SAP data base administration
- Optimization of the R/3 release change
- The ABAP/4 Development Workbench
- Global time management for companies operating internationally
- SAP Business Workflow
- Application interfaces
- Distributed applications using ALE
- The R/3 implementation environment
- New practical experience reports from Yamaha, Seattle Times, etc.
- List of abbreviations
- Updated bibliography
- Additional screen captures and graphics
  All screen captures have been updated for Release 3.x.

We have received support from many people in putting together both this English version and the German ones. Our thanks go to our colleagues at SAP and to the many readers of earlier editions for their helpful discussions, comments and advice. Further thanks go to Audrey Weinland, who translated our German manuscript into English, to our publisher Addison-Wesley both in Germany and the UK, and to our families, without whose patience and understanding this book could not have become a reality.

Rüdiger Buck-Emden　　　*Jürgen Galimow*
June 1996

Trademark notice

4004™ is a trademark of Intel Corporation.

Adabas™ is a trademark of Software AG.

AIX™, AS/400™, CICS™, CICS/6000™, DB2™, IBM PC AT™, IBM 6000™, IMS™, MVS™, Nctview™, OS/2™, OS/400™, PowerPC™, SP2™, S/370™, VM™ and /370Model 168™ are all trademarks of International Business Machines Corporation.

CORBA™ is a trademark of Object Management Group.

Encina™ is a trademark of Transarc Corporation.

Excel™, LAN Manager™, Microsoft Project™, MS-DOS™, OLE™, SoftWindows™, Visual Basic for Applications™, Visual C++™, Windows™, Windows NT™, Windows 95™ and Word for Windows™ are all trademarks of Microsoft Corporation.

HP9000™, HP-UX™, Omniback II™ and OpenView™ are all trademarks of Hewlett-Packard.

IDMS™ is a trademark of Cullinet Corporation.

Informix™ is a trademark of Informix.

Lotus Notes™ is a trademark of Lotus Development Corporation.

Macintosh® is a registered trademark of Apple Computers Incorporated.

Motif™ and OSF/1™ are trademarks of Open Software Foundation.

NetWare™ and UNIX™ are trademarks of Novell Inc.

ObjectStore™ is a trademark of Object Design Inc.

OpenLook™, NFS™, Solaris™, SunNet Manager™ and SuperSPARC™ are all trademarks of Sun Microsystems Inc.

Open VMS™ is a trademark of Digital Equipment Corporation.

Oracle™ is a trademark of Oracle Corporation UK Limited.

Pentium™ and 80x86™ are trademarks of Intel Corp.

PVCS™ is a trademark of Intersolv.

SINIX™ is a trademark of Siemens AG.

Top End™ is a trademark of NCR.

UNIX™ is a trademark of Novell Inc.

X Window™ is a trademark of Massachussets Institute of Technology.

CONTENTS

4 WHAT IS THE R/3 SYSTEM? 89

5 THE TECHNICAL ARCHITECTURE OF THE R/3 SYSTEM 93

6 APPLICATION DEVELOPMENT WITH THE ABAP/4 DEVELOPMENT WORKBENCH   135

Chapter 1
Radical Changes in Business Data Processing

1.1 Information management as the deciding competitive factor

Industrial enterprises are currently confronted with fundamental changes in the overall industry framework. Short innovation cycles, worldwide competition, and high costs are compelling companies to structure business operations rationally. Enterprise-wide information management plays a decisive role in this process.

To secure their ability to compete long term, companies must pay particular attention to the following tasks:

- optimization of all business processes along the entire net-value-added chain (business re-engineering (Hammer and Champy, 1993));

- use of the most modern data processing technology for optimization of enterprise-wide information management (technology re-engineering).

These two tasks must be considered together. Only a comprehensive approach that includes both business re-engineering and technology re-engineering will lead to success in the long run. Successful companies are characterized by the fact that, networked with customers and suppliers, they use the most modern information technology to make available products or services of the highest quality, in all sorts of varieties and with minimal delay, in response to customer demands. The customer stands at the center and selects the supplier who can best meet his or her requirements in terms of functionality, quality, delivery time, and price (Davidow and Malone, 1992).

While in the past business data processing (DP) principally provided administrative support for individual function areas like accounting or materials management (function orientation), these days intensified competition is forcing the optimization of business processes along the entire net-value-added chain. Comprehensive DP support for business processes, oriented toward customer needs, helps shorten lead times, reduce inventory, and improve deliverability and flexibility. This in turn minimizes costs, improves quality, and provides decisive advantages in competition for customer orders.

To live up to this increased responsibility, data processing in companies must undergo fundamental changes. Flexible organizational structures and technologies that allow for quick adjustment of hardware and software solutions to meet changing demands are necessary. Central DP departments must become partners with and consultants to the other departments, which control a growing share of DP investments in the enterprise and use decentralized information processing. The Gartner Group (Flynn, 1993), for example, assumes that the amount expended by end users and individual departments on DP investments is in many companies already as high as or higher than the entire budget of the central DP department.

1.2 Requirements for enterprise-wide information management

DP departments that are locked into a traditional, centralized way of thinking will always have difficulty ensuring adequate service in decentralized companies oriented toward business processes. In fact, cooperation between the DP department and the other departments is crucial to meet the functional, technical, and administrative requirements of information management that are presented here.

1.2.1 Functional requirements

- Online integration of all business applications and data in the company. Classic custom solutions with data exchange between applications only at certain points in time (batch solutions) are obsolete.
- Consistent representation of operational volume and value flows.
- Timely provision of all data and information relevant for operational business processes.
- Universal support of business processes, both internally and in the three-way relationship of customer/firm/vendor.

- Fast and easy adaptation of business applications to individual requirements and business processes that are changing ever more rapidly (customizing).
- Functional expandability of business applications with powerful development tools.
- Data and program integration of desktop applications such as MS Excel, MS Word, and Lotus Notes with core business applications using open interfaces. The gap between these two system worlds must be bridged, since it hampers the flexibility of business data processing and the productivity of employees.
- Easy interaction between people and machines with intuitive, consistent user interfaces.

1.2.2 Technical and administrative requirements

- Limitation of costs of DP infrastructure.
- High portability of application software. With a life span of ten or more years, business applications clearly have a longer service life than hardware components. The usefulness of application software must be guaranteed even if hardware, software, and communication technologies change.
- Easy adaptability (scalability) of the hardware and software installation when load profiles change, for example due to increasing numbers of users or implementation of additional applications.
- Open system architecture with adherence to widespread standards.
- Short, predictable response times for online applications.
- High throughput for background jobs.
- 24-hour availability of the entire system.
- Easy system administration.
- Short downtimes during release changes.

Integrated standard business application solutions that adhere to client/server principles can meet the requirements listed and thus provide the foundation for necessary changes in business information processing.

1.3 Re-orientation of in-house software development

The current changes in business data processing are accompanied by costs that are climbing disproportionately for business application software developed in-house. Cost-effective development and maintenance of extensive business application solutions by software development teams within companies is hardly possible anymore, due to the functional complexity of and rapid changes in business processes. Complicating the situation is the fact that in most cases, adaptation of these custom solutions to ever more quickly changing demands is not planned and is therefore not possible. The alternative to in-house development of business software is the use of standard application systems, which, as industry-neutral solutions, cover a wide spectrum of functions and business processes and which can be adapted through customizing techniques to companies' individual requirements, operations, and data structures. These standard application solutions are supplemented by some suppliers with software development tools for custom components not included in the standard, and with tools for modeling data, functions, and processes (see Section 3.10).

1.4 Component software as a new solution

It is becoming less and less possible for producers of integrated software solutions to quickly, efficiently, and inexpensively develop all of the functions and modules desired by customers. This goal can only be reached by reusing existing software components. For example, reusable components fulfill certain business functions, display data graphically, or handle all word processing and spreadsheet calculation. They can be developed in-house as well as acquired from external suppliers and can be combined as desired. Universal implementation of such modules requires that it must be possible to integrate them with the core application via standardized interfaces.

Non-proprietary, generally accepted interfaces for the integration of application modules have long been sorely lacking. Now, however, with Microsoft's OLE (Object Linking and Embedding, see Sections 3.3.6 and 3.9.2) and CORBA2 (Common Object Request Broker Architecture, see Section 3.9.1) from OMG (Object Management Group), there are two widely distributed solution approaches available for technical integration of heterogeneous software components.

The principle of component software is already changing the software industry. Standard business software packages increasingly use modules from other manufacturers. This is true, for example, of desktop applications such as word processing, spreadsheet calculation, and graphics processing. But the development will not end at the desktop. In the fall of 1994, leading suppliers of standard business software, among them SAP, founded a committee with the OAG (Open Application Group) that is tasked with working out non-proprietary interfaces for business applications. Based on the exchange formats expected for business objects, for example, a production planning solution from Manufacturer X will in

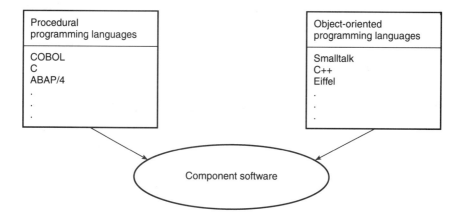

Figure 1.1 Programming languages for component software.

the future be able to run with an accounting solution from Manufacturer Y. This gives users the flexibility they need in selecting tailor-made application solutions.

One aspect should not be forgotten in the discussion of component software: component software does not necessarily have anything to do with object-oriented programming (OOP, see Section 3.9). Software components can be implemented with classic, procedural programming languages as well as with object-oriented programming languages (Figure 1.1). A program developer who incorporates a foreign software component into his or her application will in most cases be interested less in whether the implementation of the software component was object-oriented than in whether the software component fulfills the documented functionality with the corresponding response time. And this functionality must be very carefully delineated in the interface description of every component.

1.5 New fundamental technologies for business data processing

For more than 20 years, business data processing was dominated by centralized concepts and alphanumeric screens. Today, new fundamental technologies like client/server computing, graphical user interfaces, multimedia concepts, and powerful networks provide the basis for clearly improved functionality and quality.

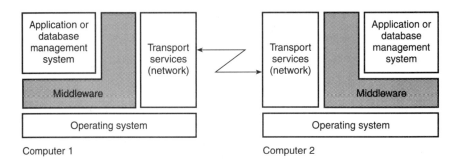

Figure 1.2 Middleware as a separate software layer.

The software that sits between the business applications and the hardware and operating system plays a special role in the development of new client/server systems. This software, which remains transparent to the user, is called "middleware" (Figure 1.2).

Essential tasks of middleware in client/server environments are:

- isolate applications from specific, heterogeneous hardware interfaces and system software interfaces;

- provide open communication interfaces for distributed applications;

- control and monitor distributed transactions;

- access different, distributed data sources;

- provide object management functions.

In an April 1994 article, the American publication *Software Magazine* sketches the new field of competition for software suppliers with the headline "Middleware Emerges As Next Battlefield" (Harding, 1994) and quotes the consulting firm META Group: "Middleware is the key enabler for second generation client/server." In *Distributed Computing Monitor*, the Patricia Seybold Group writes about the same topic: "Middleware provides the crucial underpinnings of client/server applications" (Rymer, 1994). Powerful middleware creates the basis for cooperative client/server solutions that go far beyond simple distribution concepts with remote access to special database servers.

The Gartner Group divides the middleware available today into two classes (Schulte, 1994):

- Middleware for data management:
  - Remote file systems, for example Sun's NFS
  - Database tools and interfaces

- Middleware for the support of distributed functions:
    - Basic communication functions (APPC, CPI-C, Sockets, and so on)
    - Remote Procedure Call
    - Database expansions (replications, two-phase commit, and so on)
    - Transaction monitors
    - 4GL runtime environments
    - Object management.

The quality of the middleware has a strong influence on the performance of client/server applications, as well as on their portability and openness. This makes the features of the middleware, in addition to those of the application itself, some of the most important criteria in the evaluation and selection of client/server solutions. For this reason, this book devotes Chapters 3 and 5 to middleware for client/server systems and middleware of the R/3 System, respectively.

1.6 Topics covered in this book

This book clarifies why flexible client/server systems with master–slave relationships between program modules can best meet the applications' requirements of scalability, portability, openness, and high performance.

The book is divided into two sections. The first part includes Chapters 2 and 3 and gives an overview of the technical foundations of client/server architectures. The second part of the book, Chapters 4 through 8, shows how these technical possibilities have become a reality in the SAP R/3 System.

Chapter 2 clarifies what exactly "client/server computing" is. Chapter 3 deals with the technical foundations for client/server systems. Chapter 4 provides a short overview of the R/3 System, while Chapter 5 discusses the architecture of the system's middleware. Chapter 6 describes the development tools that were included when the business applications of the R/3 System were created. In addition to an overview of functionality and basic principles, Chapter 7, "The Business Applications of the R/3 System," concentrates on general application topics such as consistent business process support, business workflow, and the distribution of applications. In Chapter 8, the essential steps for implementation of the R/3 client/server system in an enterprise are discussed and practical examples are provided.

This book is based on Release 3.x of the R/3 System.

1.7 Who should read this book?

This book addresses all technically oriented readers who are faced with the acquisition, implementation, and use of business application systems. Decision makers, personnel responsible for DP, and DP specialists will gain insight into the current status of client/server technology and its implementation in the SAP R/3 System.

Chapter 2

What Is Client/Server Computing?

2.1 Client/server computing is a software technology

The term client/server computing is used in various ways. At least two perspectives must be distinguished to understand this term: the hardware-oriented view and the software-oriented view.

The PC network operating systems of the 1980s, such as MS Net (Microsoft), Netware (Novell), and LAN Manager (Microsoft), embodied the hardware-oriented interpretation of the client/server idea. This view is heavily oriented toward the computers involved: desktop systems, usually personal computers (PCs) on users' desks, are connected by local area networks (LANs) to special background systems, which are used, for example, as file servers or print servers. In a hardware-oriented view, general usage of the term designates the desktop systems as clients and the background systems as servers.

Restricting the term client/server computing to certain hardware configurations is clearly short-sighted. This very narrow interpretation limits the ability to take full advantage of the benefits of this approach.

It is as software architecture that client/server computing reaches its full potential. The underlying concept becomes clear when one considers the block structure of modern programming languages. These draw a distinction between main programs and subroutines. Subroutines make certain services available to the main program. At run time, the main program calls subroutines and waits for them to end before it continues with the next program step. These are known as synchronous subroutine calls. Subroutines can themselves call other subroutines for certain tasks.

The calling principle for subroutines is expanded in the client/server approach to include both programs that operate on different computers and asynchronous calls. The calling program is called the master, or client, and the called program is called the slave, or server. In principle, client and server programs can be installed on a single computer, or they can be installed on different computers, linked by corresponding communication protocols. During asynchronous calls, the calling program does not wait for the called program to end, but continues immediately with processing. This form of processing is interesting, for example, for systems networked over WANs (Wide Area Networks). In such cases, one cannot assume that the recipient or the necessary communication links will be available continuously.

The software-oriented view of client/server computing is becoming increasingly important, particularly for distinguishing modern business application software from monolithic mainframe solutions. For example, COBOL (Common Business Oriented Language), the programming language widespread in the mainframe world, knows no block structuring. In contrast, client/server applications, with their extensive modularization, are characterized by a master–slave relationship between the individual software modules. Typically, certain program modules are used for graphical presentation, for individual application functions, and for data storage. In addition, modern business application systems contain independent services, for example for background processing or message exchange.

As software architecture, client/server computing forms the basis for cooperative processing of entirely different software components and can be implemented either centralized or in highly distributed, networked installations with a multitude of different servers.

2.2 Examples of client/server configurations

Client/server systems are installed in various forms. Basically, one can distinguish five types of client/server configuration (see Figure 2.1):

- Centralized system

- Distributed presentation

- Database access across computer boundaries

- Three-layer client/server systems with distributed presentation, distributed application logic, and database access across computer boundaries

- Multilayer client/server systems with cooperative processing.

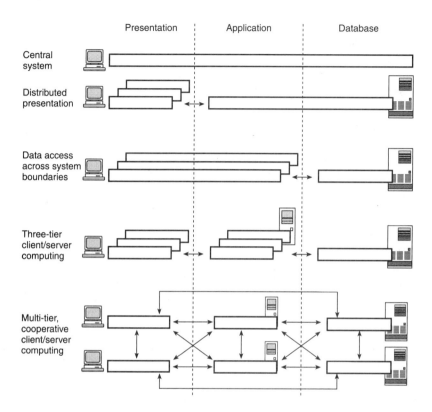

Figure 2.1 Basic client/server configurations.

In a centralized system, presentation, application logic, and database run on a single computer.

In distributed presentation, the processing associated with graphical display of the user interface is shifted to separate presentation computers close to the user. Application logic and database functions run jointly on a central server.

In database access across computer boundaries, separate servers are installed for the database and the database management system (DBMS). Presentation and application logic are situated together on separate workstations. Communication between the workstations and the database servers usually takes place with Remote SQL (Structured Query Language, see Section 3.5).

In comparison to the client/server types discussed so far, three-layer client/server systems offer clearly improved flexibility in load distribution. Special computers are implemented separately for presentation, application logic, and database services. This makes possible a homogeneous load distribution on individual servers with clearly improved response times. In addition, relatively inexpensive computers can be implemented as application servers, since they do not need graphical screens, and they need little or no hard disk storage capacity.

The greatest flexibility is provided by multilayer client/server systems with distribution of the different application and system services on the servers best suited for their tasks. Communication between the servers is based, according to requirements, on synchronous program-to-program communication, asynchronous message exchange, or Remote SQL.

2.3 Use of client/server systems

Conventional mainframes are characterized by limited and expensive resources like MIPS (million instructions per second) and storage capacities. On these systems, applications and users find themselves having to compete for tight computing resources. For this reason, applications must be developed in such a way that they put the least possible burden on the available resources. Thus the focus of development is neither the requirements of the end users nor the services and functionality of the application, but solely the distribution of limited resources. The results are application systems, currently widespread on mainframes, that have only very limited online use, no graphics support, limited functionality in processing-intensive tasks, and variable, frequently unacceptable response times.

The rapid pace of innovation in processor and memory technology makes it possible today to place the entire field of business data processing on a new foundation. Innovative PC, workstation, and multi-user systems, developed on the basis of open interfaces and standards, offer a price/performance ratio that is revolutionary in comparison to traditional mainframes, and allow for the first time the implementation of application solutions that put the end user at the center of the design.

Client/server applications are better adapted to the requirements of end users. Compared to monolithic mainframe solutions, they are distinguished by a much greater flexibility in system configuration. This has decisive advantages. One example is the design of the user interface. Mainframes are optimized to serve a large number of online users in parallel with relatively few MIPS. This is possible only if each user's online session places a minimal burden on the entire system. That is why alphanumeric user interfaces with block-mode terminals are the standard in mainframe environments to this day. Applications for the new generation of computers are not as strongly influenced by limited resources. In open systems, graphical user interfaces with icons, windowing, and mouse abilities have been around for a while. MS Windows, OSF/Motif, and Apple Macintosh are impressive examples. The advantage of these interfaces lies in their intuitive operation, their easy learnability, and the increased productivity of the user due to the ability to perform tasks in parallel in separate windows.

The user interface is, of course, only one aspect of the new possibilities offered by the client/server approach. Additional advantages, discussed in detail in the chapters that follow, are integration of desktop applications with business data processing, expanded functionality, easy scalability, portability, a high degree of availability, and improved response times. Applications developed accordingly can distribute the system load on separate servers for presentation, application logic, and data storage. Where required, the software-oriented client/server principle also enables the installation of selected servers for certain tasks. Experience shows that with such an allocation of tasks, a homogeneous load on individual computers is possible. This reduces the internal system overhead for process and buffer management, improves throughput and performance, and saves costs.

In a survey by the Gartner Group (Comport and Zbikowski, 1994), users named the following main reasons for introducing client/server solutions (the percentage of those naming the reason is shown in parentheses):

- Direct access to required data (23%)

- High flexibility of information processing (22%)

- Direct control of the operating system (12%)

- Reduced costs (11%)

- Increased productivity (9%).

Client/server computing offers a series of advantages. One must consider, however, that the introduction of these systems also places completely new requirements on the employees involved. In addition, the costs for maintaining the entire system usually climb with increased decentralization.

2.4 Client/server computing and open systems

Portability to different system platforms and integration capability across application boundaries are requirements that greatly influence the decision for a particular software solution these days. In contrast to closed, proprietary systems, which are based solely on proprietary interfaces, these are called open systems.

The POSIX (Portable Operating System Interface) specification of the 1003.0 team of the IEEE (Institute of Electrical and Electronics Engineers) contains a general definition of open systems. According to that definition, open systems are characterized by the fact that they allow for cooperation and portability of applications, data, and user interfaces due to their use of international standards for interfaces, services, and data formats.

Open systems are often mentioned in the same breath as client/server computing, although this is not entirely accurate. A client/server solution can, of course, also be implemented in a completely proprietary environment. In practice, however, client/server installations connect hardware and software from vastly different sources. And that is only possible with open systems that are based on standards that are generally recognized and widely used.

2.5 The role of conventional mainframes

With the availability of high-performance, inexpensive PCs, workstations, and multi-user systems, the question for users of conventional mainframes becomes whether and how to take advantage of the new possibilities brought about by client/server computing in the existing DP infrastructure. Mainframe investments in the millions cannot be written off overnight. What are needed are concepts for securing investments that ease the passage from monolithic, mainframe-oriented data processing to the world of client/server computing.

The first step in this direction is the use of graphical interfaces on PCs and work-stations that are integrated into classic mainframe environments as mainframe workstations. The next level of integration is cooperation between application programs on desktop systems and mainframe systems. In this type of cooperation, application components with high interaction rates, for example graphical manipulation of data, are shifted to workstations, while database and processing-intensive components run on the mainframe. Communication between the programs takes place over special interfaces for program-to-program communication (see Section 3.3.6). Examples are CPI-C (Common Programming Interface – Communication), RPC (Remote Procedure Call), and OLE (Object Linking and Embedding).

A high-performance variation of workstation/host integration based on program-to-program communication is the installation of satellite applications on decentralized workstations. Satellite solutions are function expansions of existing host applications. The systems are linked through job and data interfaces. Satellite systems have separate data storage, provided by the mainframe. Using it, they can work temporarily independent of the mainframe, although they are linked synchronously or asynchronously by program-to-program communication with the corresponding host application. Satellite systems exist, for example, in the areas of logistics (production control station, quality control station, plant maintenance control station, decentralized warehouse management system, decentralized shipping), accounting (consolidation, treasury workstation, executive information system), and human resources (decentralized time management).

Generally, there is no simple solution for moving from a centralized DP organization to the world of open systems and client/server computing. The implementation and use of productive DP solutions is therefore a strategic management task. Alternative concepts to traditional DP processes limited to monolithic centralized systems are required. The scenario that follows provides an example of this evolution.

Scenario:	• Mainframe user with many non-integrated custom solutions. Data exchange through batch interfaces.
Recommendation:	• Development of a company-wide open systems strategy.
	• Installation of integrated standard software (client/server solution).
	• Optimization of all company-specific business processes by adjustment (customizing) of the standard applications.
Example:	• A large, decentralized, German manufacturer of products with variants, with a multitude of different, poorly integrated applications on 15 computers (MVS, BS2000, UNIX), cuts its yearly DM 20 million budget for maintenance and operation of the custom applications in half through the uniform installation of the standard software R/3 from SAP.

The expectation, tied in many ways to the replacement of monolithic mainframe applications by flexible client/server software, that central computer center operations, too, would henceforth be relegated to the past, has generally proven not to be realistic in large companies. Decentralization of server systems, especially, must be very well planned and well founded to really prove useful and not just increase maintenance costs. More than one company that banked on decentrally installed servers in the first wave of client/server euphoria has already reversed that step and installed the servers in the central computer center. This allows the strength of the client/server approach, which is installing hardware flexibly and according to need, to be combined with the security and maintenance advantages of a centralized DP operation. The trend toward centralized installation of server systems is being strengthened by new, modular, high-performance computers such as IBM's SP2 (Winkler, 1994). These innovative multiprocessor systems contain a variable number of individual processors and can therefore be expanded very flexibly. Their architecture enables the operation of complete, large client/server installations within a single computer case.

2.6 Downsizing, rightsizing, upsizing, smartsizing?

The terms downsizing and rightsizing are often used in connection with the introduction of client/server systems. By downsizing, we mean replacing mainframes with medium-sized computers (midrange systems) without changing the structure of the implemented applications. A typical example of downsizing is the porting of an MVS application to a VMS or OS/400 system. Downsizing can lower the direct DP costs in the short term with the use of low-cost hardware, although it does not offer new application quality.

Downsizing projects can be carried out fully independent of the introduction of client/server systems. In client/server solutions, the term "downsizing" only applies to the outer measurements of the computers used. If, on the other hand, one considers the resource requirements and especially the functionality of newer, more powerful client/server applications, one must speak of upsizing. The reasons for this lie, for example, in demanding graphical user interfaces, in the use of relational database systems, and in the provision of newer, more processing–intensive application functions. To take this into account, one also speaks of "rightsizing" or "smartsizing" in connection with client/server projects. In every case, the goal is to use computers that are optimally suited for the applications in question.

2.7 Porting to client/server platforms

Whether the topic is downsizing, rightsizing, or client/server computing, porting and/or the portability of business application software to new hardware and system software environments are essential factors in the equation. In practice, the costs for a porting project become lower, the more the software to be ported is oriented toward open system standards.

2.7.1 Typical porting projects

Porting of application software is accomplished either on new hardware platforms or just in new system software environments on the existing hardware platform. In the commercial area, the following typical porting projects to new hardware platforms can be distinguished today:

- **Mainframe to midrange system**

  Porting of monolithic mainframe applications to midrange systems, for example under OS/400, MPE, VMS, or UNIX, without changing the application structure (for example, no client/server concept, no graphical user interface, and so on). This type of porting project can, in the short term, help lower direct costs in the computer center. The costs per workstation today are still lower for midrange systems than for mainframes. In this type of downsizing, however, the usefulness to the end users in the departments is small, because the functionality of the application is usually not changed. The decision to go ahead with such a project must therefore be weighed carefully, also keeping in mind that the cost advantage per workstation in midrange systems will likely decrease in the future as compared to mainframes.

- **Mainframe to client/server system**

  Porting of monolithic mainframe applications to distributed environments, including, depending on need, mainframes, midrange systems, workstations, and PCs. Adherence to client/server principles with defined communication relationships between masters (clients) and slaves (servers) creates the conditions for distribution of the application load on different system platforms and is the basis for far-reaching interoperability at system and application level.

  Such porting is not possible without delving deep into the application structure and is often like a new implementation. However, it is the only way to achieve a higher quality of application software, with distribution of data and applications, with separate available processing capacities, and with graphical user interfaces. In this case, fewer cost advantages are realized in the computer center than in the departments, where they are brought about by shorter training periods, better usage of application functions, and higher employee productivity.

- **Client/server solution to new system platforms**

  Porting of applications that were developed for open, distributed environments to additional system platforms. In this type of porting, the user gains a high degree of flexibility in the selection of system platforms, together with far-reaching interoperability, even in heterogeneous system environments.

  Since client/server applications usually sit on standard interfaces, the effort involved in porting application programs to additional system platforms is often low. What plays a larger role are tasks like performance optimization and the integration of special tools, for example, for system, network, and database management.

  Usually, porting to a new hardware platform is linked to the implementation of new system software. This can be, for example, software for the operating system, the database system, the network software, the development environment used, or the management tools implemented. Those interfaces between the application software and the underlying system software that are not isolated by corresponding middleware must be adapted in this case.

2.7.2 Procedure for porting projects

The procedure for porting commercial application software to new system platforms is influenced heavily by the goals to be reached by porting. The following steps are necessary in any case:

(1) Clarification of the objectives being pursued by porting. Is the focus cost reduction in the computer center, or usage increase in the departments? Is a quick and dirty port to a different platform base desired, or should highly portable, powerful software emerge? Should client/server principles and a graphical user interface be implemented as part of porting?

(2) Consideration of whether porting should be accompanied by function expansions of the existing application software.

(3) Consideration of whether reworking of the application software and the application data structures can be linked to the port, with adherence to clear interfaces between platform-specific and platform-independent components. Such a structure can considerably simplify future porting projects, since then only an adjustment of the platform-specific components is necessary.

(4) Clarification of the target platforms for porting. Which hardware, operating systems, database management systems, network software should be supported?

(5) Consideration of whether the applications to be ported use certain tools, for example for database management, network management, or backup, and whether these or comparable tools are available on the target systems.

(6) Definition of the standards and interfaces (APIs, Application Programming Interfaces) to be considered during porting in relation to the operating system, database, presentation, communication, programming language, and so on.

(7) Definition of the interfaces that the ported application software should provide for foreign applications.

(8) Description of an application software architecture as a summary of all internal and external interfaces to be considered in porting. Adherence to the interfaces recorded in this architecture description can simplify future modifications, enhancements, and additional porting projects considerably.

(9) Estimation of the porting effort to be expected.

(10) Estimation of the resource requirements (CPU, disk, main memory, network) and the performance (transaction performance) of the ported application software on the new system platform.

(11) Transfer (migration) of the application programs and data structures using the interfaces defined in the application software architecture. Modifications to and reprogramming of system-dependent program modules. Character conversion for programs and data (for example, from EBCDIC to ASCII coding).

(12) If necessary, adjustment of the ported applications to the new tool environment.

(13) Testing and debugging.

(14) Performance optimization, through use of platform-specific properties if necessary. The exploitation of platform-specific properties can, however, prove problematic in future porting projects. Good encapsulation that hides platform-dependent interfaces in only a few modules is absolutely necessary here.

(15) Determination of the resource requirements for live operation. In practice, for example, the transfer of data inventories stored in traditional file systems into relational database management systems leads to markedly increased disk storage needs. Graphical user interfaces and the distribution of data and applications likewise lead to increases in resource needs.

(16) Completion of documentation.

(17) Training of employees in the departments and in system maintenance.

The steps listed here for a porting project do not usually run in this exact order. In fact, depending on the results and decisions in the individual phases, there can be cyclical feedback. As in any software project, the earlier potentially wrong decisions can be revised, the lower the total costs of porting will be.

Porting of commercial application software requires careful preparation. The objectives to be pursued by porting must be clearly defined. It is absolutely necessary to analyze the total usefulness that can be achieved. In this process, the expenditures for hardware and software, training, and system maintenance must be considered, as well as the potential cost savings in the departments. Usefulness analysis of porting mainframe applications shows that a new concept that incorporates client/server principles frequently does better than the retention of monolithic system structures on lower-priced platforms.

Chapter 3

Technical Foundations for Client/Server Systems

Client/server systems are not based on a single technological innovation. Rather, very different development currents in various areas of data processing are united. In particular, progress in the areas of hardware technology, networks, system software, user interfaces, multimedia applications, object orientation, and software development tools has contributed to the present status of client/server systems:

- **Hardware technology**: The rapid pace of innovation in microprocessors and memory chips has created the conditions that today allow us to implement client/server solutions that no longer lag behind large mainframe installations in their capabilities (Sections 3.1 and 3.2).

- **Networks**: High-performance networks for local and long-distance areas offer the infrastructure required for data exchange in distributed client/server environments (Section 3.3). The Internet and the World Wide Web (WWW) are forcefully driving the rate of innovation.

- **System software**: Operating systems and database management systems with open, standardized interfaces create the software conditions for heterogeneous linked systems (Sections 3.4 to 3.6).

- **User interfaces**: Graphical user interfaces, first developed in PCs and workstations, are now available as elements of client/server concepts for business solutions, too, where they make an essential contribution to the merging of individual PC-oriented data processing with centralized business applications (Section 3.7).

- **Multimedia applications**: Multimedia applications are characterized by integrated processing, display, and transmission of documents that contain not only text, but also photographic, graphical, audio, speech, or video information. Client/server systems with inexpensive, decentralized processing capacities and high-performance communication channels provide the technical foundation for innovative multimedia solutions (Section 3.8).

- **Object-oriented concepts**: In general, the object-oriented approach starts with isolated objects organized into classes, which control unique interfaces and communicate using messages. Concepts that build on this can easily be embedded in client/server environments, since there, too, masters and slaves exchange information across predefined interfaces. A distinction is made between object-oriented user interfaces, object-oriented system architectures, object-oriented programming languages, and object-oriented database management systems (Section 3.9).

- **Software development tools**: Powerful software development tools for client/server applications shield the applications programmer from the technical details of distributed, networked systems and provide the foundation for high quality and productivity in the development process (Section 3.10).

- **Standardization**: The continuing trend toward open systems and standards has made it possible to combine heterogeneous hardware and software components from completely different manufacturers into integrated client/server systems (Section 3.11).

The client/server approach should by no means be considered just another short-term fad in a quickly changing DP world. Surveys have repeatedly shown that client/server solutions are only just gaining extensive market penetration. The Gartner Group, for example, assumes that by 1998 over 80% of all new, commercial multi-user applications will be client/server solutions (Brown et al., 1994). Even now, under the terms "World Wide Web" (see Section 3.3.9) and "social computing," PDAs (Personal Digital Assistants), intelligent Smart Phones, and Interactive TV/Video are laying the foundation for the next technology push in client/server systems (Bluestein and Hill, 1993).

3.1 Microprocessors and memory chips

Since 1971, when Intel created the first microprocessor – the Intel 4004, based on 4-bit technology – for the Japanese desk calculator manufacturer Busicom, IC (Integrated Circuit) technology has developed feverishly. The dramatic increases in the power of microprocessors (CPU, Central Processing Unit) and main memory (RAM, Random Access Memory) have in just 20 years created a situation in which most enterprises are busily implementing or using client/server systems (Figures 3.1 and 3.2).

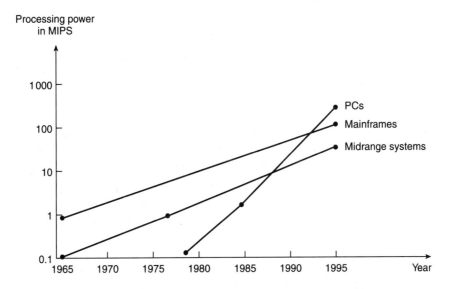

Figure 3.1 Increases in processing power.

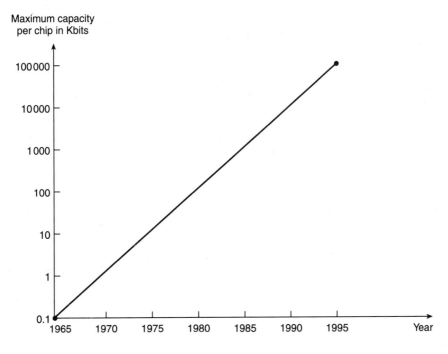

Figure 3.2 Increases in chip capacity.

Computer manufacturers currently use main memory modules that implement inexpensive, but in comparison to the clock rates of modern microprocessors also relatively slow, DRAM (Dynamic Random Access Memory) technology. At the moment, 16 Mbit can be integrated on a single chip, and 64 Mbit chips already exist in laboratories. The first products are expected in 1996. To be able to supply the processor with instructions and data quickly enough, despite the high access times on the main memory, special buffer memories are used as command and data caches. These are implemented either internally, on the processor chip, or externally, through fast – but in comparison to DRAM relatively expensive – SRAM components (Static Random Access Memory).

A defining cause of the current switch from centralized data processing to new, flexible concepts is the fact that in the past the processor power of traditional mainframe systems could be improved by only about 25% annually, due to the bipolar ECL (Emitter Coupled Logic) technology used, whereas for PCs, workstations, and server systems, which use primarily NMOS or CMOS (N-Type or Complementary Metal Oxide Semiconductor) microprocessors, annual increases in power by a factor of 1.5 to 2 are the norm. The prognosis formulated in 1964 by Intel founder Gordon Moore concerning chip packing density, which describes the maximum amount of single-block circuits (transistors) possible on an IC component, is still valid today:

Chip packing density $= 2^{\text{(current year} - 1964)}$

According to this arithmetic formula, the integration density of integrated circuits that is technically achievable doubles annually. The higher the integration, the more functions can be implemented on a component and the shorter the communication paths are between individual logic elements. This allows switching processes to be executed more quickly and system clocking to be raised. As a result, the processing power of individual IC components is improved considerably.

In 1984, Bill Joy, one of the founders of the workstation pioneer Sun Microsystems, in accordance with Gordon Moore's conjecture, coined the following statement, still more or less accurate today, regarding the capability of microprocessors, measured in MIPS (Million Instructions Per Second, see Section 3.1.1):

$\text{MIPS} = 2^{\text{(current year} - 1984)}$

According to Moore's and Joy's predictions, the technically possible integration density and power of microprocessors doubles each year. The IBM PC provides an impressive example of the validity of these assumptions: in 1984, a PC consisted of 170 ICs for logic processing and 72 ICs for 2 Mbytes of main memory. The performance of these systems was less than 1 MIPS, the clocking was 4 to 8 MHz. Today, a PC contains just one IC for the logic and one IC for 2 Mbytes of main memory. In that same period of time, the processing power has increased more than a hundredfold. The current version of Intel's Pentium processor works

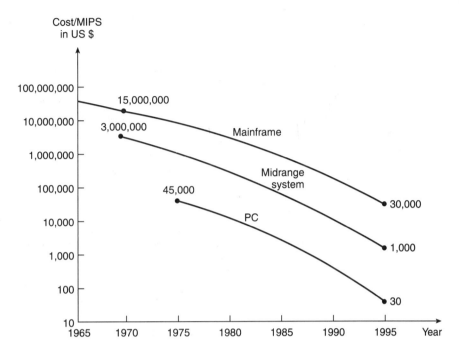

Figure 3.3 Computer prices in US dollars/MIPS.

at 100 MHz and has a capability of more than 100 MIPS. The 100 MHz version of the PowerPC 604 from IBM and Motorola can already achieve approximately 200 MIPS. The Intel processor P6 has a capability of 250 to 300 MIPS, with full binary compatibility with earlier generations of the Intel processor family.

The annual performance jumps in IC technology are accompanied by a likewise dramatic reduction in computer prices/MIPS (Figure 3.3) and main memory prices. Modern RISC processors can be obtained for a few hundred US dollars. For one Mbyte of main memory, one need hardly invest more than 10 US dollars. The resulting price/performance ratio allows modern computers to be much more generously equipped with resources than were systems in the past – to the benefit of the end user, for whom previously impossible functions such as universal graphical user interfaces are now available.

3.1.1 Measuring processor power

The selection of a computer system is often based on processor power. As long as the computers being compared have the same command set, consideration of the pure MIPS (Million Instructions Per Second) number, which indicates how many commands the computer can execute per second, can be sufficient. If the computer architectures and command sets are different, however, this approach is not as helpful. Instead, the run time of test programs known as benchmark programs is measured. With such measurements, it is important to remember that in addition to CPU speed, the main memory speed, disk speed and bus speed, the buffer strategy, and the quality of the code created by the compiler also influence the results. Also, for all benchmark programs, the critical question must be asked: To what extent does the artificial load correspond to the future application load? This makes meaningful statements possible.

The following measurements are frequently used to judge processor power:

- **VAX MIPS**: The Digital VAX 11/780, popular especially in the university environment in the 1980s, is defined as a reference machine with a performance of 1 MIPS. To determine the performance of another computer, the run time of an integer benchmark program is measured both on that computer and on a VAX 11/780. The quotient of the two values is the performance in VAX MIPS.

- **Dhrystone MIPS**: Dhrystone MIPS is a special case of VAX MIPS. A special integer program, the Dhrystone benchmark, is used as a benchmark program. Computer manufacturers usually calculate the MIPS numbers they publish according to this procedure.

- **SPECmarks**: Dhrystone benchmark programs are relatively small, in most cases fit completely into the main memory buffer (cache), and can easily be accounted for in compiler optimizations. To gain more realistic performance numbers, the manufacturers' association SPEC (System Performance Evaluation Cooperative) has published a collection of benchmark programs. The current 1992 version contains 6 integer and 14 floating-point programs. The mean values of the run times of the integer and floating-point programs are published by computer manufacturers under the designations "SPECint92" and "SPECfp92" (Table 3.1).

Table 3.1 SPECint92 performance of selected processors.

Processor	Manufacturer	Clocking (MHz)	Performance (SPECint92)
Pentium	Intel	100	100
SuperSPARC	Sun	60	89
PowerPC 601	IBM, Motorola	80	88
R8000	Mips	75	108
PA 7150	HP	125	136
Alpha 21064	DEC	275	175

- **TPC Benchmarks**: For transaction-oriented data processing, the manufacturers' association TPC (Transaction Processing Council) has defined various TPC benchmarks (TPC-A, TPC-B, TPC-C). TPC-A re-creates a simple online transaction application with a large number of active users and a realistically large database. TPC-B differs from TPC-A in that terminal I/O performance and the ability of the system to support a large number of active users are not considered. In contrast to TPC-A and TPC-B, TPC-C also uses processing-intensive transactions with complex database operations. TPC values are being increasingly used by manufacturers to evaluate the performance of server systems.

3.1.2 CISC and RISC processors

The continuing microprocessor performance improvements have not been caused solely by the dramatic increases in integration density. Of equal importance has been the exploitation of new architecture principles, for example the RISC (Reduced Instruction Set Computing) concept presented in this section, caching (see Section 3.1), and pipelining (see Section 3.1.3).

The processors in traditional computer architectures like the VAX 11/780 (Digital), the S/370 (IBM), and the PC AT (IBM) are based on the CISC (Complex Instruction Set Computing) principle. CISC processors can process a very large number of instructions with many different addressing possibilities. These machine instructions are interpreted by microprograms, which form a separate software layer beneath the machine language level. Several CPU clock cycles are required for the execution of most instructions.

CISC processors were the processor manufacturers' answer to main memory technology in the early years of data processing. This technology was characterized by high prices, high access times, and small storage capacities. The natural consequence was the development of compact application programs with complex command sets that took up little space in the main memory and could be interpreted by microprograms.

With today's decisively improved price/performance ratio of DRAM (Dynamic Random Access Memory) main memory technology, the original limitations that led to the CISC design no longer apply. Research in IBM labs at the beginning of the 1980s showed that the use of CISC instructions by application programs occurs in an 80/20 distribution. From 80% of the commands of an application software program, compilers create object programs that use only 20% of the commands offered by CISC processors. As a result of this research, since the 1980s various manufacturers have been developing processors with a clearly reduced instruction set that implement only the most important commands in the hardware, loyal to the KISS maxim: Keep It Simple, Stupid. More complex instructions are constructed from these simple commands by optimizing compilers.

The idea of RISC processors, originally devised in the 1960s by the forefather of the supercomputer, Seymour Cray, was thus brought to life for "normal" data processing as well. The essential characteristics of RISC processors are:

- Minimization of the command set and addressing possibilities

- Large set of registers

- Execution of most instructions in one clock cycle

- Load/store architecture, in which only LOAD and STORE commands can access the main memory or the main memory cache directly

- Command execution without microprograms.

For a while, it seemed as though RISC processors might displace the traditional CISC design, but today the two approaches are coming closer together. CISC technology is also continuing to develop; both RISC and CISC systems are increasingly following the same implementation guidelines. It is only logical that modern processor designs should unite the best of both worlds. Intel and HP, for example, recently announced cooperation in the development of a new 64-bit processor architecture, which is supposed to combine the advantages of Intel processors and PA-RISC processors. In contrast to 16-bit processors, which have an address space of only 4 Gbytes, 64-bit processors have an address space of 16 Gbytes.

3.1.3 Pipelining and superscalar design

By taking advantage of parallelisms at the instruction level, processing power can be increased considerably. In the processor design shown in Figure 3.4, commands are processed in several stages and partially overlapped. Although this procedure, known as pipelining, cannot shorten the execution time of an individual instruction, it can still markedly improve the total throughput.

At the beginning of the 1980s, pipelining technology was still rarely implemented, and then only in special mainframes and supercomputers. Today, the use of pipelining procedures for improving the performance of computer processors is common. Pipelining can clearly improve the throughput of the processor at constant clock rates. A requirement for the parallel execution of commands, however, is their independence. While non-pipelined systems typically finish one instruction every 5 to 10 clock cycles, modern pipelined RISC systems can complete one instruction per clock cycle. In practice, however, dependencies such as those in control transfer instructions often result in somewhat lower values.

Simple pipelining designs allow parallel execution of two or three commands. If the pipeline is implemented at a deeper level with a higher degree of parallelism between the individual instructions, this is called superpipelining.

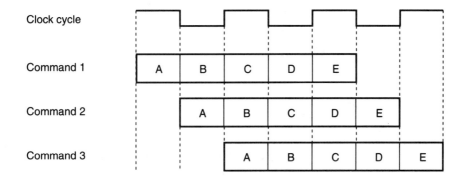

A: Read command cache
B: Read register contents
C: Execute commands
D: Access data cache
E: Write register contents

Figure 3.4 Example of a pipelining design.

Almost all RISC processors process integer and floating-point operations in parallel. Superscalar design, in which function units are duplicated, offers another possibility for performance improvement (Figure 3.5). This allows the processing of several homogeneous commands to begin in a single clock cycle. For instance,

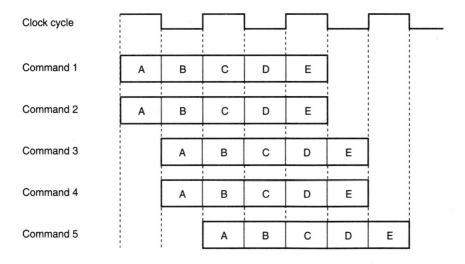

Figure 3.5 Example of a superscalar design.

Intel's superscalar Pentium processor controls two ALUs (Arithmetic Logical Units) for processing integer commands. Other examples of superscalar design are the SuperSPARC processor from Texas Instruments and the processors of IBM's PowerPC series.

3.1.4 Multiprocessor systems

Multiprocessor systems (MP systems) have more than one central processing unit (CPU). MP systems have existed since the beginning of the 1970s, when IBM installed two processors in the system /370 Model 168. Today, with the availability of powerful, inexpensive microprocessors, multiprocessor systems are offered by all of the major system manufacturers.

As the name implies, multiprocessor systems have several central processors, with either one common or several independent main memories. Single-processor systems, in contrast, have only one CPU and one main memory. The implementation of multiprocessors can considerably shorten the processing time of application programs. The software requirements for this are a multiprocessor-capable operating system and application programs that are developed in such a way that individual parts can operate in parallel on different processors. Multiprocessors offer few advantages for monolithic application programs, for example those developed as a single UNIX process, since this process must run sequentially on one CPU, while the remaining processors remain inactive.

The multiprocessor systems available today can, from a hardware point of view, be divided into

- loosely coupled MP systems, and

- tightly coupled MP systems.

Loosely coupled MP systems (Figure 3.6) consist of several computers, each with its own CPU and main memory, as well as common resources like a central storage disk peripheral (shared disk) or just a high-speed communication link (shared nothing). A complete operating system runs on each computer. The individual processors use a bus or switch system to communicate between themselves. In bus systems, a jointly used channel is available for all communication connections between processors. In contrast, switch systems can switch individual one-to-one channels between processors. An example of a bus-connected MP system is Digital's VAX cluster, in which several VAX systems are connected by one input/output bus (I/O bus). An example of an MP system with switch communication is the IBM SP2 system.

Loosely coupled MP systems create a high level of availability and flexibility, but are also relatively expensive, since basically complete computers are installed. Communication over external lines between the computers can be slower than with an internal system bus. In addition, the software that synchronizes data accesses

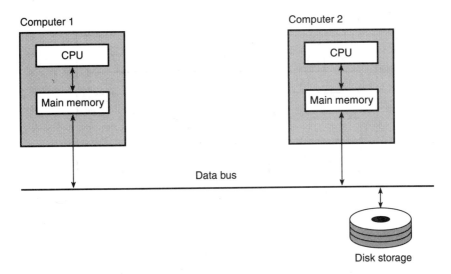

Figure 3.6 Loosely coupled multiprocessor system.

is relatively costly. The alternative to loosely coupled MP systems that is in widespread use today is tightly coupled multiprocessor systems (Figure 3.7), which are based on a common main memory (shared memory) and a common operating system. The main memory is accessed with a high-speed memory bus.

Examples of tightly coupled MP systems are RM600 (Siemens Nixdorf), HP9000 (Hewlett-Packard), the SPARC systems from Sun, and the MP servers from AST, Sequent, and Compaq.

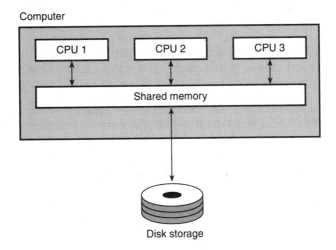

Figure 3.7 Tightly coupled multiprocessor system.

Computer

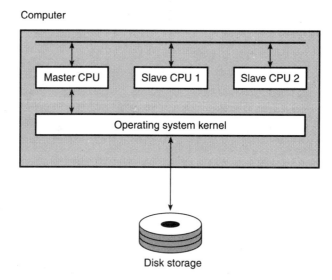

Disk storage

Figure 3.8 Asymmetrical multiprocessing.

In addition to the hardware-oriented classification of MP systems into tightly and loosely coupled architectures, there is another, software-oriented classification. This distinguishes

- asymmetrical MP systems, and

- symmetrical MP systems.

In asymmetrical multiprocessor systems (Figure 3.8), a single processor is designated as the lead CPU, on which the core of the operating system runs. This lead CPU distributes processing jobs to the remaining, dependent CPUs and is the only one with access to operating system resources, such as storage disk peripherals. This makes asymmetrical MP systems suitable for certain types of processing only, such as processing-intensive simulation tasks. For applications with high data traffic, however, asymmetrical MP systems are less suitable, since the central lead CPU can quickly become a bottleneck.

In contrast, in symmetrical multiprocessor systems (Figure 3.9), also called SMP systems, all CPUs have equal rights and have access to a common main memory (shared memory). Each processor can execute the functions of the operating system core and can thus also access the disk subsystem independently of a central lead CPU. For this reason, SMP systems are of particular interest in commercial data processing. Examples of operating systems that support symmetrical multiprocessing are UNIX System V, Release 4 and Windows NT.

Multiprocessor systems are an interesting platform alternative for large R/3 installations. Because of R/3's flexible architecture (see Section 5.5.4), individual R/3 processes can easily be installed on different processors.

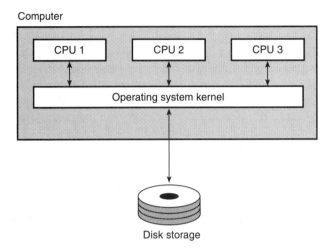

Figure 3.9 Symmetrical multiprocessing.

3.2 New disk storage technologies

While microprocessor clock rates have improved in the past 10 years by a factor of more than 10, and CPU performance has improved by a factor of more than 100, the average seek time for magnetic storage disks has improved by a factor of only 2, to about 5 to 10 milliseconds. In contrast, important innovations in this area have been increased density and the resulting miniaturization, a clearly improved price/performance ratio, and the use of parallelisms to improve access times and data security (RAID, Redundant Array of Independent Disks, see Section 3.2.1). In addition, optical disk storage technology has gained importance for certain tasks.

These days, magnetic disk storage in the 5.25-inch format can store 10 Gbytes or more. Ten years ago, the IBM PC XT shone with a 10 Mbyte disk in the 5.25-inch format. In addition to the 5.25-inch format, widespread drive formats today include 3.5-inch and 2.5-inch. In the PC area, prices per gigabyte of disk capacity are already under 1,000 US dollars.

Examples of magnetic disks are:

- **Seagate "Elite 9"**
  5.25-inch, 9 Gbytes, 11 ms average seek time, approximately 3,500 US dollars

- **Seagate "Barracuda"**
  3.5-inch, 2 Gbytes, 5.6 ms average seek time, approximately 2,000 US dollars.

3.2.1 RAID technology

RAID (Redundant Array of Independent Disks) solutions combine many low-priced magnetic disks into a memory subsystem that works like a single virtual disk with regard to the server operating system. The individual disks can be operated in parallel. The RAID concept was engineered in the second half of the 1980s by a research team at U.C. Berkeley with the goal of improving the seek times, storage capacity, and reliability of disks.

Today, all major server manufacturers offer RAID solutions. These basically consist of three components (Figure 3.10):

(1)   Disk array of magnetic storage disks

(2)   Hardware controller for control of the disk array

(3)   Management software that controls read and write access to the disk array.

Depending on where the management software resides, a distinction is drawn between "hardware RAID" and "software RAID." In hardware RAID, the management software is implemented in the controller. This procedure is somewhat more expensive than software RAID, but it makes possible seek times that are independent of the server's CPU load. In software RAID, the programs of the management software are run by the server system. Software RAID has the disadvantage of server-dependent seek times and cannot always make use of all of the hardware properties for performance optimization.

RAID solutions are implemented differently, according to the goals set. There are six different standard RAID levels, RAID 0 to RAID 5. Of particular practical importance are RAID 0, RAID 1, RAID 3, and RAID 5.

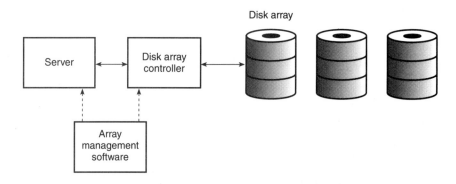

Figure 3.10 The essential parts of a RAID solution.

- **RAID 0**: Data Striping Array (DSA) without parity. In RAID 0, data to be stored is broken down into blocks according to the sector size of the disks and distributed in parallel across the disks. RAID 0 offers a high read/write performance without improvement in data storage reliability.

- **RAID 1**: Mirrored Disk Array (MDA). RAID 1 stores each data block twice, once on the data disk and once on the mirror disk. On the one hand, this leads to high data security; on the other hand, however, it also leads to 50% storage overhead.

- **RAID 3**: Parallel Disk Array (PDA). In RAID 3, data is written byte for byte in parallel to the same physical sector on the disks involved. On one particular disk, a checksum is also stored for error correction. If a disk fails, its information contents can be recovered from the checksum. This mode of operation is shown in Figure 3.11.

  Since data blocks in RAID 3 are basically distributed across several disks, this is also called Parallel Disk Array. RAID 3 has only minor storage overhead and offers high security and high data transfer rates, especially when accessing large data blocks.

- **RAID 5**: Independent Disk Array (IDA). Like RAID 0, RAID 5 stores data, according to the sector size, block by block and in parallel on the disks of the disk array. In addition, a checksum is established for error correction. However, test information is not stored on a particular disk like in RAID 3, but is instead distributed across all of the disks in the disk array.

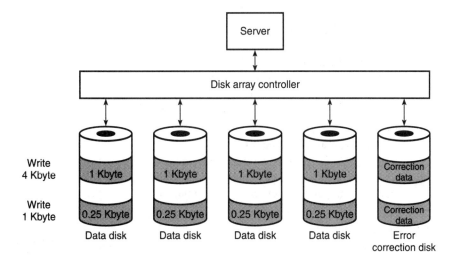

Figure 3.11 Parallel Disk Array (RAID 3).

RAID 5 is of particular interest for access to small data blocks, since several such accesses can be processed in parallel. For this reason, RAID 5 is also called Independent Disk Array. RAID 5 offers the benefits of minor storage overhead and high security. Additionally, RAID 5 allows for high data transfer rates, especially in applications with many transfers of small data blocks (for example, online transaction applications).

Hardware manufacturers also offer, in part, systems with additional RAID levels, for example RAID 5 Plus, RAID 6, and RAID 7. These are proprietary approaches for additional improvement of reliability and the data transmission rate. There is, however, no generally recognized definition for these procedures.

The details of RAID technology are hidden from the applications by the operating system. Applications like the R/3 System can therefore profit from the advantages of this technology without being directly affected themselves.

3.2.2 Optical storage disks

Optical storage disks are characterized by their use of laser technology for storing and reading data. Since the mid-1980s, they have been gaining importance for commercial applications, because they offer an inexpensive and space-saving method for storing large amounts of information. If parallel online access to many disks is required, disk changers (jukeboxes) can be installed, which these days can already manage more than 100 disks.

Optical storage disks, depending on type, present an interesting alternative to paper archives, magnetic disks, magnetic tapes, and microfilm. A general distinction is made between three types of optical storage disk:

- **CD-ROM**: CD-ROM is a read-only storage disk with a diameter of 5.25 inches. It is based on the same technology as audio CD. CD-ROM was standardized in the ISO 9660/High Sierra standard. Philips, Sony, and Microsoft developed an expanded specification based on this, CD-ROM-XA, which encompasses all current CD formats (CD audio, CD-I, CD-ROM, photo CD).

  To produce a CD-ROM, data is stored digitally on the medium in a spiral form, in one track that is several kilometers long. Approximately 650 Mbytes can be stored on one CD-ROM, which corresponds to approximately 300 000 pages of text or 2000 scanned images. CD-ROMs can be manufactured very inexpensively in mass production and are thus particularly suitable for the distribution of large volumes of data, for example reference books, catalogs, or software and its documentation.

- **WORM**: Optical WORM (Write Once Read Multiple) disks can be written to exactly once by the user and are therefore particularly suitable for archiving original documents. WORM drives are available in various formats. There is as yet no general standard for them. However, a standard is currently being prepared for CD WORM disks and will be published as ISO standard 13490.

- **MO**: Magneto-optical (MO) storage disks combine the advantages of laser technology with those of magnetic storage technology. Like a magnetic disk, they can be written to often. For storage of large volumes of data, therefore, they compete directly with magnetic disks. There is as yet no standard for MO.

In a cost comparison of various storage media, the paper solution turns out to be the most expensive. Table 3.2 gives an overview.

Table 3.2 Storage capacity and costs per Mbyte for different storage media.

Medium	Storage capacity in Mbytes	Costs per Mbyte in $
A4 paper	0.002	10.00
Hard disk	500	1.33
WORM 5.25"	800	0.53
MO	650	0.4
CD-WORM	650	0.05
CD-ROM	650	0.003

3.3 Networks

Client/server computing is usually associated with distribution of data and applications on different computers, even when it is understood as a software concept (see Section 2.1). Message exchange between the distributed computers takes place over a communication network that is made up of communication links (twisted cable, coax cable, fiber optic cable, radio ranges, and so on) and, if necessary, special switching systems. The communication network, together with the linked computers, forms the computer network (see Figure 3.12).

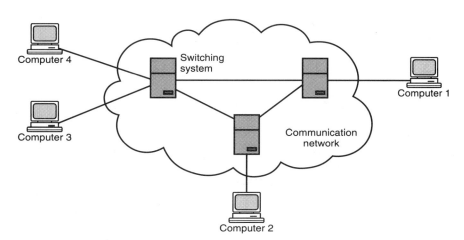

Figure 3.12 Structure of a computer network.

Computer networks can be implemented as point-to-point networks or as broadcast networks, in which many participants monitor a common transmission medium. Different network architectures, called network topologies, are possible. Typical broadcast networks include, for example, bus networks like the familiar Ethernet. Point-to-point networks can be found in ring, star, or tree topology or as arbitrarily meshed structures. Examples of point-to-point networks are the Token Ring and the public German Datex-P network.

Computer networks are traditionally divided into LANs (Local Area Networks) and WANs (Wide Area Networks).

- LANs are used for internal data exchange within a limited geographical area (for example, company property) and are privately owned by the operator. LANs can be implemented as broadcast networks (for example, Ethernet) or as point-to-point networks (for example, Token Ring). Typical LAN transfer rates these days lie between 4 and 100 Mbit/s.

- WANs are implemented as point-to-point networks and handle computer networking over long distances. In Germany, WAN services are offered by the postal service and, as part of the deregulation of postal services, increasingly by private enterprises. Typically used WAN transfer rates are between 9.6 and 64 Kbit/s. WAN links in the Mbit/s range are also offered, but are still relatively expensive. Examples of wide area networks are Datex-P/X.25 and ISDN (Integrated Service Digital Network), as well as Frame Relay Networks in the US.

The distinction between LANs and WANs, which is still valid today, will lose meaning in the future, because the basis technology planned for broadband ISDN, ATM (Asynchronous Transfer Method), provides a procedure that can be implemented in local area networks as well as in wide area networks. For this reason, experts like the Gartner Group (Sundt, 1992), when referring to ATM, speak in terms of an AAN (All Area Network).

3.3.1 The ISO reference model

To standardize the discussion of computer networks, their architecture and implementation, the ISO (International Standards Organization) published at the beginning of the 1980s the ISO reference model for open computer networks, under the name "Reference Model for Open Systems Interconnection – OSI" (Effelsberg and Fleischmann, 1986; Sheldon, 1994). OSI defines a general architecture for computer networks consisting of seven layers and determines which protocols and services can be implemented in the individual layers (Figure 3.13). Today, the ISO reference model represents a generally recognized architecture for networks.

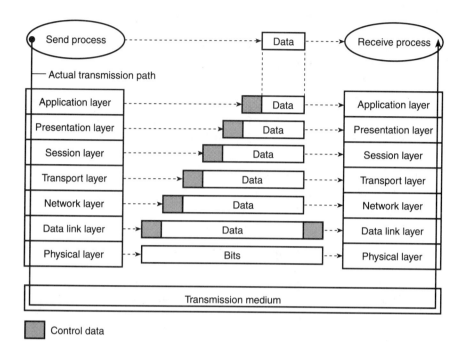

Control data

Figure 3.13 Communication in an OSI network.

The ISO reference model defines the following layers for network protocols:

(1) **Physical Layer**: The physical layer deals with the physical transmission of bit streams between computers and the computer's interface to the transmission medium.

Examples of Layer 1 device interfaces are

 – CCITT V.24

 – CCITT X.21

 – Access units for LANs (for example, ISO 8802-3 Ethernet).

(2) **Data Link Layer**: The data link layer is responsible for block-oriented data transfer between two directly adjacent computers. This layer must recognize and, if necessary, correct errors, as well as implement procedures for flow control (speed adjustment between sender and receiver).

Examples of implementations of Layer 2 in the LAN area are

 – ISO 8802-2 Logical Link Control (LLC)

 – ISO 8802-3 CSMA/CD Media Access Control (MAC)

 – ISO 8802-5 Token Ring Media Access Control (MAC)

 – ISO 9314-2 FDDI Token Ring Media Access Control (MAC).

WAN examples are
- CCITT X.25 Link Access Protocol (LAP)
- CCITT Q.992 Frame Relay
- CCITT I.440 ISDN Data Link Protocol.

(3) **Network Layer**: The task of the network layer is the transmission of data packets between nodes over several hops. This includes, for example, path selection (routing), multiplexing of several node connections over a connection, and error handling and flow control between nodes.

Examples of implementations of Layer 3 are
- CCITT X.25 Packet Level Protocol
- CCITT I.450 ISDN Network Protocol
- ISO 8473 Connectionless Network Protocol.

(4) **Transport Layer**: While the data link layer is responsible for connections between computers, the transport layer has the task of enabling links between application processes on different computers. The programming interfaces to the transport layer are therefore comparable to those of inter-process communication.

Widespread interfaces for Layer 4 are
- X/Open XTI (Extended Transport Interface)
- Sockets with TCP/IP (Transmission Control Protocol/Internet Protocol, see Section 3.3.4)
- Novell SPX/IPX (Sequence Packet Exchange/Internet Packet Exchange).

Additionally, in the 8073 standard the ISO has defined a separate transport protocol conforming to OSI standards. These protocols have as yet found little acceptance in the marketplace, however.

(5) **Session Layer**: In contrast to the transport layer basic services, the session layer offers powerful functions for synchronization and organization of communication between two application processes. OSI-conforming protocols of this layer do not have much market penetration.

Current programming interfaces that can be assigned to this layer are
- Remote Procedure Call (RPC)
- APPC/LU6.2
- CPI-C
- Named pipes.

(6) **Presentation Layer**: The presentation layer provides a common representation of information during communication between application processes across computer boundaries. Before data transfer, the presentation layer connection partners determine which common language should be used in the transfer. This way, even mainframes and UNIX systems that use EBCDIC or ASCII character display internally can communicate with each other.

(7) **Application Layer**: The application layer makes general, high-grade services available to application processes for communication in distributed environments. The end-user applications themselves, however, are not an element of the ISO reference model.

Examples of application layer services are
- ISO 8571 File Transfer, Access and Management (FTAM)
- CCITT X.400 Message Handling System (MHS)
- CCITT X.500 Directory Service (DS)
- ANSI X12 Electronic Data Interchange (EDI).

A number of important network protocols, such as TCP/IP (Transmission Control Protocol/Internet Protocol) and IBM's SNA (System Network Architecture), were in existence before the ISO published its reference model. These protocols therefore cannot conform to the OSI architecture in all details. Pure OSI protocols have little meaning in contrast to the ISO reference model, with the exception of some services of Layer 7, like X.400 and EDI.

3.3.2 Cabling strategy

These days, cabling is hierarchically structured. A distinction is made between horizontal floor cabling, vertical building cabling, and horizontal site cabling. In the backbone area (vertical building cabling, horizontal site cabling), more and more fiber-optic cable with the FDDI (Fiber Distributed Data Interchange) protocol, in conformance with the ANSI standard X3T9.5, is being laid. In the floor area, cabling using twisted-wire lines according to IEEE 802.3 10BASE-T and IEEE 802.5 is replacing use of traditional coaxial cabling. Cabling with fiber optics according to IEEE 802.3 10BASE-F or FDDI is equally possible.

The decision to use a certain kind of cabling should not be reached independently of the desired topology and the planned method of access to the transmission medium. In local floor networking, bus topology with CSMA/CD according to IEEE 802.3 as the access method and ring topology with the token access method (IEEE 802.5) are the most widespread today. In both cases, the most flexibility is offered by physical cabling with twisted-wire lines that run in a star formation to a central distributor that is named according to the technology used, for example switch or hub.

Generally, large networks are set up in a structured fashion. For connection of subnetworks, the following repeaters, bridges, routers, and gateways are used:

- **Repeaters**: Repeaters are signal amplifiers that operate on OSI layer 1. They connect homogeneous networks (for example, two Ethernets).

- **Bridges**: Bridges connect LANs with the same protocol on Layer 2a (Logical Link Control, LLC). They are characterized by filter functions that enable a reduction in the volume of data to be transferred in the individual subnetworks.

- **Routers**: Routers link networks with the same protocol on Layer 3. Like bridges, routers offer filter functions, but they also interpret the network addresses of Layer 3. This makes them more flexible than bridges, since they can determine the optimal transport paths from among several possible paths to the receiver. They are, however, also sometimes slower, because of the internal processing necessary for this.

- **Gateways**: Gateways can connect networks with completely different protocol structures, for example TCP/IP networks and SNA networks.

3.3.3 Ethernet, Token Ring, and FDDI

The IEEE 802 standard and the ISO 8802 standard specify the lower two layers of the ISO reference model for LANs, taking into consideration, among other things, the most important LAN access techniques, which are CSMA/CD (Carrier-Sensed Multiple Access/Collision Detection) for bus networks (Ethernet) and the Token access procedure for ring networks (Token Ring, FDDI). These are described below.

- **CSMA/CD** was developed for Ethernet access control. Conceived by Xerox at the beginning of the 1970s, today's Ethernet is still the widespread Version 2 defined by Digital, Intel, and Xerox (the DIX group) in 1978. Version 2 was the basis for the IEEE 802.3 standard and the ISO 8802-3 standard.

  The CSMA/CD procedure is an access method that works by detecting and handling collisions. It includes three activity parts: carrier sensing (checking if the line is free), collision detection (listening on the line during the transmission process and canceling upon recognition of conflicts), and backoff algorithm (restarting after a conflict). CSMA/CD offers advantages for traffic volume that fluctuates greatly in time and quantity. Unlike in a Token Ring procedure, a maximum wait time for fulfillment of a transmission request cannot be provided, since with every send attempt a send-ready station must compete with all other stations for transmission rights. A high network load can lead to a high collision rate with diminishing throughput. In this case, the network must be divided into several subnetworks.

  CSMA/CD networks can be installed relatively inexpensively and have established themselves as the standard in the area of open systems. The transmission performance of most CSMA/CD networks is 10 Mbit/s. In addition, with 100BASE-F and 100BASE-T (Fast Ethernet), there are two standards conforming to IEEE 802.3 for 100 Mbit/s Ethernet over fiber-optic cable or twisted-wire lines.

  As a new guideline, under the designation IEEE802.12, IEEE has worked out the 100VG-AnyLAN standard. The goal is not to lose any transmission bandwidth through high collision rates, even with a high network load. 100VG-AnyLAN can transmit Ethernet and Token Ring data formats with a transmission speed of 100 Mbit/s over fiber-optic cable and twisted-wire lines. The network topology is always a star with a central node, at which every transmission request must be announced in advance. This ensures that collisions are basically impossible. For the allocation of transmission rights, different priorities can be allocated to individual computers (DPAM procedure, Demand Priority Access Method).

• In the **Token procedure**, access control is handled by a particular bit pattern. As long as no station wants to send, this bit pattern, the so-called free token, circles around the logical or physical ring. A station wanting to send can append a packet and the address of the receiver to this free token. The resulting packet is transmitted over the ring to the receiver. The receiver copies the packet into its receiver buffer and places a delivery notice into the packet. As soon as the packet returns to the sender, the sender takes the message from the net, generates a new free token, and gives it to the next station in the ring.

The essential advantages of the Token procedure are its simplicity, its low protocol overhead, and the ability to calculate the maximum wait time for a transmission request. In the worst case, a send-ready station must wait for transmission rights until all other stations in the ring have exercised their transmission rights exactly once. Token Ring installations are usually somewhat more expensive than Ethernet installations, for example. The transmission performance of Token Ring networks is 4 or 16 Mbit/s.

• **FDDI** (Fiber Distributed Data Interface) is a local high-speed network specified by the ANSI X3T9.5 team based on fiber-optic technology. As an alternative, transmission over copper lines (CDDI, Copper Distributed Data Interface) is also offered. Today, FDDI is used primarily as a backbone network for connecting local subnetworks. The essential features of FDDI are:

– High transmission performance (100 Mbit/s)

– Large network expansion (to 100 km)

– High noise immunity

– Fault tolerance (reconfigurable double ring)

– High start-up loading.

In FDDI, access to the transmission medium is controlled by a Token Ring procedure (Early Token Release) according to ISO 9314-2.

Next to the LAN types most widespread today, Ethernet, Token Ring, and FDDI, ATM will play a decisive role in the future.

3.3.4 The TCP/IP protocol family

TCP/IP (Transmission Control Protocol/Internet Protocol) is a protocol family that covers Layers 3 to 7 of the OSI reference model. TCP/IP provides a generally recognized industry standard for communication between open systems. Worldwide, some 100 companies offer TCP/IP products. The TCP/IP protocol family is continually undergoing development by way of RFCs (Requests for Comments) under the administration of the IETF (Internet Engineering Task Force) committee, which belongs to the Internet Activities Board (IAB).

The roots of the TCP/IP protocol family go back to the 1970s and are tightly connected to the beginnings of the worldwide ARPA (Advanced Research Projects Agency) network. The general breakthrough of the TCP/IP protocol family was brought about by its incorporation in the Berkeley 4.2 version of UNIX and the publication of all TCP/IP protocols, including program sources, as public domain software.

The TCP/IP protocol family consists of the following individual protocols:

*   **Layers 1–2**:
    No unique specification. TCP/IP protocols can be implemented in LANs as well as in WANs.

*   **Layer 3**:
    IP   (Internet Protocol)
    ARP   (Address Resolution Protocol)
    ICMP   (Internet Control Message Protocol)

*   **Layer 4**:
    TCP   (Transmission Control Protocol)
    UDP   (User Datagram Protocol)

*   **Layers 5–7**:
    FTP   (File Transfer Protocol)
    SMTP   (Simple Mail Transfer Protocol)
    Telnet   (Remote Login)
    SNMP   (Simple Network Management Protocol)

The **Internet Protocol** (IP) has the task of transporting datagrams from the sender over several networks to a receiver. Datagrams are packets that can be transmitted without a pre-existing link between sender and receiver. This is also called connectionless data exchange.

The **Address Resolution Protocol** (ARP) changes Internet addresses into hardware addresses.

The **Internet Control Message Protocol** (ICMP) is responsible for the exchange of error messages and other control information in the network. ICMP messages are created by the TCP/IP network software itself and sent as IP datagrams.

The **Transmission Control Protocol** (TCP) is a Layer 4, connection-oriented, end-to-end protocol.

Like TCP, the **User Datagram Protocol** (UDP) is based on IP and offers application processes the possibility of using connectionless datagram services.

The **File Transfer Protocol** (FTP) allows the exchange of files between different systems. FTP is based on the transport protocol TCP and the interactive terminal protocol Telnet.

The **Simple Mail Transfer Protocol** (SMTP) offers a simple mail service. SMTP is based on a client/server architecture with a central SMTP message router (SendMail) and decentralized client programs (SMTP Mailer), which are responsible for the preparation, storage, reading, and sending of messages. Communication between the Mailer and the message router proceeds on the basis of POP3 (Post Office Protocol) or the new IMAP4 (Internet Mail Access Protocol) protocol. The use of SMTP and POP3 in the R/3 System is discussed in Section 7.2.6.

The **Network Terminal Protocol** (Telnet) makes services available for communication between terminals on one side and interactive application processes on the other.

The **Simple Network Management Protocol** (SNMP) provides services for management of TCP/IP networks (see Section 3.3.7).

Sockets and TCP/IP are not only used in many custom distributed applications, but they are also the basis for such well-known services as Sun's distributed file system NFS (Network File System), MIT's X Window (see Section 3.7.1), and the Internet service WWW (World Wide Web, see Section 3.3.9). The entire network communication of the R/3 System is based on this interface, too.

3.3.5 Linking computers over trunk lines

There are various possibilities for linking computers over trunk lines:

- Dedicated lines

- Leased line services (telephone, Datex-L, ISDN)

- Packet switching services (Datex-P/X.25, Frame Relay, ATM).

The use of dedicated lines is recommended if a large, continuous data stream is expected between sender and receiver.

Computer links over analog telephone lines are very flexible, since they can be set up with a modem (modulator/demodulator) from any telephone jack. They are, however, relatively unreliable and have the additional distinction of having low transmission performance. Analog telephone connections should therefore be used only in special situations.

The universal, service-integrating digital ISDN (Integrated Service Digital Network) network is the standardized digital network defined by CCITT in the I.x Series for end-to-end dial-up connections. The base connection offers two data (B) channels with 64 Kbit/s each and one signal channel with 16 Kbit/s. The primary multiplexing connection includes 30 data channels with 64 Kbit/s each and one signal channel with 64 Kbit/s. ISDN is a flexible, powerful, and economical possibility for linking computers over trunk lines.

Packet switching services are available in various forms (Figure 3.14). X.25 is currently the most frequently used service. In this procedure, messages are broken down into packets with a fixed maximum length. The packets are transmitted individually through the network, like normal parcel post. Datex-P, the X.25 network of German Telekom, supports standard data transmission rates of up to 64 Kbit/s. For certain users like the German Research Network (DFN, Deutsches Forschungsnetz), 2 Mbit/s links are also available.

As a further development of X.25, the Frame Relay transmission procedure today enjoys enormous popularity, especially in the US. Like X.25, Frame Relay works with packets of fixed maximum length. The packets can accept up to 8 Kbytes of user data. The protocol overhead of Frame Relay is greatly reduced in comparison to X.25, because X.25 was developed over 20 years ago for data transfer over unreliable, analog telephone lines. That made extensive error correction mechanisms necessary, which are no longer necessary with the low error rates of today's long-distance lines. In Frame Relay, correction of transmission errors is left to the higher protocol layers, allowing transmission rates to reach up to 45 Mbit/s.

Frame Relay is not well suited for voice transmission because very large and very small packets are transmitted together on the network. The probability that a long data packet will be transmitted between two short voice packets is very high. Distortion of voice transmission due to the delay resulting from this cannot be

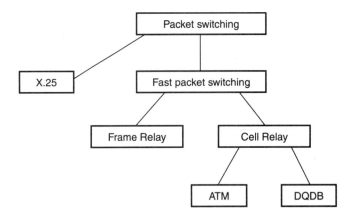

Figure 3.14 Packet switching procedure.

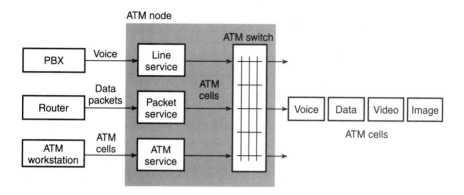

Figure 3.15 Asynchronous Transfer Mode (ATM).

excluded. As an alternative for links that must be suitable for the transmission of not only data, but also image and sound information, Cell Relay protocols were developed, which are based on a fixed packet size. Of importance here are DQDB (Distributed Queue Dual Bus) for locally restricted MANs (Metropolitan Area Networks) and particularly ATM (Asynchronous Transfer Mode).

As early as 1988, the CCITT selected ATM as the basis for the planned universal broadband network B-ISDN (Broadband-Integrated Service Digital Network). In contrast to X.25 and Frame Relay networks, ATM breaks down messages to be transmitted into cells of equal size, 53 bytes. The transmission medium in ATM is used in asynchronous time multiplexing (Figure 3.15).

In addition, each packet receives a channel by which allocation to the respective link takes place. The core of ATM networks is formed by ATM switches, onto which network participants attach themselves, using, for example, 155 Mbit/s or faster lines. Network participants do not share a common transmission medium, like in a LAN; instead, they simply deliver their data cells to the ATM switch. The total transmission bandwidth available in the network therefore increases with every new participant. ATM switches control an accumulated processing capacity of 10 Gbit/s or more. Owing to these properties, ATM is also suited for applications with high data transmission volume, for example in the multimedia area, both in LANs and WANs (All Area Network, AAN).

The TCP/IP protocol, too, can be transmitted over trunk lines, for example on the basis of X.25, Frame Relay, ATM, and ISDN links, or over telephone lines on the basis of the SLIP protocol (Serial Line IP Protocol, see Stevens (1990)) or PPP (Point-to-Point Protocol).

TCP/IP is the standard protocol of the global Internet (see Section 3.3.9).

3.3.6 Program-to-program communication

Protocols for program-to-program communication enable direct dialog between independent applications on a single computer or on different computers.

Widespread base interfaces for program-to-program communication today are, for example, Sockets, XTI, APPC, and CPI-C. They offer functions for the initialization of links, connection establishment and breakdown, and the control of the data transmission itself. DDE, OLE, and RPC are protocols on a logically higher level that relieve the applications programmer of most aspects of network communication. Protocols that are oriented even more toward the application are X.400 and EDI.

- **Sockets**: Sockets, first introduced with Berkeley UNIX 4.2BSD, represent a general interface to the transport layer. Besides being used for access to TCP, UDP, and IP, Sockets, conceived as a generic communications interface, can be implemented for local interprocess communication as well. Owing to their widespread use, Sockets are considered the industry standard for access to the transport layer of open systems.

- **XTI**: Based on the work of AT&T in the definition of a transport-level interface (TLI) for the UNIX V.3, X/Open system published in the XPG3 (X/Open Portability Guide, version 3), the XTI interface (Extended Transport Interface) is an OSI-conforming interface to the transport layer. The functionality of XTI resembles that of the Socket interface.

- **APPC**: In 1983, IBM defined APPC (Advanced Program-to-Program Communication) as the programming interface to the SNA (System Network Architecture) LU6.2 protocol. APPC supports communication between transaction programs that are installed on a single computer or on different computers in an SNA network.

- **CPI-C**: The definition of the APPC interface still leaves a lot of freedom when it comes to implementation. That led to APPC products from different vendors, though equal in semantics, displaying considerable differences in syntax. With CPI-C (Common Programming Interface – Communication), IBM attempted to achieve standardization in the framework of its SAA (Systems Application Architecture) architecture. Meanwhile, X/Open has taken up CPI-C as the standard for program-to-program communication between UNIX systems and mainframes in the Portability Guide XPG4. The basic CPI-C commands, which are summed up in the so-called "starter set," are presented in Table 3.3.

- **Remote Procedure Call**: Remote Procedure Calls (RPCs) expand the call mechanism for procedures familiar from standard programming languages in such a way that procedure calls are possible even across computer boundaries (Figure 3.16). The tasks linked to communication over the network, such as data conversion, packetization of data, and so on, are invisible to the

Table 3.3 CPI-C starter set calls.

ABAP/4 call	CPI-C function	Description
CMINIT	Initialize_Conversation	Determine communication parameters
CMALLC	Allocate_Conversation	Set up link
CMACCP	Accept_Conversation	Accept link
CMSEND	Send	Send data
CMRCV	Receive	Receive data
CMDEAL	Deallocate_Conversation	Break down link

applications programmer and are handled on both sides of the RPC link by special modules (stubs) that can be created either automatically or manually, according to their implementation. In contrast to Socket communication, which is based on an unstructured byte stream, RPC data is exchanged in typed and structured form. The communication relation between client and server can be synchronous or asynchronous, depending on the manufacturer.

The following components belong to an RPC service:

- **Stubs**: Interface modules between client or server and the runtime system
- **Binding protocol**: Localization of a server by the client
- **Data representation**: Common data representation for client and server
- **Transport protocol**: Transport service over the network
- **Control protocol**: Status tracing for RPC calls.

There is no clear standard for RPC at this time. Familiar products come from Netwise (RPC Tool), Sun (ONC RPC), and OSF (DCE RPC). SAP has integrated RFC (Remote Function Call) for synchronous and asynchronous communication in the 4GL language ABAP/4 (see Section 5.3).

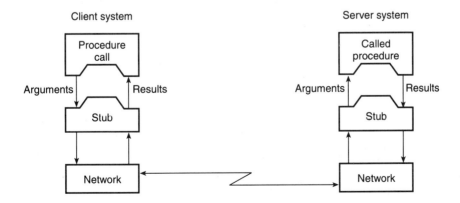

Figure 3.16 Operation of an RPC communication.

- **DDE**: Windows users can define dynamic links between applications with the help of DDE (Dynamic Data Exchange). The display of just-processed documents is automatically updated across application boundaries. DDE links can also be set up across computer boundaries.

- **OLE Automation**: OLE (Object Linking and Embedding) is a family of technologies developed by Microsoft that enables the non-proprietary co-operation and integration of independent software components (see Section 3.9.2). Program-to-program communication is supported by OLE Automation, an interface technology for cross-application macro programming. OLE Automation makes it possible for applications to manipulate objects from other applications. For example, a word processor can cause a spreadsheet to manipulate cells of a table embedded in a word processing document.

  A network-capable version of OLE (Distributed/Network OLE) is part of Windows 95 and Cairo, the successor to Windows NT.

- **X.400**: An MHS system (Message Handling System) is used for asynchronous exchange of messages between applications, even across computer boundaries. With the X.400(84) standard, the CCITT published the first MHS standard in 1984. The current version, X.400(88), is recognized today as the worldwide standard for MHS systems. X.400 is enhanced by a global address service standardized in X.500.

- **EDI**: The term EDI (Electronic Business Data Interchange) encompasses all approaches for automated, paper-free data exchange between business entities. With EDIFACT (Electronic Data Interchange for Administration, Commerce, and Transport), the ISO has defined a standardized EDI protocol in the ISO 9735 standard. In a defined syntax, EDIFACT determines the structure in which trade information is stored in files for automated data exchange. Applications must either implement this standard syntax themselves or let their information be adapted by special converters available on the market. Additional current EDI standards are, for example, ANSI X12, VDA (Verband der Deutschen Automobilindustrie), and Odette (Organization for Data Exchange by Teletransmission in Europe).

3.3.7 Network management

Safer and smoother network operation requires powerful network management. A network management system should fulfill the following tasks:

- **Network control**: Initialization and termination of activities, activation and deactivation of resources such as individual servers

- **Error management**: Error detection, diagnosis, restart, and so on

- **Configuration management**: Network and protocol configuration

- **Network tuning**: Optimization of behavior

- **User management**: Addressing, access control, accounting, and so on.

For heterogeneous, open network environments, SNMP management solutions (Simple Network Management Protocol) are usually used these days. Additional approaches to standardized network management in open system environments are provided by CMIS/CMIP (Common Management Information Services/Common Management Information Protocol) for OSI networks and DME (Distributed Management Environment) by OSF. SNMP is maintained and continually under development by the Internet committee IETF (Internet Engineering Task Force). The current version, SNMPv2 (Figure 3.17), includes the following areas:

- Protocol services

- Security concepts

- Communication between management stations

- Error signaling

- Object and name administration

- Management information bases (MIBs).

The SNMPv2 architecture has the following components:

- **SNMP manager**: SNMP managers are network management stations in which information from the individual network elements flows together. The data models of a network management system are called MIBs (Management Information Bases). A MIB consists of object classes and the associated instances. In the MIB all parameters sent by an SNMP agent and requested by the SNMP manager are determined. SNMP can be expanded at any time by the definition of new MIBs. Of special interest are proprietary enterprise MIBs. The management stations evaluate the MIBs and, if necessary, start required actions.

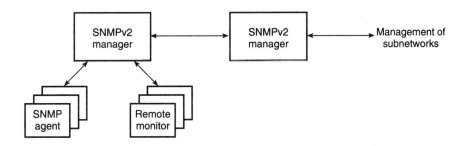

Figure 3.17 SNMPv2 network management.

- **Network elements**: Network elements are servers, gateways, routers, bridges, and so on, in which special SNMP agents are implemented. SNMP agents collect the MIB data and send it over the SNMP protocol to the SNMP manager.

- **SNMP remote monitors**: SNMP monitors, or LAN probes, are based on the RMON-MIB (Remote Monitoring Management Information Basc). Remote monitors collect data from subnetworks and take over the preprocessing of this data. The SNMP manager is thereby relieved of the duty of communicating with many individual SNMP agents.

Widespread products that support SNMP are, for example, OpenView (HP), Netview/6000 (IBM), and SunNet Manager (Sun).

3.3.8 DCE

DCE (Distributed Computing Environment) was created by the OSF (Open Software Foundation) with the goal of providing an inclusive set of basic services for the development, operation, and management of distributed applications in heterogeneous environments. DCE covers the following areas:

- **Remote Procedure Call**: Call of procedures across computer boundaries. Based on HP's NCS (Network Computing System) and Digital's NCA (Network Computing Architecture).

- **Naming**: Directory service for copying user-oriented object names onto system-oriented addresses in the network. Based on Digital's DECdns and SNI's DIR-X/X.500.

- **Security**: Authentication and authorization of users as well as access protection for messages. The basis is Kerberos (Schill, 1993) from MIT (Massachusetts Institute of Technology). The basic principles of Kerberos are shown in Figure 3.18.

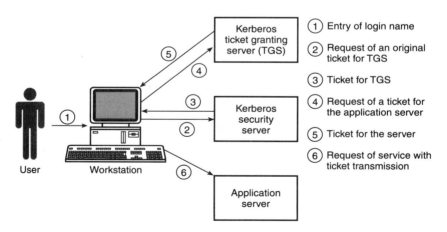

Figure 3.18 Basic principles of Kerberos.

Kerberos starts from the fundamental premise that desktop systems are not secure. For every service request, therefore, it demands identification from a client. In the process, the following principles apply:

- Users need identify themselves only once at the beginning of their processing session.
- Passwords are never sent unencrypted over the network.
- Only the Kerberos security server knows all passwords.

- **Threads**: Threads support parallel operations within an address range without costly process exchanges and are of particular interest for the set-up of fast servers that must process many inquiries in parallel. DCE implementation is based on Digital's Concert Multithread Architecture (CMA).

- **Time service**: Time services are required for synchronization of local system clocks in a network. Users of such services are, for example, various security procedures. DCE uses Digital's DECdts Time Service.

- **Distributed file system**: DCE's distributed file system allows transparent access to the local file systems of the different computers in a network. The basis is Transarc's AFS (Andrew File System).

Currently, DCE components are offered by all leading system manufacturers as part of their system software. Increasing distribution in the area of commercial application systems is expected, especially for the RPC, Naming, and Security services.

3.3.9 Online information services and the Internet

Globally distributed online information and communication services are in increasing demand these days, especially for business communications. The exchange of electronic messages (electronic mail) is becoming the standard means of communication between customers and vendors. Customers retrieve information from their vendors using online databases and can order products and services directly over the network (electronic commerce, see Section 7.5.6). In open or closed discussion forums, customers exchange dialog on special topics with each other or with their vendors.

Today, important platforms for suppliers of online information and communication services are

- The Internet (World Wide Web)

- CompuServe

- America Online

- Telekom Online (formerly Datex-J/BTX)

- Europe Online.

The Internet and the World Wide Web

The Internet is a global system of computers and computer networks. Developed from the US Defense Department's ARPANET (Advanced Research Projects Agency Network), which was originally conceived for military purposes, the Internet, coordinated by the Internet Activity Board (IAB), includes over 15 000 individual networks with more than a million computers and over 30 million end users (Angell and Heslop, 1995).

The Internet is not a centrally installed and managed computer network; rather, it is more of a hierarchy of many individual networks. Local and regional computer networks are switched together into increasingly larger systems and, as a combined whole, form the Internet. Special Internet service providers give the end user access to the Internet over partially separate networks. Examples of Internet service providers in Germany are EUnet, Xlink, and DFN (Deutsches ForschungsNetz). Communication between the individual networks takes place over fast backbone networks, such as the American ANS (Advanced Network and Services, Inc.) network.

Computers on the Internet use the TCP/IP transport protocol for data transmission. For the identification of communication partners, every computer on the Internet receives a unique, hierarchically structured IP address, for example 155.56.123.12. Since such numerical addresses are difficult for people to deal with, there are text addresses as well, like pc01.sap-ag.de, which are converted into IP addresses by the DNS (Domain Name Service) service of the Internet.

The terms "Information Super Highway" and "Data Highway" are often associated with the Internet. The reason for this designation becomes clear when one considers the many millions of users and the abundant communication services offered to users by the Internet. The most well-known Internet services are:

- **Electronic mail**: Sending and receipt of electronic messages (for example, to ruediger.buck-emden@sap-ag.de).

  Anyone who sends a mail message with the text "SUBSCRIBE SAP-R3.L" to the Internet address LISTSERV@MITVMA.MIT.EDU can be included in an independent R/3 mailing list.

- **Network News (USENET)**: Distributed conferencing system with more than 10 000 subject areas (newsgroups). Topics related to SAP's R/3 System, for example, are discussed in the newsgroup de.alt.comp.sap-r3.

- **FTP (File Transfer Protocol)**: Sending and receipt of files.

- **WWW (World Wide Web)**: Distributed, hypertext-based multimedia information service.

The World Wide Web (WWW), developed in 1989 at the European nuclear research center CERN (Conseil Européen pour la Recherche Nucléaire, European Laboratory for Particle Physics) in Geneva is currently the fastest-growing information service of the Internet. More and more commercial and professional suppliers, among them SAP (Figure 3.19), are using the WWW as a presentation, information, and communication system for their customers. The WWW offers its users comfortable navigation capabilities between distributed stored multimedia documents (see Section 3.8). The physical location for these multimedia documents is totally unimportant to the user. The basis for navigation is hypertext links (hyperlinks) between the documents, which are activated simply by clicking on the appropriately marked areas within the document (see Section 3.7).

The layout of WWW documents is specified with the help of embedded HTML (HyperText Markup Language) formatting commands. A Web client program (browser) is required for displaying WWW documents. Well-known client programs are Microsoft's Explorer, Mosaic from NCSA (National Center for Supercomputing Applications) at the University of Illinois (see Angell and Heslop (1995)) and Netscape Navigator.

The servers in the WWW that are responsible for document storage communicate with WWW clients using the HTTP (HyperText Transport Protocol) protocol. Individual WWW pages can be addressed directly by their URL (Uniform

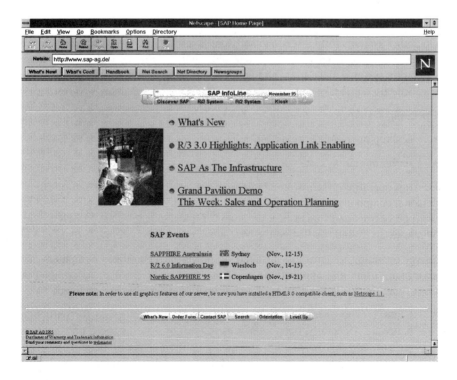

Figure 3.19 SAP's Home Page on the WWW.
© SAP AG

Resource Locator) address. For example, the German and American home pages of SAP (Figure 3.19) can be reached using the URL addresses http://www.sap-ag.de and http://www.sap.com.

CompuServe

Next to the Internet, CompuServe has for years been offering commercial online information services such as electronic mail, file transfer, and information and discussion forums on various topics. More than 3.5 million members are hooked up to CompuServe worldwide. Several hundred hardware and software suppliers, among them SAP, provide their customers with information about new developments, product strategies, and service in their own computer support forums. CompuServe users can call up general information about SAP using GO SAPAG. In addition, SAP customers can use SAP's Online Software Service (OSS) over CompuServe.

3.4 Operating systems

Operating systems form a separate software layer that lies between the hardware and the machine language on the one side and the middleware on the other. Operating systems make users and applications independent of the details of the hardware used and take over the management of users, processes, and resources.

Operating systems can generally be divided into

- desktop operating systems, and
- server operating systems.

Desktop operating systems are single-user operating systems that run on users' personal computers and are optimized for supporting individual applications like word processors and spreadsheet programs. Typical examples are MS-DOS with Windows 3.x, Windows 95 and the Macintosh operating system, System 7.

Server operating systems are installed on powerful, centralized computers and give many users and applications access to the resources of those computers. Over time, four different classes of server operating system have evolved:

- **Class 1**: The operating systems of Class 1 are engineered for particular hardware. Generally, open interfaces to foreign systems based on standards are not foreseen. Installation and administration of these operating systems is costly and requires trained department specialists. Examples of Class 1 operating systems are MVS, VSE, and VM (all from IBM), BS2000 (SNI), VMS (Digital), and MPE (HP).

- **Class 2**: Many vendors of Class 1 operating systems are currently introducing open variants of their hardware-specific operating systems. These are characterized by integration of open, recognized standard interfaces, for example for program-to-program communication. Examples are MVS Open Edition (IBM), BS2000 Open Systems Direction (SNI), OpenVMS (Digital), and MPE/iX (HP). The operating system implemented for Intel 80x86 processors, OS/2 (IBM), also belongs in this class.

- **Class 3**: Class 3 includes the many different UNIX operating systems. The success of UNIX lies largely in the fact that it is the first mostly hardware-independent operating system that can be adapted quickly to different hardware environments. In addition, UNIX offers many generally recognized standard interfaces, which facilitate communication and porting. Disadvantages of UNIX are the expense of installation and administration and the fact that all manufacturers offer their own UNIX variants, which are only partially compatible. Examples are AIX (IBM), HP-UX (HP), OSF/1 (Digital), SINIX (SNI), and Solaris (Sun).

- **Class 4**: With Windows NT, Microsoft now offers a new operating system class for server systems. Windows NT has a modern micro-kernel architecture, in which only the operating system core is hardware-dependent. This makes Windows NT very easily portable to different hardware platforms, including symmetrical multiprocessor systems. In contrast to UNIX, there is only one version of Windows NT, which is identical on all platforms.

A particular need that Microsoft considered in the development of Windows NT is the reduction of installation and administration expenses. Under the code name Hermes, the Systems Management Server (SMS), a powerful environment for network-wide system management, was created.

Windows applications can use a multitude of open interfaces. These are summed up in OLE (Object Linking and Embedding, see Section 3.9.2) and in WOSA (Windows Open Services Architecture). WOSA consists of

- Services for general applications
- Services for vertical applications
- Communication services.

The general WOSA application interfaces include ODBC (Open Database Connectivity), MAPI (Messaging API), TAPI (Telephony API), and LAPI (License API). Communication services are offered for SNA (Windows SNA API), TCP/IP (Windows Sockets), and Remote Procedure Call (Windows RPC). WOSA services for vertical markets are "WOSA Extensions for Financial Services" and "WOSA Extensions for Real Time Market Data."

It is to be expected that in the near future Microsoft will continue to develop both OLE and WOSA in parallel, with the main emphasis probably on OLE. The question that remains open is when the entire WOSA functionality will also be accessible over OLE interfaces.

In general, it seems obvious that the pace of innovation of the market-dominating operating systems was rather restrained in the past. The most important server operating system today, UNIX, was conceived at the end of the 1960s and was not meant to be a universal server operating system. Windows NT sets new standards here, particularly in terms of user friendliness, which affects simple installation and administration.

Windows applications have enormous market acceptance. To make these applications runable on UNIX systems, too, some companies have created emulations, for example WABI (Windows Applications Binary Interface) from the Sun spin-off SunSelect and SoftWindows, from Insignia Solution. With these emulations, Windows applications can be used on UNIX computers without any customizing effort. In fact, WABI is now supported not only by Sun, but also by HP and IBM. To improve the competitiveness of UNIX systems, several manufacturers are running projects, under such names as "Common UNIX API," "COSE" (Common Open Software Environment, see Section 3.8), and "Common Desktop Environment" (CDE), for standardization of the various UNIX variants with their incompatible user interfaces and APIs. X/Open is planning a certification procedure for products conforming to CDE.

3.5 Database management systems

As a rule, business applications work with large amounts of data. Master data and transaction data often take up many gigabytes of disk storage. To be able to handle such data volumes comfortably, powerful storage and access methods are necessary.

3.5.1 Requirements for data storage

An essential requirement for computer-aided data management systems is guaranteed data independence, defined as isolation of the applications and the users from

- the physical properties of the storage devices used;

- the physical organization of the data on the device or storage medium;

- the system-internal strategy for accessing the stored data.

Simple file and data management systems, like those first offered in the 1960s as part of the operating systems of the time, could not completely fulfill these requirements. They provided only physical data independence (device independence) for individual files, which they did by taking over the control and monitoring of external devices, the blocking and unblocking of records, the occupancy and release of storage areas, and the control of overflow and index areas. The applications programmer still had to take care of the access paths to the data, the search process for reading and changing data, and the use of auxiliary data like indexes and pointers.

At the end of the 1960s, the early physical file access methods were enhanced by "logical" procedures, which simplified in particular the search process and the management of access paths. Familiar examples are ISAM (Indexed Sequential Access Method) and VSAM (Virtual Storage Access Method). But even these could not make the applications programmer completely independent of the physical organization of the data and the internal access strategy. It is precisely for the management of data that is stored in different files but logically interconnected that classic file systems offer inadequate support.

At the beginning of the 1970s, with the goal of meeting the requirements for the most extensive data independence possible, powerful access operations, and data management across file boundaries, the first hierarchical database management systems (DBMS) with network-like structure were developed. They introduced the concept of navigation to data using logical access paths, even across file boundaries. Hierarchical database management systems, such as IBM's IMS (Information Management System) can optimally support only treelike access paths branching out from the root segment, but they offer very high performance. More general access paths, on the other hand, can be implemented with network-oriented database management systems. Network-oriented database management systems were standardized by the CODASYL (Conference on Data Systems Language, see Groff and Weinberg (1994)) group. Examples are SNI's UDS (Universal Database management system) and Computer Associates' IDMS (Integrated Database Management System).

Even hierarchical and network-oriented database management systems cannot create complete data independence. Specifically the independence of applications from the internal access strategy is not assured due to the necessity for navigation. Additionally, only certain access paths predetermined by the system administrator can be used. This situation did not change until the middle of the 1970s, when the first relational database management systems (RDBMS) were implemented, based on the works of Edgar F. Codd (Codd, 1970). Examples of relational database management systems are Oracle 7 from Oracle, Informix Online from Informix, DB2 from IBM, ADABAS D from Software AG, and System 10 from Sybase.

3.5.2 Foundations for relational database management systems

Relational database management systems are characterized by their logical simplicity. All of the data, as well as the relations between the data, are stored in two-dimensional tables (Figure 3.20). Every table has a primary key, by which table entries can be uniquely identified. The definition of data, tables, and table

Employee-in-department table

Department number	Personnel number
.	.
.	.
0815	1234
0815	4711
.	.

Employee table

Personnel number	Last name	First name
.		
1234	Doe	Jane
4711	Public	John
.		

Department table

Department number	Department name	Department head
.		
0815	Purchasing	4711
.		

Figure 3.20 Relational tables.

relations takes place in the database catalog (Data Dictionary) of the database management system. Tables can be expanded as desired, without existing applications having to be changed. This largely ensures the desired data independence.

Tables in relational databases are organized in a flat manner with elementary data fields that have no additional internal structure. Every field depends only on the primary key. This is known as normalization of tables or storage in normal format. Only storage in normal format guarantees that insertions and deletions always update the data set consistently.

Access to the data stored in a relational database takes place with simple, largely self-explanatory expressions that follow the SQL standard (see Section 3.5.4). For example, from the table in Figure 3.20, all of the employees with the first name Jane can be chosen with the following statement:

SELECT   personnel number, last name
FROM   employees
WHERE   first name = 'Jane'.

The relational join operation makes it possible to analyze several independent tables together, according to certain criteria. In this way, the following instruction delivers a list of all departments and their respective department heads:

SELECT   department name, last name
FROM   department, employee
WHERE   department.department head = employee.personnel number.

Furthermore, end users and application programmers have the ability to access the subset of stored data relevant to them using predefined, external views, independent of predefined access paths and the internal table organization. For example, the following statement defines a view of the Employee table, which contains only the names, but not the personnel numbers, of the employees:

```
CREATE VIEW    names
AS SELECT      last name, first name
FROM           employees.
```

Relational database management systems offer extensive functionality, but also have their limitations:

- One example is support for complex, structured data objects. Material master records, which in a relational database must be distributed among a multitude of tables due to normalization, are not recognized by the database management system as business objects. The logical relationship between the individual tables must be ensured by the application.

- To ensure consistent writing and reading of data by parallel users, database management systems offer the capability to temporarily lock data for exclusive use (locking, see Section 3.5.3). Since relational database management systems do not recognize complex, structured objects, they cannot lock them. This means that appropriate locking mechanisms must be provided by the application.

Object-oriented database management systems (OODBMS) try to go beyond these limitations of relational database management systems. How far they succeed is discussed in Section 3.5.5.

3.5.3 Locks in relational database management systems

To enable parallel use and changing of a common data set, multi-user database management systems have some highly developed locking mechanisms. These ensure that database contents such as balances in debit and credit accounts cannot be changed by several users at the same time and thereby falsified.

Database management systems can place locks at different levels. In the simplest case, a transaction that wants to change a database entry locks the entire database. This strategy is very easy to implement, but it leads to unacceptable response times, because all other active transactions must wait, even if they want to access entirely different parts of the database. A better locking granularity is achieved with locks at table level and block level (page level). Locking at page level involves locking individual disk blocks, for example in sizes of 2, 4, or 16 Kbytes.

The highest degree of parallelization is offered by locks at the level of table rows (row level). This procedure, not yet offered by all database management systems, enables parallel access to different table rows of the same table, even if these rows are stored in the same disk block.

Most commercially available database management systems recognize various types of database locks. Differentiation into read locks (shared lock) and write locks (exclusive lock) is widespread. Read locks allow several parallel transactions to have joint read access to certain database contents while concurrent write access is excluded. However, if a transaction wants to change data in the database, it must place a write lock that excludes any parallel access by other transactions.

To improve the response time behavior of database systems, many manufacturers introduced additional lock levels that go beyond the crude differentiation into write locks and read locks. These include, for example, reading of data that has been changed by a parallel transaction but has not yet been released (read uncommitted). This procedure, also known as a "dirty read," ensures that write accesses to data never get lost and the database remains in a consistent state long-term, but it cannot avoid the fact that inconsistent data is read out short-term. Therefore, the software developer must decide from application to application if such a dirty read procedure delivers data of the required quality. This applies to application development with the ABAP/4 Development Workbench of the R/3 System, too (see Chapter 6).

3.5.4 SQL standards for relational database management systems

The standard for data query and data manipulation in relational database systems is set by the SQL (Structured Query Language, see Figure 3.21) language specified in the ISO 9075 norm.

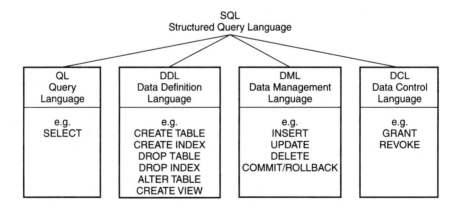

Figure 3.21 The structure of SQL.

The first SQL norm of 1987 was lacking important elements, which were consequently developed by the database manufacturers as proprietary extensions. In the new, 1992 version, SQL2, additional functions were added, for example standardization of dynamic SQL and access to remote databases (Remote SQL). The anticipated standard SQL3 is expected to contain additional complex data structures like bills of materials, language elements for database procedures (stored procedures), and mechanisms for event control (triggers). The most important concepts from SQL2 and SQL3 are briefly presented in the following list:

- **Static and dynamic SQL**: It is not always possible to fully describe a SELECT command during program development. This is the case, for example, if the user of a program is supposed to enter WHERE conditions interactively on the screen at run time. To meet this requirement, SQL commands can be executed not only statically, but also dynamically. In static SQL, the SQL commands are prepared by a pre-translator in such a way that the compiler can process them in the translation run that follows. This processing occurs independently of the execution that follows later. In dynamic SQL, on the other hand, the SQL commands are not prepared and compiled until the point of execution of the application program. Dynamic SQL is flexible and saves storage space, but uses more processing time at run time.

- **Stored procedures and triggers**: Stored procedures and triggers are procedural expansions of relational database concepts. With the help of stored procedures, application functions that have a high interaction rate with the database can be executed within the database system. Stored procedures are explicitly called by the higher-level application program. Triggers differ from stored procedures solely in that they are started by predefined events.

  Currently, stored procedures and triggers must be written in proprietary languages, which makes porting applications that use these techniques to other database environments very difficult. Additionally, intensive use of stored procedures and triggers can lead to a heterogeneous load that is unfavorable for the performance of the database computer.

- **Remote SQL**: With Remote SQL, access to relational databases becomes possible in distributed client/server environments, too. Database accesses are transmitted by the database system, fully transparent to the application, from the client to the server. In most cases, the transport protocol is TCP/IP.

- **Two-phase commit protocol (2PC)**: 2PC is the procedure used in distributed database systems to synchronize distributed transactions. 2PC consists of two phases:

- Prepare phase

- Commit phase.

In the prepare phase, all servers involved in the distributed transaction are polled to see if they can close their part of the current, distributed transaction. If all the computers involved agree, all of the database changes associated with the transaction are made on all computers permanently (COMMIT), otherwise the original condition is restored (ROLLBACK).

Distributed databases with 2PC can only partially fulfill the requirements of distributed applications. One problem is that distribution of data is possible only at table level. Also problematic is the fact that 2PC makes the unrealistic assumption that all of the computers and communication lines involved are always available. When one component is lost, all processing stops. In contrast, centralized database systems are more reliable, easier to administer, and cheaper to install and maintain.

• **Data replication**: Data replication is a possible alternative to distributed transactions based on 2PC. In this procedure, copies of data are distributed asynchronously by a lead system to the satellite systems. Data replication offers various advantages. Data access is considerably faster than with 2PC, because the data is stored locally. Also, processing can continue even if an individual component is lost. Procedures for data replication are offered, for example, by Oracle, Sybase, and others.

Relational database systems are generally recognized these days as base technology for business applications. Applications that exclusively use the SQL standard for query and manipulation of data are extremely portable, but in general offer very poor performance. Therefore, all leading manufacturers have implemented their own, performance-raising concepts in their database products. To nevertheless guarantee extensive interoperability of database products and applications by different manufacturers, the SQL Access Group (SAG), a union of leading American manufacturers, proposed various enhancements of SQL to the ISO. The ODBC interface (Open Database Connectivity) advanced by Microsoft is also based on these specifications.

3.5.5 Object-oriented and object-relational database management systems

Relational database management systems (RDBMS) have their advantages over database management systems that are organized in a hierarchical and network-like fashion, especially where independence of data and flexibility of data access are concerned. On the other hand, they offer hardly any support for complex, structured data objects, such as those common in technical or business applications. The representation of a complex data object in a number of normalized, relational tables calls to mind the driver of a car who doesn't put his whole automobile in the garage, but rather disassembles it and stores the individual components. No driver would go to such lengths, especially if he considered the fact that he would have to re-assemble the automobile before he could drive it again.

Like the driver who puts always away his automobile in drivable condition, object-oriented database management systems (OODBMS) also try to manage complex objects as a whole in the database. For example, an OODBMS can recognize a complete text document (book) that consists of different objects (chapters), which themselves consist of different objects such as sections, figures, and so on. By way of a class hierarchy, the database management system recognizes the type of every (sub) object. Every (sub) object disposes over its own methods (for example, for on-screen display) with the corresponding messages for activation.

Object-oriented database management systems are identified by four basic elements:

- Object model

- Object definition language (pattern definition in the database)

- Object manipulation language (expansion of existing object-oriented programming languages)

- Object query language.

Suppliers of relational database management systems occasionally dispute the necessity of OODBMS. They believe that relational database management systems can fulfill object-oriented demands with the introduction of large binary storage objects (BLOBs, Binary Large Objects). A problem, however, is the fact that relational database management systems cannot interpret the contents of a BLOB, since they know nothing or only very little about the internal structure of a BLOB.

Object-oriented database management systems, such as the ObjectStore product by Object Design Inc., have been commercially available for several years. Critics of OODBMS solutions argue that they essentially represent the hierarchical database concepts of the 1960s, disguised in new terminology. Access to objects stored in an object-oriented database proceeds, like in hierarchical database management systems, by navigation using references (pointers). Additional points of criticism of OODBMS products in existence today include:

- Insufficient support for multi-user environments

- No standardized query language

- No sophisticated security system.

One possible answer to these criticisms is the object-relational approach, such as that being pursued by UniSQL, Illustra, and HP (Odapter) (Davis, 1995). All three suppliers are attempting to integrated object-oriented procedures into the relational database environment.

Despite all of the discussion concerning object-oriented database management systems, the past has shown that new data management software spreads very slowly in companies. It took nearly 20 years for relational database management systems to become a generally recognized industry standard. Everything points to the fact that relational database management systems will remain first choice for some time to come. Object-oriented and object-relational database management systems, on the other hand, will first establish themselves as platforms for special applications.

3.5.6 Data warehouses and multidimensional database management systems

Transaction applications (OLTP, Online Transaction Processing) are distinguished by a multitude of parallel users, who read and change records in a common data set. Typical examples of such applications are "order entry," "financial accounting," and "invoicing." In addition to these record-oriented transaction applications, quantity-oriented analysis applications (OLAP, Online Analytical Processing) are gaining importance these days. The task of OLAP applications is to give decision makers in companies answers to strategic, multidimensional queries, for example "what were our sales of product X in time period Y in the countries A, B, and C in comparison to last year?" (five-dimensional query). The essential distinguishing characteristics of OLTP and OLAP applications are presented in Table 3.4.

Theoretically, OLTP and OLAP applications can be implemented on the basis of a common data set. However, because of the different processing profiles and to avoid mutual hindrances, it is recommended that the two worlds be separated, and that a separate data set with its own physical data storage be established for OLAP applications. This is called a data warehouse (PRISM, 1993) for OLAP applications.

A data warehouse can accept information from different sources. Before the transfer of data into the data warehouse, is it necessary to standardize this information, for example by implementing consistent names, measurements (for example, meters, inches, or yards), coding (for example, male/female or 1/0), key structures, and so on.

Table 3.4 Characteristics of OLTP and OLAP applications.

	OLTP	OLAP
Typical operation	Data change	Data analysis
Processing paradigms	Program-driven	User-driven
Data volume per access	Small	Large
Processing level	Basic data elements	Aggregates
Time frame	Present	Past, present, future

A data warehouse should support information applications that perform complex business analyses, forecasts, and data consolidations. This includes quick processing of multidimensional queries, a simple query language, support for any views, and different aggregate formats, as well as provision of special analysis functions such as time series analyses with calculation of moving averages. Currently still under heavy discussion is whether such queries can be covered by a traditional relational database management system, or if a new type of multidimensional database management system is required. Unlike relational database management systems, multidimensional database management systems do not store data in two-dimensional tables, but in multidimensional cubes. They are being promoted especially by the OLAP Council, which was founded in 1995 (Strange, 1995).

SAP's data warehouse concept is discussed in Section 7.2.5.

3.6 Transaction processing

The identifying characteristic of transaction processing systems is the consistent changing of a common data inventory by several online applications running in parallel. The first transaction systems were developed for airline reservations; today transaction processing is state-of-the-art for every online business application (OLTP Processing, Online Transaction Processing). Typical examples of business transactions are credit and debit entries in accounting, which are only meaningful together; in the same way, the creation of an order and the reservation of the associated materials go together.

Formally, a transaction is a sequence of processing steps that fulfills the ACID conditions (Atomic, Consistent, Isolated, Durable):

- **Atomic**: Transactions are indivisible. They fulfill the all-or-nothing condition. If a transaction is canceled, for example due to a system error or operator action, all incomplete changes to the database are reversed. This is an absolute requirement in financial applications, in which debit and credit entries must always be posted together.

- **Consistent**: By definition, successfully completed transactions leave the database in a consistent – meaning logically correct – state.

- **Isolated**: The isolation of transactions means that processing sequences have results that are independent of transactions that may be running in parallel. If two transactions want to change the same data simultaneously, one transaction must wait for the other to end.

- **Durable**: Successfully completed transactions cause lasting changes to the database. System errors that crop up later do not lead to the loss of these changes.

Since the 1960s, transaction applications have been developed on mainframe systems. Transaction monitors like IBM's CICS (Customer Information Control System) guarantee adherence to the ACID conditions.

Transaction monitors follow a typical assembly-line approach: business operations are divided into very simple, recurring tasks that operate under the control of the transaction monitor and are combined by the application logic into rigid operations. Applications based on transaction monitors are called TP-heavy.

Functions that were executed exclusively by transaction monitors in the past are today often elements of relational database systems. An example is secure transaction processing. As an alternative to TP-heavy applications, TP-lite applications are being increasingly offered, which carry out the transaction processing exclusively through use of database means. One problem with TP-lite applications, however, is that they function only in cooperation with relational databases. They also assume that a homogeneous database environment from a single manufacturer is being used.

For several years now, transaction monitors have also been available for open system platforms. Examples are Tuxedo (Novell), Top End (AT&T/NCR), CICS/6000 (IBM), ACMS (Digital), and Encina (Transarc/IBM). X/Open has defined a model in which distinctions are made between application (AP), resource manager (RM), for example of a database, and transaction manager (TM) (Figure 3.22). Without special transaction management services, applications can communicate directly with the resource manager, for example by using SQL. For communication between application and transaction manager, the APTM protocol was defined, and for message exchange between transaction manager and resource manager, the XA protocol was defined. Market penetration of these protocols is, however, still shallow. The APTM protocol, in particular, is being replaced by manufacturers' own interfaces. This makes porting of applications between different transaction monitors very difficult, even in the world of open systems.

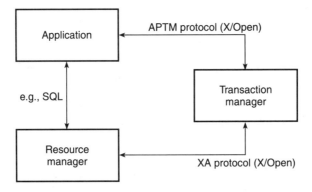

Figure 3.22 The X/Open model for transaction processing.

Another alternative on which secure transaction processing can be based is the use of portable 4GL development environments with a transaction-supporting runtime environment (middleware). Examples are Forté's "Cooperative Solutions" and SAP's "ABAP/4 Development Workbench." These systems allow the creation of portable, system-independent transaction applications, which can also run in heterogeneous environments. In addition, they have the potential to react flexibly to the current demands of business transaction processing. These days, the focus of business transaction processing is the automation of entire business process chains, not small, isolated processing steps. Long-lasting transactions and flexible, workflow-oriented processing sequences must be supported, as well as distributed, heterogeneous client/server installations. For this, suitable middleware is required that combines transaction management, workflow management, message queuing, and security management into a general, process-oriented transaction management.

3.7 Graphical user interfaces

The change in commercial data processing associated with the introduction of graphical user interfaces (Figure 3.23) can be compared to the re-orientation of DP when punch cards were replaced by alphanumeric terminals. Graphical user interfaces are easily and quickly learned, offer productivity advantages due to comfortable use and windowing technology, and are the basis for a multitude of new application types, such as graphical production control stations and graphically interactive planning systems.

The foundation for today's graphical user interfaces was laid in the 1970s with the development of the legendary Star system (Johnson et al., 1989) at Xerox PARC (Palo Alto Research Center). In 1984, Apple for the first time offered to the mass market a desktop system based on that work, the Macintosh. Microsoft followed with the introduction of Presentation Manager for OS/2 and Windows for MS-DOS. Graphical user interfaces for UNIX were developed on the basis of X Window, for example by OSF (Motif) and Sun/AT&T (Open Look) (see Section 3.7.1).

Graphical user interfaces are designed by manufacturers according to certain style guides, in which the interface model and the design of windows, menus, operating elements, and system messages are determined. Familiar style guides are

- CUA – Common User Access (IBM)

- Human Interface Guidelines (Apple)

- OSF/Motif Style Guide (OSF)

- Windows Interface (Microsoft).

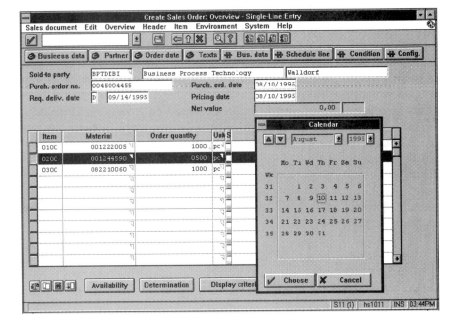

Figure 3.23 Example of a graphical user interface.
© SAP AG

All of the style guides listed are first and foremost technical manuals and focus less on the question of ergonomic design of graphical user interfaces. This aspect must therefore be addressed in supplemental documents. For this reason, for example, SAP has developed the SAP Style Guide on the basis of the style guides listed (Eberleh, 1994).

The design of ergonomic user interfaces should conform to generally recognized standards and norms. Of special importance are the EU90/270 EG guidelines of the European Union, which determine the requirements for ergonomic workstations, and the ISO 9241-10 norm, which defines and comprehensively documents seven design criteria for ergonomic software:

- Task appropriateness

- Intuitiveness

- Controllability

- Conformance to expectations

- Robust error handling

- Customizability

- Learnability.

Another important aspect of the user interface is the design of the help functions and the online documentation. Hypertext and hypermedia techniques are increasingly being applied here (see Hofmann and Simon, 1995). One example is Microsoft's help system WinHelp, for Windows systems. Hypertext systems process documents whose logical elements are linked in non-sequential fashion. This corresponds to the familiar organization of encyclopedias, with cross-references to supplemental information. Hypermedia systems go a step further. In addition to textual information, they can also store, link, and display multimedia documents.

In general, all graphical user interfaces have a similar look and feel. The programming interfaces, however, differ considerably in some cases. To make porting to a new system environment simple, applications should be engineered as independently as possible from a certain graphical user interface. Some 4GL environments, such as the ABAP/4 Development Workbench, offer the application developer a programming interface that is completely independent of the GUI being used. A change in the front-end remains invisible to the application and the application developer.

3.7.1 X Window

In most DP environments, applications that want to display data graphically on screen call certain library functions or system software functions. These functions perform the desired task (for example, draw_line) and do not return flow control to the calling application until afterwards.

A stronger separation of application logic and graphical screen display is made possible by special user interface servers. The most well-known example of a user interface server is X Window (Jones, 1991), developed in the mid-1980s at MIT (Massachusetts Institute of Technology) for graphical screen display in heterogeneous, networked UNIX system environments. In an X Window system (Figure 3.24), the task of the library or system software function mentioned above is taken over by a special application, the X server. The X server has total control over the screen. An application that wants to create a certain display on the screen is called an X client. When a display is desired, the X client sends an appropriate request in the form of a message to the X server. Communication between the X client and the X server proceeds asynchronously, meaning that the X client does not have to wait for the completion of its request by the X server, but instead immediately regains flow control of its program. The X server can respond to a message from the X client with its own message, but it does not have to.

The set of all possible messages between the X client and the X server is called the X protocol. An X server can simultaneously serve several X clients.

The functions of the X protocol are available in the Xlib library for developers who want to implement X clients. Supplemental toolkits, such as OSF/Motif Toolkit and X View Toolkit (AT&T, Sun), are available for creation of entire applications with menus and pushbuttons.

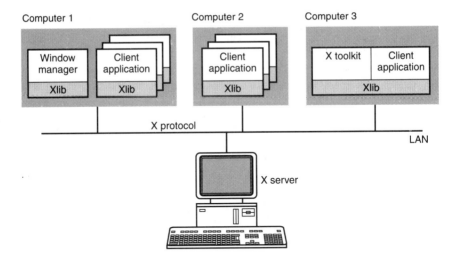

Figure 3.24 X Window environment.

X Window is an event-controlled system. X clients typically wait for a message from the X server to which they must react (for example, a call to refresh a window that became visible after another window was deleted). This method distinguishes X Window from procedural solutions in which the application prescribes a strict flow and interaction pattern.

The X server creates exclusively graphical displays according to the X protocol requests of the X clients. User functions such as controlling the size, position, or display sequence of stacked windows, however, are provided by a special X client, the window manager. Well-known window managers for X Window are OSF/Motif and Open Look (AT&T, Sun).

X clients are typically UNIX computers. An X server can be a UNIX workstation or a non-programmable X terminal. In addition, for several years now, X servers have been offered for DOS PCs and Macintosh computers. All variations of X clients are supported by the R/3 System.

Despite its elegant concept and its incorporation in the standardization process of ANSI and X/Open, X Window was unable to prevail against Microsoft Windows in the mass market.

3.8 Multimedia systems

Since the beginning of the 1980s, multimedia systems have been the object of computer science research, and today they are available in many products (Burger, 1995). They expand the classic, alphanumeric format of data processing with new information types like

- Graphics

- Images

- Audio

- Speech

- Video.

Documents put together using these information types are called multimedia documents (Figure 3.25).

To be able to edit, store, and transmit multimedia documents, the technical conditions first had to be created, along with the corresponding tools. Powerful

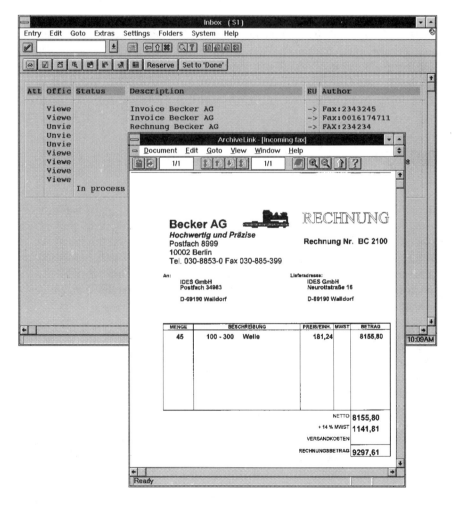

Figure 3.25 Multimedia processing with image integration.
© SAP AG

computers, new volume storage like optical disks, and broadband transmission networks make implementation of comfortable multimedia applications possible today.

An interesting application area for multimedia technology is, for example, electronic sales and information sites. These systems, also called kiosks, are marked by a high degree of user friendliness that is oriented toward the needs of the occasional user. Information input typically takes place using touch-sensitive screens (touch screens). Any multimedia information types can be used for information output. Kiosks can serve, for example, as interactive information systems at expositions, fairs, and so on, or they can serve as sales terminals that are available 24 hours a day.

As part of the COSE (Common Open Software Environment) initiative, HP, IBM, SunSoft, and other manufacturers are working on both a common communication interface for multimedia documents, called DMS (Distributed Media Service), and an integrated multimedia tool environment under the name of DIME (Distributed Integrated Media Environment). Since the spring of 1994, COSE has belonged to the OSF (Open Software Foundation).

3.9 Objects and components

Client/server applications are based on the implementation of individual services using special software modules. Clients can retrieve services of the service modules with dedicated interfaces. Further development of this approach is visible in object- and component-oriented procedures, which are based on consistent isolation of data and its processing methods within special software modules as well as message exchange between these modules over uniquely defined interfaces.

The object-oriented approach is characterized by the depiction of objects from the real world in program-internal software objects (Figure 3.26). Software objects have at their disposal data accessible only to them (attributes), and methods for manipulating this data. The communication between objects, meaning the calling of methods in the target object, takes place exclusively by message exchange (messaging). For this, every object has a uniquely defined interface at its disposal. When suitable software technologies such as CORBA (Common Object Request Broker Architecture, see Section 3.9.1) and OLE (Object Linking and Embedding, see Section 3.9.2) are used, message communication between objects is possible across application and computer boundaries, too.

In pure theory, the objects of an object-oriented software solution must fulfill the following requirements:

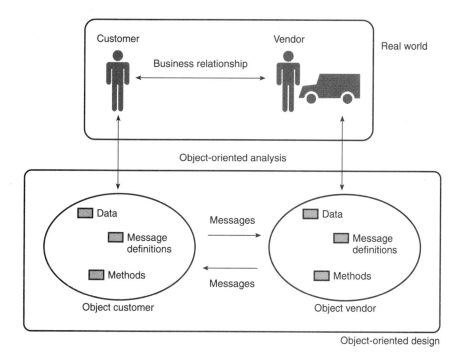

Figure 3.26 Object-oriented modeling of the real world.

- Objects are encapsulated (encapsulation). Data and implementation type of the methods of an object are known only to this object. Access to the data and methods of an object is only possible over the prescribed interfaces, with the help of messages.

- Objects are organized into classes (classification). Classes define the acceptable methods and data attributes for a certain set of objects. The objects belonging to a class are also called instances of this class.

- Data structures (attributes) and methods of a class are inheritable by subclasses (inheritance). In this way, different special classes can be derived very easily from a basic class. A basic "vehicles" class, for example, can be specialized into the subclasses "street vehicles," "rail vehicles," and so on.

- A message that is sent to different objects can produce different reactions (polymorphism). For example, the sending of a "display" message to objects of the "text document" and "multimedia document" classes starts different processing steps in each case. A prerequisite for this is late, dynamic binding (late binding) of the method program to the method call at run time.

Not all software architectures and programming languages that call themselves object-oriented fulfill all of the basic theoretical requirements for class hierarchy, inheritance, encapsulation, and polymorphism. In these cases a better term to use is object-based systems.

In different programming languages, objects can be constructed and communicate with each other according to different rules. To make programming-language-independent definition of objects possible, these rules are recorded in general object models. Well-known object models are Microsoft's COM (Component Object Model), IBM's SOM (System Object Model), and OMA (Object Management Architecture) from OMG (Object Management Group).

The term object orientation is used in many different ways, as seen in the following terms:

- Object-oriented user interfaces

- Object-oriented software architectures

- Object-oriented programming languages

- Object-oriented database management systems.

These four approaches are briefly outlined here:

- **User interfaces**: Object-oriented user interfaces offer the user familiar objects from the working world (letters, spreadsheets, filing cabinets, and so on) with corresponding operations (methods) for processing. The methods are tied directly to the objects and can, for example, be activated simply with the mouse, using Point&Click. A distinction between data (objects) and programs that process this data is becoming less and less of a necessity.

- **Software architectures**: Object-oriented software architectures are based on dynamically creatable and deletable software objects that fulfill the basic requirements mentioned above for an object-oriented software solution. It must be taken into account that the program conversion of an object-oriented software architecture is not necessarily tied to an object-oriented programming language. Object-oriented solutions can be implemented using 3GL and 4GL languages, too, building on object-oriented analysis and design methods.

  Implementation of object-oriented software solutions can proceed in several steps. Specifically, the object-oriented development process is divided into:

  - Object-oriented analysis (OOA)

  - Object-oriented design (OOD)

  - Programming

  - Testing and maintenance.

Object-oriented analysis is concerned with the following questions:

– How do I find the right objects for my application?

– Which objects from the real world need to be represented as software objects?

– Into which classes should my objects be organized?

Object-oriented design is the middle step between object-oriented analysis and object-oriented programming. While object-oriented analysis views the problem at hand exclusively from a specialized, application-oriented perspective, object-oriented design considers implementation perspectives. Object-oriented design ascertains how the objects, classes, and structures determined in the object-oriented analysis can be represented in an actual hardware and software environment.

Well-known OOA and OOD methods were developed by Rumbaugh et al., Coad/Yourdon, and Grady Booch (Schäfer, 1994).

• **Programming languages**: With special language elements, object-oriented programming languages (OOP) make possible the definition of classes and objects, inheritance of class attributes, and message exchange between objects. Object-oriented programming languages are used with the following goals:

– Reuse of program pieces

– Intuitive programming

– Short development cycles

– Simple program changes

– Easy program maintenance.

The use of object-oriented programming languages can greatly improve the implementation and maintenance of applications. On the other hand, inappropriately created inheritance and class hierarchies carry the danger, especially in the case of very large applications, of unnecessarily hampering flexibility in later development steps. Examples of object-oriented programming languages are C++ and Smalltalk.

• **Database management systems**: The relational database management systems widespread today have the disadvantage of having to represent complex, multidimensional and hierarchically structured objects of the real world in two-dimensional tables. Object-oriented and object-relational database management systems, on the other hand, try to achieve a more direct correspondence between objects in the real world and their representation in the database (see Section 3.5.5).

Software objects must be distinguished from software components. Software objects are structuring, technical modules that are only useful within a particular programming language. Software components, in contrast, represent complete, operational software modules that can be integrated using generally recognized, cross-language interfaces. The goal is to make software components from different manufacturers as easy to combine, say, as the components of stereo systems. The interfaces required for this sort of component interoperability are available, for example, with Microsoft's OLE/COM (Object Linking and Embedding/Common Object Model), OMG's CORBA (Common Object Request Broker Architecture) and IBM's OpenDoc/DSOM/SOM (Distributed System Object Model) (see Section 3.9.1 through 3.9.3).

Software objects and software components are playing an increasingly large role in the further development of the R/3 System (see Chapter 6).

3.9.1 CORBA

Distributed applications need mechanisms for ensuring the accessibility of all of the software components that exist in different places on the network. Pioneering work in this regard has been done by the non-profit organization OMG (Object Management Group), founded in 1989 by Digital, HP, HyperDesk, NCR, and Sun. The OMG's goals are the specification and distribution of commercially available, object-oriented, and object-based technologies. Together with X/Open, the OMG in 1992 defined a Common Object Request Broker Architecture (CORBA), whose core is an Object Request Broker (ORB) for exchange of transparent message relations between distributed software components. An ORB uses message interfaces to transmit requests from client components to server components or to deliver results. The interfaces themselves are specified with the CORBA Interface Definition Language (CORBA IDL).

CORBA is an object-based, not object-oriented, technology. Topics such as class hierarchies and the inheritance of data attributes and methods are not addressed by CORBA. Moreover, CORBA is only familiar with interface inheritance. An ORB that fulfills the CORBA specification can be used in an object-oriented environment as well as in a non-object-oriented environment, in which the individual software components are implemented in a traditional 3GL or 4GL, for example.

CORBA is a part of the OMG's Object Management Architecture (OMA) (Figure 3.27). OMA objects (application objects) use general services (common services) such as help, time, printing, and security services. In addition, there are special services (object services) such as naming, or copying and deleting of objects. These services are used by the Object Request Broker itself to complete its tasks.

No interoperability between ORBs by different manufacturers has been achieved on the basis of the first CORBA specification of 1992. This imperative requirement for non-proprietary, component-oriented software solutions was not taken into account until the recently passed CORBA 2 specification.

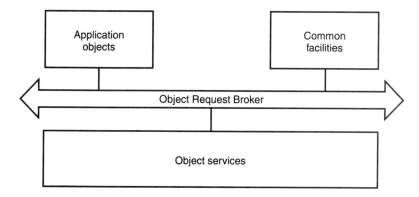

Figure 3.27 OMG's Object Management Architecture (OMA).

3.9.2 OLE/COM

Microsoft's solution for the construction of documents and applications from reusable components is OLE (Object Linking and Embedding). The current version of OLE, OLE2, is based entirely on the object-based Microsoft model COM (Common Object Model) (Figure 3.28). Unlike other products, OLE does not follow the CORBA specification.

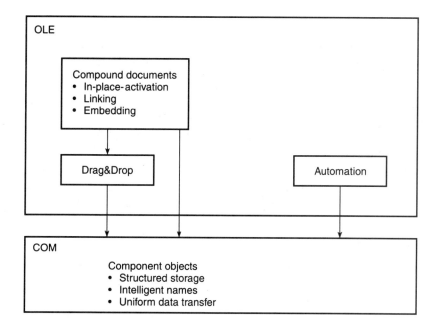

Figure 3.28 COM as the basis of OLE.

The basic principle of COM is programming-language-independent specification of reusable objects by definition of their interfaces. Although COM is familiar with message interfaces and encapsulation, it is not familiar with inheritance. Objects that are implemented in accordance with the COM specification are called Component Objects.

OLE itself is best described as "component oriented." The elements of OLE are:

- **Compound documents**: Compound documents are documents that contain objects from different applications. They are therefore also known as compound objects. Applications that create objects for compound documents are called servers. The compound documents themselves are created by container applications. Objects can be either embedded in a compound document (embedding) or inserted with a reference (linking). To the extent supported by the container application, data objects of a compound document can be edited, displayed, recorded, or played, without having to change to another window. This is called in-place processing or visual editing.

  Of particular importance for the looming market for reusable software components are OLE Custom Controls (OCX). These are embeddable objects that support in-place processing and OLE communication and are sold, for example, by software houses.

- **Drag&Drop**: Mouse-controlled procedure for data exchange between different applications, windows, and objects.

- **Automation**: Procedure for cross-application programming, with whose help applications can manipulate the objects of other applications (see Section 3.3.6).

OLE is delivered by Microsoft with all operating systems as a freely available base technology. Developers who want to implement OLE-capable applications can use the required program libraries (Dynamic Link Libraries, DLLs) for free.

Microsoft is continually developing OLE. Support for OLE by the operating systems UNIX and MVS (IBM) has already been announced. In addition, Microsoft is planning OLE extensions for company-wide applications with

- Network OLE (network communication between components, based on DCE RPC)

- OLE Transaction (transaction processing)

- OLE DB (access to any desired data sources).

3.9.3 OpenDoc/SOM

As an alternative to the compound document concept established by Microsoft with OLE, IBM, in cooperation with Apple, Novell, and others, is trying to establish OpenDoc as a platform-independent compound document standard (Figure 3.29). Characteristics of OpenDoc are:

- Compound document concept

- Drag&Drop support

- In-place processing

- Network capability.

OpenDoc is based on IBM's SOM/DSOM (System Object Model/Distributed SOM) object model. SOM offers a method for programming-language-independent formation of class libraries and a corresponding runtime environment.

SOM is made network-capable by DSOM. DSOM includes all SOM classes that enable calling of SOM objects in foreign address spaces. The DSOM class library meets the CORBA specification of the Object Management Group (OMG).

SOM was originally developed by IBM as an object model for OS/2. Today, SOM is also available for AIX, Windows, and Mac System 7. Support for additional platforms is planned. SOM/DSOM allows inheritance, encapsulation, and polymorphism and is thus more object-oriented than, say, Microsoft's COM.

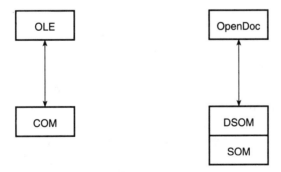

Figure 3.29 OLE and OpenDoc.

3.10 Development tools for client/server applications

Powerful development tools are required for the creation of client/server applications, and they should be integrated in a uniform working environment. In addition to the actual programming language, the following components belong to such a tool environment:

- Editors

- Interface builders for the creation of graphical user interfaces

- Report builders for the programming of any and all database analyses

- Test and monitoring tools for program optimization

- Debuggers for error analysis

- Repositories for management of development objects and descriptive metadata

- Modeling tools

- Tools for the management of software development projects

- Software management tools.

Repositories, modeling tools, and software management tools are relatively new concepts and are briefly discussed here.

- **Repositories**: Repositories hold the development objects created with modern development environments, such as programs, screens, documentation, and so on, as well as all of the accumulated metadata, that is, descriptions of the individual development objects. Repositories are tailor-made by the manufacturers for their development tools and methods. Data exchange between different repositories is possible through standards like CDIF (CASE Data Interchange Format) from EIA (Electronics Industry Association). Texas Instruments and Microsoft have recently agreed on common development of a non-proprietary, open standard for repositories.

- **Modeling tools**: Modeling tools provide the necessary overview of business objects and processes. This is the basis for both optimization of business processes and successful introduction and company-specific customization of standard business application solutions. The Gartner Group assumes that evaluation costs can be reduced by at least 30%, and implementation costs by at least 8%, if the application software is documented by logical models (Brown and Rin, 1994).

- **Software management tools**: Software management tools are required by large teams of developers and in the use of software in distributed environments. They must cover three task areas:

– **Source code management**
Control of access at source code level, including version management.

– **Configuration management**
Management of the individual components of an application.
Creation of executable modules.

– **Software distribution**
Distribution of executable modules on target computers in the network.

Software management tools are either part of modern 4GL software development environments or are offered separately, for example by Intersolv (PVCS) or Legent (Endevor) (Conway, 1994).

3.10.1 Classification of programming languages

The area of programming languages changes quickly and is becoming increasingly unwieldy. To facilitate an overview, programming languages are divided into different generations.

The first generation of programming languages emerged in 1950, at the beginning of the computer age. At the time, there were no compilers or interpreters. The machine language used could not be ported to other system platforms, since the commands were oriented directly to the hardware addresses.

With the introduction of symbolic addressing at the end of the 1950s, the second generation of programming languages was introduced. Symbolic addresses were copied by assemblers onto hardware addresses.

The combination of several computer instructions into a more powerful command led to the emergence in the 1960s and 1970s of the third-generation programming languages, like COBOL. The third-generation catchphrase was high-level programming, meaning programming on a logical level independent of machine properties. Over the course of time, various third-generation programming languages were standardized. This made programs more easily portable to other systems.

From the first third-generation languages, new languages were soon developed that went far beyond the simple combination of machine language commands in their principles. The terms structured programming and data type emerged. These programming languages made it possible to design larger programs in a clear fashion, by allowing them to be divided into individual function modules. An example of an early language that supports these possibilities in its language concept is Modula-2. The concept of function modules already made the reusability of program code possible, since the modules could be translated separately and incorporated in other programs.

With the fourth-generation languages available since the end of the 1970s, definition and identification are increasingly difficult. These languages, also called 4GL languages, are powerful programming languages with full development environments or development tools. It is the goal of these 4GLs to quickly and easily create efficient and easy-to-maintain applications. Typical terms from this generation are rapid prototyping and rapid application development (RAD).

In general, one can assume that the choice of a 4GL development environment will result in a moderate productivity gain of 2.5 to 1 in relation to conventional 3GL languages. The Gartner Group (Brown and Rin, 1994) gives these reasons for this productivity gain:

- Interface builders with a graphical user interface

- Libraries of predefined function modules

- Dictionary- or repository-based validation of field contents and customization of field and report formats

- Optimized software creation in a complete, interactive development process (edit, compile, debug, test)

- Isolation of the application from system-specific programming

- Support of rapid prototyping.

Most fourth-generation languages and development environments are tied to a platform and a database system. This is one of the reasons why there are no standards in this generation. The transition to the next language generation, the fifth, has not yet occurred. It is the highly developed 4GL development environments, for example those of Compuware/Uniface, Forté, and SAP (ABAP/4 Development Workbench, see Chapter 6), that should jump the generation gap. The emphasis in this transition is on the portability and openness of the languages or development environments. Object-oriented concepts play an increasingly large role.

The porting of applications developed with highly developed 4GL languages is possible without modification of the software. Target and development platforms can be either mainframes, larger midrange systems, or PCs. Additional aspects of these development environments are the efficient use of reusable program components, the use of CASE (Computer Aided Software Engineering) tools, and the support of different database systems. Complete transition to the fifth generation will not take place until standards and de facto standards are introduced with extensive interoperability between the development environments of different manufacturers.

3.10.2 Selection of client/server development tools for company-wide applications

The development of client/server applications is becoming easier and easier – when viewed superficially. Powerful GUI (graphical user interface) builders enable fast creation of sophisticated graphical user interfaces. Visual methods support fast and comfortable linking of these user interfaces to the database management system. But that alone is not enough for the development of high-end applications, that is, of applications that support or even make possible the core operations in companies.

High-end applications have many layers of functions, operate with large numbers of users, transaction rates, and data volumes, are implemented in distributed, heterogeneous system environments, and cooperate with very different foreign applications. Development tools for high-end applications should have a graphical user interface and be easy to learn and use. In addition, the following aspects should be considered in the selection of a tool.

Aspects that affect the development environment itself

- How is the representation of objects and operations from the real world as internal program structures carried out? Which modeling procedures are supported for the representation of business data and processes?

- What capabilities are there for prototyping?

- How are individual reports developed?

- How is the creation of multilingual, international applications supported?

- Does the programming environment offer support for special application requirements, for example automatic currency conversion for internationally designed applications?

- What sorts of interfaces are there to other programming languages and applications?

- What sort of tools for measurement and analysis are available for optimizing the behavior of developed applications?

- Can true client/server applications be realized, with flexible distribution (partitioning) of application modules on different computers?

- How is the work of large development teams supported?

Aspects that affect the runtime environment for the developed applications

- What is the situation with regard to the scalability of developed applications in light of a growing volume of data and transactions?

- Can the runtime environment guarantee the required response times even with a high load?

- How portable are developed applications? Are different operating systems, database management systems, and graphical user interfaces supported?

- Does the runtime environment fulfill the requirements for security and reliability?

- Does the runtime environment offer sufficient support for application management, from installation, to distribution, to monitoring and optimizing of high-end applications?

Finally, a number of strategic company aspects influence the decision for a high-end development environment:

- Planned development platforms (hardware, system software)

- Planned target platforms (hardware, system software)

- Know-how and profile of the employees in question

- Existing and planned applications to be possibly integrated

- Price considerations

- Planned time frame

- Stability and future prospects of the tool supplier.

3.11 The importance of standards for client/server systems

3.11.1 What are standards?

Standards are generally recognized rules for the design of systems, components, and interfaces. Standards emerge through majority use and not by being proclaimed by an official authority.

In the DP world, the term open systems was developed for systems whose creation took into consideration generally recognized standards for interfaces, services, and data formats. Standards and common interfaces are of major importance, especially for client/server systems, which integrate many components from different manufacturers.

The standards used today in the DP area can be classified into

- industry standards (for example, TCP/IP, NFS, SNMP)

- official standards (for example, from ISO, CCITT)

- standards from the non-profit organization X/Open

- standards from market-oriented groups (for example, OSF, OMG, OAG).

National as well as multinational and international groups participate in the standardization process. In general, various degrees of maturity can be seen in the published standards and norms: official standards drafted at the drawing board are often overtaken by evolutionary standards defined by use and dissemination. An example is the success of the TCP/IP protocol family as opposed to the OSI protocols. Often, several standardization approaches for the same problem exist side by side. In contrast, in some other areas like repository structure (see Section 3.10), there are to date no generally recognized standards.

3.11.2 Use of standards to benefit the user

Standards create independence, create a basis for portable applications, and set the conditions for the integration of heterogeneous systems.

As a rule, DP personnel in companies do not pursue the goal of greater independence from hardware and software vendors because they want to install a colorful, cluttered diversity of hardware and software modules by different manufacturers in their computer centers and departments. Rather, they need the security of knowing that today and in the future they can effectively connect several systems and speed the flow of information both in their company and across company boundaries. The most important aspect of DP strategies in the 1990s is the ability to meet the needs of the end users better, more quickly and in a more up-to-date fashion. That is why there is a series of good reasons for the users' wish for greater independence from the proprietary interfaces that their hardware and software suppliers offer them:

- Applications and data should be easily transferable to different system environments.

- Company-wide relevant data should be accessible from any application and every computer.

- Applications should present themselves to the user with the same look and feel, independent of the hardware and software vendors. For this, conformance to generally recognized, non-proprietary design guidelines is necessary.

- Modifications and expansions to the existing hardware and software infrastructure should be integratable, independent of specific vendors.

- Effective communication between various hardware and software components should be guaranteed even with the use of products from different
  manufacturers.

Despite all of the advantages of standardized systems, it is clear that not all
innovative solutions can always follow recognized standards. Innovations and
standards are even mutually exclusive in some ways, since completely new ideas
and technologies do not immediately find general acceptance. Only successful
competition with alternative concepts can lead to broader dissemination and
official or industry standards.

Chapter 4

What Is the R/3 System?

According to a June 1995 study by IDC (International Data Corporation), "Client/server Applications: Forecast and Leading Vendors Final Estimate for 1994," SAP with its R/3 System is the most successful supplier of client/server applications (IDC, 1995). With R/3 product sales of over 600 million US dollars, SAP has a greater market share (9.8%) than the next three suppliers combined: Lotus (4.8%), Oracle (2.6%), and Microsoft (2.0%). The total R/3 market, including infrastructure such as hardware, database management systems, and consulting, has been estimated at over 5 billion US dollars for 1994 by AMR (Advanced Manufacturing Research) (AMR, 1994).

The R/3 System is based on SAP's more than 20 years of development experience in real-time business applications. "R/3" stands for Real-time System, Version 3. Its predecessors, "R/1" and "R/2," were likewise real-time systems, albeit for mainframes. The R/2 System is still in use today in over 2000 enterprises.

The following principles served as guidelines in the development of the R/3 System:

- Coverage of all business processes. Guarantee of consistent business data across all process stages and organizational entities.

- Consideration of customer requirements in different branches of industry and countries.

- Decoupling of application solutions from system functions by a clear layer architecture, with an application layer (see Chapter 7) and a basis layer (see Chapter 5).

- Early decision to use future-oriented technology. The R/3 architecture is based on a multilayer client/server concept with methods for control of master–slave relationships between individual software components. Special servers can be installed for certain tasks without losing the integration of data and processes across the entire system.

The applications of the R/3 System are based on an overall business model that makes possible a uniform view of all data and business processes in the enterprise. The overall model covers the following application areas (see Chapter 7):

- Financial Accounting
- Controlling
- Asset Management
- Materials Management
- Production Planning
- Sales & Distribution
- Quality Management
- Plant Maintenance
- Project Management
- Service Management
- Human Resources
- Office Communication
- Workflow Functions
- Industry Solutions
- Open Information Warehouse

The business applications of the R/3 System are supplemented by software development tools that make possible both the creation of custom solutions and the extension of the standard R/3 applications (see Chapter 6). Additional tools are available for implementing the R/3 System at the customer site and for controlling and monitoring the system under normal operation. These are described in Chapter 8 and Section 5.8.

4.1 History of the R/3 System

The milestones in the evolution of the R/3 System illuminate the close link between this solution and changes in the DP industry. Time-to-market, fast conversion of paradigm changes, and the departure from mainframe solutions required early, future-oriented design decisions. The R/3 System was developed for computer platforms which at the beginning of the project had only just emerged in the laboratories of hardware manufacturers, or which were still only objects of theoretical consideration.

1987 In May, IBM announces the SAA (System Application Architecture) concept. Essential elements of SAA were the implementation of platform-independent applications, the use of graphical user interfaces, and the integration of relational database management systems. Although SAA eventually failed, because it was limited exclusively to IBM platforms and did not want to integrate UNIX systems into the architecture, its fundamental ideas were nevertheless groundbreaking for future development. Already in 1987, SAP began to turn these concepts into the new R/3 project, though with a broader approach that included open systems. At that time, the policy decisions for the development of the R/3 System were:

- Use of relational database management systems

- New data design

- Development of the runtime environment in the C programming language

- Implementation of applications in ABAP/4

- Design Guide for the user interface, based on recognized standards.

1988 UNIX becomes the preferred development platform for the R/3 System. At this point, there are no all-inclusive business applications for UNIX. UNIX is essentially established in the area of technical and scientific applications.

The first data models are developed.

SAP has its first experiences with a client/server environment. SAP's development centers boast one of the world's largest, heterogeneous client/server infrastructures to date, with hundreds of database and application servers, several thousand PCs as presentation systems, and powerful FDDI networks and WAN links. Experience with this infrastructure was turned into methods and functions for managing all manner of different configurations in the R/3 System.

1989 The first R/3 System applications are presented at the CeBIT Conference in Hanover, Germany.

1991 Financial Accounting and the software development tools are installed at pilot customer sites.

1992 In January, the decision is made to go with an entirely graphical user interface. At this time, there are only a few business applications on the market that include graphical screen functions as a fundamental part of their architecture.

In October of this year, the first R/3 customer goes live.

1993 In April, Microsoft and SAP begin cooperation to integrate PC applications like Word, Excel, Project, and Access with the business applications. At this point, most R/3 customers already use Windows systems for presentation.

The R/3 System experiences overwhelming success in the American market during this year.

In addition to the UNIX platforms, availability of the system on Windows NT is announced. At the end of the year, porting is accomplished unusually quickly in just a few days.

With "Application Link Enabling (ALE)," SAP begins a development initiative that is groundbreaking for the design of distributed applications. ALE allows message-based, asynchronous linking of distributed, but still integrated, applications across system boundaries.

1994   SAP opens a new development center in the USA. The focus here is on development of new software technology for the R/3 System.

At the beginning of the year, with R/3 Release 2.1, a complete Kanji version becomes available for the Japanese market.

1995   In the fall, R/3 Release 3.0 is released, with a function scope and capability that exceed those of the mainframe system R/2. OLE Automation is supported. The first standard ALE solutions are implemented.

With the integrated Reference Models, the Procedure Model, the Implementation Guide, and the "Business Navigator," a complete infrastructure is available for carrying out R/3 implementation projects.

With its "Business Object Repository," "Open Object Interface," and expansion of the ABAP/4 language, the R/3 System embodies initial object-oriented concepts.

Configure to Order (CTO) is a development initiative that is begun with Release 3.0. The goal is system-supported, custom configuration of customer systems. Using this method, system implementation for mid-sized companies, for example, can be further simplified.

With the new generation of IBM's AS/400 computer, the R/3 System supports an additional, widely distributed platform.

At the end of 1995, over 4000 systems are installed, with approximately 350 000 users.

Chapter 5

The Technical Architecture of the R/3 System

5.1 Principles of the basis architecture

The R/3 System is based on a software-oriented, multilayer client/server architecture (see Section 2.1). For this reason, the R/3 System has a modular structure with methods for controlling master–slave relationships between individual software components. Special servers linked by communication networks can be used for certain tasks without losing the integration of data and processes in the overall system (Plattner et al., 1993).

The structure of the R/3 System follows a layer model with largely independent function layers connected by interfaces. The main layers portrayed in Figure 5.1 are:

- Basis layer

- Application layer.

The basis layer contains the middleware of the R/3 System (see Section 1.5). This middleware makes the applications independent of the system interfaces of the operating system, database system, and communication system used and ensures optimal handling of the business transactions. On the basis layer sits the application layer, which implements the business functions and processes of the R/3 System. The basis layer is written in the C and C++ programming languages, while the application layer is written in the 4GL language ABAP/4 (see Chapter 6).

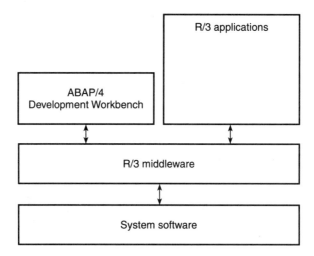

Figure 5.1 Layer architecture of the R/3 System.

The R/3 System follows internationally recognized standards and open interfaces:

- **TCP/IP** as the transport protocol in networks (see Section 3.3.4).

- **RFC** (Remote Function Call) as the open high-level programming interface (see Sections 3.3.6 and 5.3.2). With the help of RFC, application functions on other computers can be called.

- **CPI-C** for program-to-program communication beyond computer boundaries (see Sections 3.3.6 and 5.3.1). With CPI-C, any number of communication operations between computers can take place.

- **SQL** and **ODBC** for access to the R/3 System business data stored in relational databases (see Sections 4.5.2 and 5.6).

- **OLE/DDE** and **RFC** for integration of PC applications (see Sections 3.3.6, 3.9.2 and 5.3.2).

- **X.400/X.500** as the open electronic mail interface (see Sections 3.3.6 and 7.2.6).

- **EDI** for the exchange of trade data at the application level (see Sections 3.3.6 and 7.5.5).

- **ALE** (Application Link Enabling) for online integration of decentralized applications through the exchange of business objects (see Section 7.5.7).

- **Open interfaces** for particular applications like CAD (Computer-Aided Design), optical archiving, and technical subsystems in the production area, for example for plant data collection (see Sections 7.5 and 7.5.4).

Because of the open architecture of the R/3 System, there are virtually no portability restrictions.

- The R/3 System can run at full capacity on all major UNIX platforms, on Windows NT (Microsoft), and on AS/400 (IBM).

- Various database systems can be used, for example Informix Online, Oracle 7, ADABAS D from Software AG, IBM's DB2/6000, and Microsoft's SQL Server 6.0.

- The graphical user interface of the R/3 System (SAP GUI) can run on various desktop systems, such as OS/2 Presentation Manager, OSF/Motif, Macintosh, and Windows.

The multilayer architecture of the R/3 System makes possible the decoupling of the application logic from the presentation and the database, which is the pre-requisite for load distribution in client/server configurations, even in very large installations with several thousand users. Implementation of separate servers for particular tasks makes optimal use of the performance potential and the different cost structures of available hardware architectures. Examples of servers that execute particular tasks are:

- Database servers for the central database. As well as single-processor systems, multiprocessor systems and cluster configurations can be used.

- Powerful, inexpensive single- or multiprocessor computers for the application logic. Application servers need not have monitors or hard disks. The number of computers and processors used can be adjusted to meet performance requirements.

- Computers for additional special tasks, for example for optical archi-ving, delivery of X.400 messages, mail services, or offline background processing.

- Presentation servers under Windows, OS/2, UNIX, or Macintosh System 7.x for implementation of a graphical user interface.

The R/3 basis architecture has the following features:

- **Scalability**: The multilayer client/server architecture allows easy adjustment (scaling) of the installed computer performance, for instance in the case of amended load profiles due to increasing numbers of users or due to the use of additional application components. The installation sizes possible with the R/3 System are shown in Figure 5.2.

- **Portability**: The portability of the R/3 System secures the investments of R/3 customers in the application software and in the design of business operations, since the life of business application software, up to 10 years or more, is considerably longer than the short innovation cycles of hardware components, operating systems, and databases.

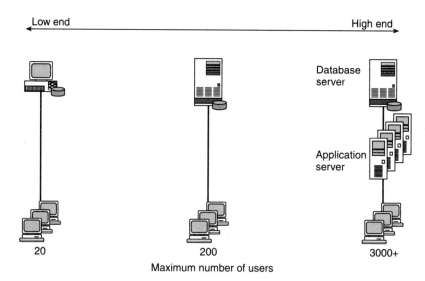

Figure 5.2 Scalability of R/3 installations.

- **Interoperability and openness**: The integration of the data and functions of R/3 applications with external applications using open, standardized interfaces like OLE (Object Linking and Embedding) and RFC (Remote Function Call) makes integrated company information management using decentralized PC applications possible.

- **Customizability**: R/3 Customizing (see Section 8.2.4) enables fast and simple modification of standard applications to meet individual requirements, both during implementation of the R/3 System and later, when business processes are altered. Development of in-house software is possible with the ABAP/4 Development Workbench, which is integrated in the R/3 System (see Chapter 6).

- **Graphical user interface**: SAP GUI is the standards-oriented graphical user interface of the R/3 System. It is optimized for typical business operations such as those in logistics or accounting. Since its design elements and logic are similar to those of PC applications, it can be learned easily and used intuitively.

5.2 R/3 configurations

An essential characteristic of the R/3 architecture is the fact that various program modules can be distributed flexibly across different computers, also known as partitioning of applications. This software-oriented client/server approach differs fundamentally from the hardware-oriented approach, in which certain computers are installed for certain tasks only (see Section 2.1). This gives users great flexibility in planning and operating their R/3 installation. Centralized configurations are just as possible as distributed solutions with a multitude of special servers (Figure 5.3).

The individual program modules of the R/3 System provide different services. The fundamental services are the following:

- **Presentation services** for implementation of the graphical user interface

- **Application services** for handling of the application logic

- **Database services** for storage and recovery of business data.

These basic services are supplemented, for example, by printing services, security services, and communication services.

In a central R/3 configuration, all processing tasks are handled by one computer. In principle, this corresponds to conventional mainframe processing, with X terminals instead of alphanumeric terminals.

Two-layer R/3 configurations are typically set up with special presentation servers that are responsible exclusively for preparing the graphical user interface. Many R/3 users use Windows PCs as presentation servers, for example.

An alternative two-layer configuration involves the installation of powerful desktop systems, on which presentation and applications run together. Such configurations are particularly well suited for processing-intensive applications (for example, simulations) or for software development.

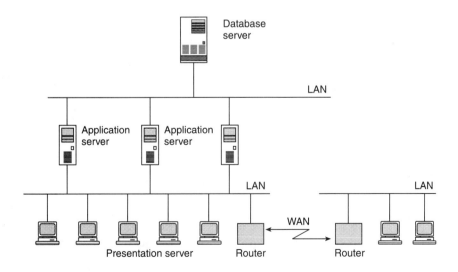

Figure 5.3 Example of an R/3 configuration.

With three or more layers, separate computers are used for presentation, application, and database. This takes advantage of the differences in cost structure when planning the performance in the front-end and back-end areas. The data from one database server is available to many application servers in parallel. Applications on different application servers exchange information using program-to-program communication protocols. To achieve the most balanced load distribution on individual computers and thereby achieve optimal performance, special application servers can be installed for individual work areas.

Owing to its largely hardware-independent system design, the R/3 System is executable on many different platforms (see Section 5.1). Both homogeneous R/3 installations, with computers and operating system from only one manufacturer, and heterogeneous R/3 installations, with different system platforms, are possible.

5.3 Network communication

The Internet protocol TCP/IP has prevailed as the standard transport protocol for open systems (see Section 3.3.4). It is available on all operating systems supported by the R/3 System. For this reason, TCP/IP was chosen for communication within the R/3 client/server system. Connection of the R/3 System to IBM mainframes is achieved through the SNA (System Network Architecture) protocol LU6.2. In principle, the R/3 architecture can be expanded to include additional protocols, for example the OSI transport protocols, since the independence of R/3 applications from the underlying system interfaces is assured even in network communications. Figure 5.4 provides an overview of the protocols used in the R/3 environment.

On top of the transport protocol implemented, the SAP presentation protocol is used for data exchange between presentation and application servers, and the Remote SQL protocol of the database manufacturer is used for data transfer between application and database servers. The SAP presentation protocol is structured in such a way as to enable linking of presentation computers to the R/3 System over a WAN (Wide Area Network), as well. However, the link between application and database servers should be established over a LAN (Local Area Network) because of the high data transfer volume associated with Remote SQL.

5.3.1 Basic services for communication

In communication over networks, a distinction is made between synchronous, that is, alternately time-dependent, and asynchronous, that is, time-independent, data exchange. People, too, can exchange synchronized (conversation) or asynchronous (letter) information. For application programming with ABAP/4, basic services for both kinds of communication are available.

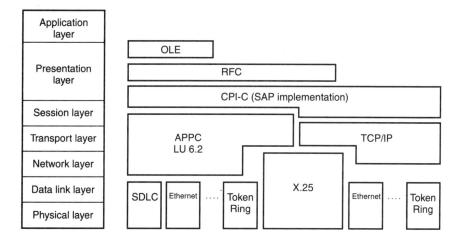

Figure 5.4 Protocol layers in the R/3 area.

Synchronous communication is accomplished with functions from the CPI-C (Common Programming Interface – Communication) standard described in Section 3.3.6. The CPI-C "Starter Set" (see Table 3.3) has been implemented, as have additional functions, for example for data conversion. Program-to-program communication basically proceeds over an internal software gateway, which takes care of the conversion from CPI-C communication to externally used transport protocols such as TCP/IP or LU6.2.

In many situations, business applications require an asynchronous communication mechanism instead of synchronous communication. This is the case, for example, if processing in the target system is to be started manually or if the target system is temporarily not in a position to accept data. In such situations, the R/3 System can temporarily store the data in queues designed for this purpose and send it at a later time. The mechanism for managing such queues is called Q-API (Queue Application Programming Interface). It can be integrated into application programs at any desired point.

5.3.2 Higher-level communication interfaces

Remote Function Call (RFC) is the protocol for system-internal and cross-system calls of special ABAP/4 subroutines identified as function modules. These are managed in separate function libraries in the R/3 System (see Section 6.2.4). A function module call across computer boundaries differs from a local call only in that a particular parameter (destination) determines the target computer on which the program should be executed (Figure 5.5). It is generally true that R/3 applications, R/2 applications, and even external applications can be used as RFC communication partners. In all three cases, RFC calls are possible in both directions, meaning:

Computer 1

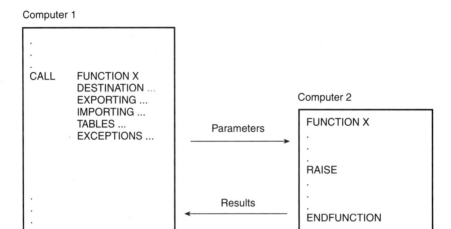

Figure 5.5 Remote Function Call (RFC).

- Call of external services from ABAP/4 programs over Remote Function Call

- Use of R/3 services by external applications with the help of RFC.

Remote Function Call is used for both synchronous and asynchronous communication (see Section 6.2.4).

Function modules can be called by external Windows systems using OLE Automation, too (see Section 3.9.2). The basis for this is the RFC Automation Server (see Section 7.5.2). For access to external OLE Automation servers, the ABAP/4 language was expanded to include an open object interface (see Section 6.2.4). OLE Automation is thus the second important higher-level program-to-program communication interface of the R/3 System, after RFC.

Additional R/3 communication interfaces are located at application level (see Chapter 7). These include EDI (Electronic Data Interchange), ALE (Application Link Enabling), and BDC (Batch Data Communication), as well as the SAPoffice interfaces for electronic mail and telematic services (teletext, telefax, and so on).

5.4 Presentation services

The layer of the R/3 client/server architecture that presents the user interface to users is the presentation layer. R/3 presentation services include modules for the representation of various document and graphic types as well as the required communication services. A dispatcher coordinates the work of the individual components of the R/3 presentation service.

The graphical user interface of the R/3 System, the SAP GUI, is portable and is offered by SAP on Windows, OS/2 Presentation Manager, OSF/Motif, and Apple Macintosh. In principle, the same functionality is provided on all platforms, that is, the look and feel of the R/3 applications are largely independent of the choice of presentation system. If a user has learned how to use the R/3 System on one platform, he or she does not have to switch thought processes when changing to another platform.

5.4.1 Ergonomic interface design

The use of R/3 applications is based on knowledge gained from ergonomics research and SAP's own ergonomics lab (Eberleh, 1994). In this laboratory, researchers and users alike test the usability of SAP software. The knowledge gained from the tests, which are standardized according to EC 90/270 and ISO 9241, flows directly into current development. For instance, every screen includes a toolbar that contains the most important standard functions. The symbols always appear in the same order. With the menu bars, too, care was taken to ensure that in different applications the user would always find the standard functions in the same position.

The design norms for the R/3 user interface are stipulated in the SAP Style Guide. This document is based on the Windows Style Guide as well as the CUA, OSF/Motif, and Apple Macintosh guidelines. All SAP applications are designed according to the SAP Style Guide. This has the advantage that the R/3 user always has a consistent work environment. Training in new applications and use of features in applications that are already available are therefore greatly simplified. The uniformity achieved with the help of the SAP Style Guide affects all parts of the interface design:

- **Online help**: Online help gives the online user documentation on using R/3 applications. It works with hypertext references, making navigation between different information units possible. Help functions that are always available offer various methods of access to the online help, for instance through the glossary or directly from within the application. On Windows presentation systems, online help is offered with the help of Microsoft's WinHelp.

- **Control elements**: In addition to input and output fields, there are check boxes, table controls (table display), pushbuttons, and radio buttons. Scroll bars are implemented wherever more information is available than fits on the screen.

- **Menus**: All functions of the R/3 applications can be reached via menus. The menus are uniformly structured system-wide: From the root menu, the user branches to one of the R/3 application areas, for example Materials Management, Sales and Distribution, or Accounting. At the next level, the application-area level (for example, Purchasing), the user chooses a concrete task, say "Change Purchase Order" or "Create Client." After that, the individual operations of the chosen task determine the content of the menu bar. For ease of use, custom user menus – which can, for example, be adapted for a certain task area – can also be defined.

- **Toolbars**: A standard toolbar contains symbols for the most often used navigation commands (Back, Exit, Cancel) and for calling online help.

- **Pushbutton bar**: The essential functions for controlling an application can be accessed with pushbuttons.

- **Input values**: Anywhere that the number of valid input values can be meaningfully limited for a field, the user can display the limited list and select an entry with the mouse.

An example of the user interface of the R/3 System is shown in Figure 5.6. It is designed so that the user can work predominantly with a mouse. The keyboard is only necessary for entering text or numbers – on the other hand, it can also be used as the sole input medium for the R/3 System.

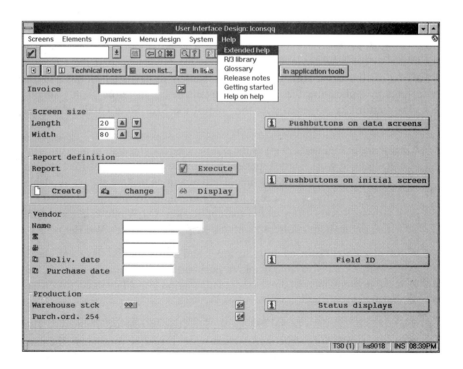

Figure 5.6 Possibilities for design of the R/3 user interface.
© SAP AG

Where more extensive abilities are required for presenting business information, the R/3 presentation uses special graphics tools. The interactive SAP Business Graphics is integrated in many R/3 applications for presentation and processing of data. The SAP Hierarchy Graphics allows the user to navigate through treelike structures. There are additional, local graphics services such as those for presenting and processing SAP enterprise data models or those for certain applications like Sales and Operations Planning. The business data presented by these in both digital and analog form can easily be processed by simple manipulation with the mouse.

5.4.2 Data exchange between presentation and application servers

The characteristics of the R/3 user interface are its hardware independence and its portability. Both are achieved by generic, platform-independent descriptions of the graphical presentation being exchanged between the R/3 presentation system and the R/3 application server instead of completely prepared screen images. Not until these descriptions reach the R/3 presentation software on the individual pre-sentation systems is the graphical interface realized with the help of the devices provided by the respective presentation environment. This results in a compact data stream between R/3 presentation systems and application servers: The volume of data to be transferred per image is typically between 1 and 2 Kbytes. The linking of presentation systems is thus easily achieved even over WANs.

5.4.3 The multilingualism of the R/3 user interface

The user interface of the R/3 System is available in various languages. Currently, those listed in Table 5.1 are supported.

Table 5.1 Language versions of the R/3 System.

Chinese (Mandarin)	Italian
Czech	Korean
Danish	Norwegian
Dutch	Polish
English	Portuguese
Finnish	Russian
French	Slovakian
German	Slovenian
Greek	Spanish
Hebrew	Swedish
Hungarian	Turkish
Japanese (Kanji)	

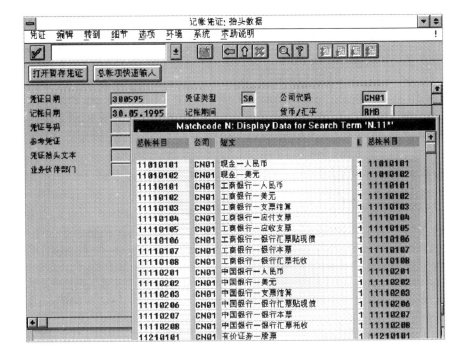

Figure 5.7 Mandarin version of the R/3 System.
© SAP AG

The desired language version is activated when the user enters a language key while logging on to the system.

To achieve the multilingualism of the R/3 user interface (Multi-National Language Support, Multi-NLS), all text portions in screen forms, help information, and so on are managed separately and integrated into the screen layout at the time of display, according to the language key. Languages like Japanese Kanji and Mandarin Chinese (Figure 5.7), whose extensive character sets require two bytes per character internally (Double Byte Character Set), can also be displayed.

The set of all representable characters is defined by the active code page of the computer in question. Single-byte code pages and double-byte code pages are widespread. Single-byte code pages represent every character with a single byte. Double-byte code pages use either a mixture of one- and two-byte representations (for example, S-JIS, Shifted Japanese Industry Standard) or a consistent two-byte representation (for example, Unicode). The code pages supported by the R/3 System are shown in Table 5.2.

Table 5.2 Code pages in the R/3 System.

Formal designation	Informal designation	Single-byte	Double-byte	Supported languages
ISO 8859-1	Latin-1	x		Western European languages (German, English, French, etc.)
ISO 8859-2	Latin-2	x		Eastern European languages (Albanian, English, Czech, etc.)
ISO 8859-3	Latin-3	x		Southeast European languages (English, Catalan, Maltesian, etc.)
ISO 8859-4	Latin-4	x		Northern European languages (English, Estonian, Lithuanian, etc.)
ISO 8859-5	–	x		Cyrillic languages (English, Russian, Serbian, etc.)
ISO 8859-6	–	x		Arabic and English
ISO 8859-7	–	x		Greek and English
ISO 8859-8	–	x		Hebrew and English
ISO 8859-9	Latin-5	x		Turkish and English
EUC (Extended UNIX Code Page)			x	Japanese and English
S-JIS (Shifted Japanese Industry Standard)			x	Japanese and English
GB2312-80	Simple Chinese		x	Mandarin and English
	Traditional Chinese		x	Taiwanese and English
KSCS601-1992	Korean		x	Korean and English

Viewed technically, the R/3 System today is implemented as a single code page solution. The individual servers for presentation, application, and database work with exactly one active code page and can therefore support all languages that can be represented with this code page. The concurrent use of German and Japanese, or the parallel use of Asian languages, is not possible at the moment. However, different servers can work with different code pages, to the extent that that makes sense.

5.4.4 Continued development of SAP presentation services

The ways in which the end user interacts with the R/3 System are continually being further developed. This is evident, for example, in the new, customizable menu visualization produced by the R/3 Session Manager, as well as in expanded

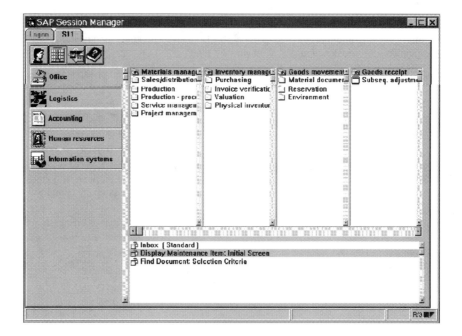

Figure 5.8 The R/3 Session Manager.
© SAP AG

forms of interaction using electronic forms, information kiosks (see Section 3.8), and the telephone.

- R/3 Session Manager
  The R/3 Session Manager is the new, central control tool for all R/3 applications (Figure 5.8). It is based on the idea of representing the entire R/3 menu tree graphically in a separate window. It is possible to display only those branches of the whole menu that the customer has selected in Customizing (company menu). In addition, every user is given his or her own user menu which contains only those transactions that are required for his or her position within the company's internal organizational structure.

  Logging on to the R/3 System is also done via the Session Manager. Customers with several R/3 Systems (for example, test system, training system, and live system) can navigate between the different systems by selecting "index cards."

- Electronic forms
  Using electronic forms, users of worldwide communication and information networks such as the Internet and CompuServe (see Section 3.3.9) have direct access to the R/3 System. By simply filling out screen forms, business information can be retrieved and R/3 business operations such as order processing can be started (electronic commerce).

- SAP Automation API

  Under the project name "SAP Automation API," SAP is currently developing various alternatives to the existing SAP GUI. Among these are multimedia kiosk systems with extremely simplified user interfaces (see Section 3.8), as well as interactive processing of telephone inquiries and orders (TIVR, Telephony Interactive Voice Response Systems). Telephone order processing means, for example, that certain R/3 operations can be started by entering tones on a touch-tone telephone, and their results are automatically transmitted to the ordering party as spoken information using a text–speech converter. The basis for these alternative R/3 user interfaces is a new R/3 programming interface that reveals the data stream between application server and presentation server to the desktop programmer who works with non-SAP tools.

5.5 Application services

The ABAP/4 programs running on the application servers of an R/3 installation implement the business logic of the R/3 applications. These programs are processed by the R/3 runtime system, which is installed on every application server (Figure 5.9).

While the R/3 runtime system itself is written in the C and C++ programming languages, all application programs in the R/3 system are written in the 4GL programming language ABAP/4. Both the ABAP/4 programs and the flow logic for each screen are processed interpretatively. The runtime environment for R/3 applications contains both of the required software processors.

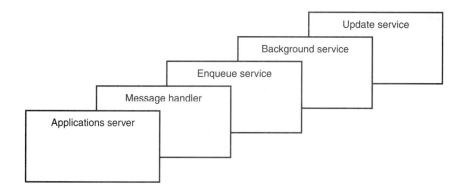

Figure 5.9 R/3 application services.

5.5.1 User sessions

A user session consists – from the point of view of the R/3 System – of a user logging on to the SAP System, selecting a series of transactions and then finally logging off.

Logon to the R/3 System always takes place over a message handler whose network address is known to the presentation server on which the user is working. The message handler is installed on one of the application servers or on the database server and has the task of coordinating the internal message exchange between the individual SAP services. The message handler delivers the address information necessary for access to the desired application server. In the process, it can perform an automatic load distribution on the application servers installed in the network. It reads the information required for this from a performance database in which the most recent performance data from all of the application servers is stored.

During his or her session, the user can pursue several activities in parallel by opening several windows (sessions). In each window, transactions can be run in any sequence (see Section 5.5.2). At any time, the user can start a new transaction in another window or continue a transaction that is already running. This allows the user to work in another application area while waiting for a system response.

5.5.2 Business transactions

The applications of the R/3 System work in a transaction-oriented fashion. An SAP transaction is a sequence of logically linked dialog steps consistent with business practices. SAP transactions can also appear nested if the ABAP/4 language element CALL TRANSACTION is used.

In addition to the application-oriented definition of a transaction, the system-oriented term "SAP LUW" (Logical Unit of Work) is also used, which denotes the sum total of the dialog steps of a transaction plus the update of the database, or posting (see Section 5.6.3). The difference between the two terms is presented in Figure 5.10.

In general, in accordance with the ACID maxim (see Section 3.6), a Logical Unit of Work is always executed completely or not at all. As a rule, SAP transactions are completed by a COMMIT WORK. The affiliated LUW ends when the posting is complete.

SAP transactions and LUWs are not necessarily carried out within a single system process. Rather, the individual dialog steps of a transaction are handled by one process or by different processes, which are called work processes (see Section 5.5.4). An asynchronous posting procedure is also available, which makes it possible for the online part of an SAP transaction and the accompanying

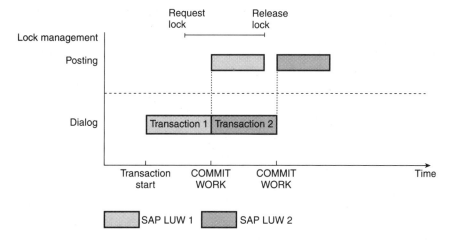

Figure 5.10 Logical Unit of Work (LUW) in the R/3 System.

database update to run in different work processes and even on different computers. This makes a distinction necessary between the atomic processing steps (LUWs) of the SAP System and those of the database management system, because database management systems do not recognize transaction operations across processes.

From the point of view of the database system, every dialog step belonging to an SAP transaction is a separate database transaction (database LUW). Updates of the database are likewise carried out as part of a database transaction. This insures the consistency of the R/3 System at all times.

Each dialog step of an SAP transaction is represented by a separate screen. The graphical screen display, together with the accompanying flow logic, is called a dynpro (dynamic program) (see Section 6.1). The logical connection of dialog steps belonging to a transaction is guaranteed by the SAP System:

• By requesting locks, an application program can require that a user session be given exclusive access to a certain business object for the duration of an SAP LUW.

• All changes to the database caused by an SAP LUW, or possibly by different screens, remain completely reversible until the SAP LUW has reached a successful conclusion.

5.5.3 Synchronous and asynchronous posting

SAP online transactions can consist of several screens (dialog steps). The dialog programs belonging to an online transaction create a log record for the database update, which is processed after conclusion of the online phase. The changes caused by a transaction are not carried out in the database until this log record is processed, the so-called posting.

The log record contains the names of the posting routines to be started as well as all of the data necessary for carrying out the database changes. If the user aborts a transaction during the online phase, or if the transaction fails for other reasons, writing to the log record ceases, and the posting along with it. Unnecessary database accesses are thus prevented.

Online transactions carry out changes to the database directly or indirectly. In a direct change, the posting program is executed by the dialog work process. The online user must wait for the conclusion of the posting before he or she can make new entries. This is called synchronous posting. Synchronous posting is recommended in cases where very high throughput is required. On the other hand, asynchronous posting, in which the online phase of a transaction and the update of the database run in different, decoupled work processes, enables good online performance even when the load on the database server is great. This is because, in asynchronous coupling of application and posting, the online response times are less dependent on communication with the database. A prerequisite is the installation of special posting work processes.

In the R/3 System, asynchronous processing of a log record can proceed in several sections, the posting components. This fragmentation allows structuring of the posting by content, in which separate posting components are set up for the update of each individual data object. A special distinction is made between primary and secondary posting components. These are called U1 and U2. The multilayer nature of the posting allows the separation of operational data changes, for example those that affect reservations or stock movements, from statistical updates, such as those from profitability analysis. The former must always be carried out as soon as possible, so they are undertaken in primary components. The latter, less time-dependent updates are declared secondary components. This gives the dispatcher (see Section 5.5.4) the ability to give them a lower priority when distributing jobs to the posting work processes. This guarantees fast execution of operative processing even under large system loads.

In general, the processing of the primary components must be completed before the secondary components of a log record can begin. The processing of the secondary components can proceed in any sequence and even in different posting processes. Distribution of the secondary components on different computers is also possible. Likewise, processing of primary components from different log records can occur in parallel.

Error situations appear during posting only in exceptional cases. Logical errors, for example incompatible entries, cannot occur during posting, since all of the related required tests were done in the online phase and errors brought to the user's attention. If errors still appear during posting, they are usually technical problems, for example a file overflow, a database buffer overflow, or something similar. These error situations can only be corrected by the system administrator.

Even in error situations, the transaction concept of the R/3 System ensures that the consistency of the data remains intact. Since errors cannot be corrected by interactive contact with the user during posting, as they can during the online phase, processing of the current posting component terminates; the changes already made in the database during the component are reversed. In the case of a primary posting component, all changes already made by other primary components of this log record are reversed, as well. In this case, the entire log record is reversed, while in the other case only the faulty secondary component of the posting is reversed.

Components that have been reversed are marked accordingly and can be processed again later, after correction of the error. The user whose online use created the log record is automatically informed by SAPmail of the termination of the posting (Mail Enabled Application).

5.5.4 Dispatcher and work processes

The R/3 runtime system runs as a group of parallel, cooperative system processes (see Figure 5.9). On every application server, these parallel processes include the central dispatcher and a variable, configuration-dependent number of work processes (Figure 5.11). There are special work processes for online processing,

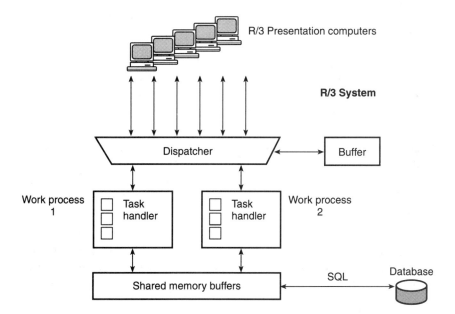

Figure 5.11 R/3 Dispatcher and task handler.

for posting of change documents, for background processing, for print spooling, and for lock management. The dispatcher distributes waiting processing jobs to the responsible work processes.

In every application server there is only one dispatcher, but several work processes. Work processes can access the database directly with SQL. In a client/server configuration of three or more layers, the database may be on another computer. All data traffic between a work process and the outside world that takes place beyond the boundaries, for example program-to-program communication or SAP GUI communication, runs through the dispatcher. The APPC (Advanced Program-to-Program Communication) server, which is part of the dispatcher, recognizes the work processes' communication orders and forwards them to a software gateway which constitutes the interface between the R/3 System and the different transport protocols such as TCP/IP or LU6.2.

Online work processes are active in shifts for the user sessions running. If, after user input, a screen is ready for processing, the dispatcher adds this job to a queue. As soon as an online work process is available, the first job from the queue is submitted to it for processing. The online work process processes exactly one dialog step, in which – among other things – a response screen is compiled that is returned to the window from which the input originated. The online work process is then free for the next user session.

Starting with R/3 Release 3.0, work processes can also become active exclusively for the processing of a complete SAP transaction. This is necessary when very many or very large data objects must be stored in the roll area, and rolling in and rolling out with every dialog step becomes too costly (see Section 5.5.8). This is known as roll-free operation with privileged work processes.

One task handler coordinates the activities within a single work process. If application logic must be processed, as is the case with dialog, posting, and background processes, the task handler activates, depending on need, the dynpro processor for processing the screen flow control and the ABAP/4 processor for the application logic.

Whenever they use data structures, both ABAP/4 programs and screens refer to the definitions of those structures in the central ABAP/4 Dictionary. For this reason, both the ABAP/4 processor and the dynpro processor depend on the overall view of the R/3 data world that is semantically and technically stored in the ABAP/4 Dictionary.

Owing to the client/server architecture of the R/3 runtime system with its special work processes coordinated by the dispatcher for logic processing, the R/3 System is also suitable for implementation in multiprocessor environments (see Section 3.1.4). Different processes can easily be installed and run on different processors of the multiprocessor system.

5.5.5 Automatic load distribution

Distributed systems with several active processors work especially effectively if the application load is distributed evenly. The load on the individual processors should be as homogeneous as possible to reach a high locality of program execution and a high buffer hit rate.

During user logon, as well as during the transaction processing that follows and during background processing, the R/3 System uses mechanisms for automatic load distribution. These are based on services that are provided by the Computer Center Management System (CCMS) (see Section 5.7.2). The basic idea is to divide the available application servers into groups in such a way that each one covers a certain task class or application area. Because each server only performs uniform tasks, the homogeneity of the application load is markedly increased. For example, when a user wants to log on to an application server group from his or her presentation computer, the presentation server first inquires of the message handler the address of the application server from this group that currently has the smallest load. Then, it creates the link to the application server thus determined.

Load distribution is also possible for distributed ABAP/4 applications that communicate through RFC (Remote Function Call, see Section 2.4.1) calls. For this, no definite target computer is specified during the RFC call; instead, a group of application servers is specified as a destination. At execution time, the R/3 runtime system consults the message handler and routes the function call to the application server that currently has the smallest load.

5.5.6 Background processing

Offline processing of background programs in the R/3 System is achieved by special background work processes. The operation is analogous to online operation. Often, background processing uses the same programs as online processing.

Any background processing can run parallel to online applications. Tools for scheduling and managing background jobs are part of the Computing Center Management System (CCMS) described in Section 5.7.

5.5.7 Spooling

Spooling means the buffered transfer of data to output media like printers, fax machines, and so on. In distributed systems, management across computers is necessary for this task.

The spool mechanism of the R/3 System can manage spool jobs network-wide and can provide printers and external spoolers with print jobs both within a LAN and over a WAN. On each computer involved, it works together with the locally available spool system. It is recommended that one of the R/3 computers be declared as a spool server, through which all spool jobs are to be processed. This way, the installation of a new printer need be declared only once, at a central location.

Data to be output over the spool mechanism of the R/3 System is temporarily stored in the TEMSE (temporary sequential) file. This data is mainly text released by R/3 applications for printing, long-distance copying (fax), or sending as electronic mail. A separate print control job provides information about details of the further use of a TEMSE data set, for example the logical name of the printer to be used.

5.5.8 Lock management

The locking mechanisms offered as part of relational database systems are not sufficient by themselves to handle extensive business data objects that extend across several relational tables (see Section 3.5.3), for example material master records or customer orders. For this reason, the R/3 System contains an additional internal lock management feature for coordinating parallel, updating accesses of the same business objects by several applications.

Lock management also ensures that transactions whose dialog steps are processed by different work processes keep the locks placed by them during process changes. This security of locks across processes is also an essential prerequisite for the decoupling of dialog and posting in the R/3 System, since the posting phase of an SAP LUW must be able to rely on the fact that certain data has not changed since the processing of the online phase. During the online phase, application programs request locks for those data objects that they want to change. Competing database accesses are recognized in the preliminary stage, so that the application program can notify the user quickly that the desired operation is not possible at this time.

If a lock is granted, it remains in effect until the end of the entire SAP LUW, assuming the application program does not explicitly give it up at an earlier point. After posting of the log record created by the online phase is completed, the posting program deletes all locks set by the SAP transaction.

R/3 lock management satisfies the requirements of distributed client/server and multiprocessor systems with local data buffers. The implementation of the R/3 locking mechanism is particularly ambitious, because each lock must be valid not only for the application server that is carrying out the locking transaction, but for all servers involved in that client/server configuration. For this reason, each installation of the R/3 System contains a central lock manager (Enqueue service), which monitors the compatibility of the locks granted system-wide. The Enqueue service can be installed on one of the application servers or on the database server.

5.5.9 Memory management of the R/3 runtime environment

The memory management of the R/3 runtime environment distinguishes two main memory types:

- Main memory that is used privately by individual work processes (private memory)

- Main memory that is available to all work processes for common use (shared memory).

In shared memory, ABAP/4 programs, dynpros, data definitions, table contents, and so on are buffered. All work processes access this data jointly and directly.

Until R/3 Release 2.2, the private main memory of the work processes contains two areas for session-specific (window-specific) data that describes the user context, that is, the current processing status of the running transaction. These are called the roll area and the paging area. Their data contents must be stored longer than the duration of a dialog step.

The data in the roll area is automatically made available to the work process when processing of a dialog step begins (rolling in). After processing ends, R/3 memory management stores the contents of the roll area on the disk or in shared memory until processing of the next dialog step begins, which might be started by a different work process. Data in the roll area is directly addressable and always occupies the same position in the virtual address space of the processing work process, even after roll procedures.

Among other things, the roll area contains:

- data describing the user, such as his or her authorizations;

- input data collected in the dialog steps of the current transaction that have already been completed;

- management information for the R/3 runtime environment.

Since roll areas are always automatically loaded into the private main memory of the processing work process, they must be configured relatively small to achieve a high throughput. Larger volumes of data, those that occur during processing of a transaction, are therefore placed in the paging area, which is organized in a paged fashion. The pages are not assigned to or withdrawn from the work process during the changeover to the next dialog step, as they are in the roll area; instead, they are assigned or withdrawn only when needed. Because the paging area is organized in pages, unlike the roll area, there is no guarantee that the data will occupy the same position in the virtual address space of the processing work process after a roll procedure.

Like roll areas, paging areas are buffered in shared memory or on disk.

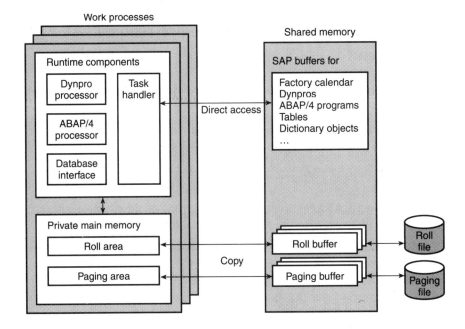

Figure 5.12 Main memory management valid until R/3 Release 2.2.

The concept of memory management valid until Release 2.2 is shown in Figure 5.12.

For R/3 Release 3.0, the memory management of the R/3 runtime environment was redesigned in order to

• improve performance behavior, and

• support complex ABAP/4 data types.

Complex ABAP/4 data types require direct access to the memory. SAP paging is therefore not suitable for these data types.

In order to fulfill the requirements, a special area in shared memory, called extended memory, replaces SAP paging. Extended memory holds the greatest portion of the individual user contexts. The user context required for the execution of the current dialog step is copied from extended memory into the virtual address space of the processing work process (mapping). This copying is always done to the same virtual address in every work process. The physical transport of data by the R/3 runtime environment no longer applies.

As a supplement to extended memory, only a small roll area is still needed, primarily for management information.

In case the roll area and extended memory are insufficient to hold the entire user context, additional, private memory is occupied (allocated). At the same time, the processing work process becomes active exclusively for the running transaction

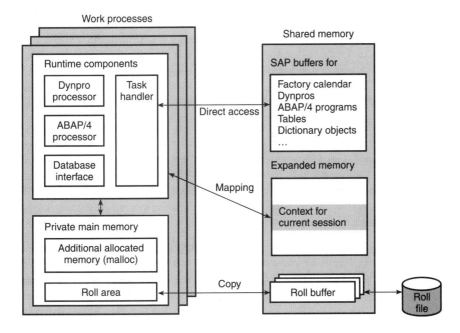

Figure 5.13 Main memory management as of Release 3.0.

until its completion. This is because the contents of the additionally allocated memory cannot be saved in a work process changeover.

The new procedure for main memory management is shown in Figure 5.13.

5.6 Database services

5.6.1 Relational database accesses

For the definition and manipulation of data, the R/3 System exclusively uses SQL language commands (Structured Query Language, see Section 3.5.2). The architecture of the system is laid out in such a way that differences in the syntax and the semantics of the SQL implementations of different database manufacturers are isolated in special R/3 modules. Therefore, in principle, all relational database systems available on the market can be supported, as long as they offer sufficient performance.

Since all relational database systems offer different SQL functionality, the ABAP/4 Development Workbench makes two SQL levels available.

- **ABAP/4 Open SQL**: The entry level is realized in ABAP/4 Open SQL. ABAP/4 Open SQL is a language extension of ABAP/4 (see Section 6.2.2) that guarantees that all applications that access the database using only these language elements can run without any changes on all database management systems supported by the R/3 System. ABAP/4 Open SQL is copied by the R/3 database interface to the Native SQL interface of the underlying database management system.

- **ABAP/4 Native SQL**: The language range available with ABAP/4 Native SQL allows use of the full functionality of the database system in question, including all proprietary enhancements. In the R/3 applications, all of the places that make use of Native SQL are encapsulated in database-specific modules, so that during porting to another database system only those places need to be reviewed.

An important advantage of SQL is the ability to address sets of records with a single database operation (array operations). This characteristic, which is decisive for performance, is used extensively by R/3 applications, because in client/server architectures a large amount of network communication can be saved by using set operations.

The data storage of the R/3 System meets the demand for open interfaces in three ways:

- All of the R/3 application data is stored transparently in tables in the relational database system. Access to this data is possible both with the SQL tools from the database manufacturer and with standardized access interfaces like ODBC (Open Database Connectivity, see Section 3.5.4).

- Openness of data access does not only mean providing the technical ability and tools for external data access. Just as important is the semantic openness of the system, without which the external user is not in a position to find the tables and columns in which the information he or she needs resides. With the enterprise data model, SAP makes documentation available that makes a simple orientation to the data structures of the business applications of the R/3 System possible (see Section 6.4.3).

- R/3 applications are not restricted to addressing only one particular database within their R/3 installation. By taking advantage of transparent distribution concepts of the database manufacturers, additional databases can also be accessed.

Next to execution of SQL instructions, parsing and access optimization consume the largest amount of resources in relational database systems. Access optimization includes, for example, the selection of access paths and the identification of suitable indexes. In the case of SQL instructions with a small hit rate, for example the reading of a certain client master record, it is entirely possible that these preparatory measures are costlier than the final acquisition of the data. This lends importance to the reuse of already optimized SQL instructions. The different database manufacturers offer a wide range of different possibilities for reusing optimized SQL instructions, from the storage of optimized SQL instructions in fixed access plans to the dynamic buffering of such instructions. In the R/3 System, these database-specific functions are encapsulated in the R/3 database interface in such a way that the applications programmer is not affected by them.

5.6.2 Optimization of client/server operation

In addition to copying Open SQL statements to the SQL interface of the database management system, the R/3 database interface has the job of optimizing database access in client/server operation (Figure 5.14). Special buffers exist for this in the shared memory of every application server, which are called the client cache due to their implementation on the client side of the database. In these buffers, often-used data from the applications is stored, so that access to the database server is no longer required for reading. The client cache reduces network traffic and the load on the database server. Technical data in particular, such as ABAP/4 programs, dynpros, and ABAP/4 Dictionary information, but also business parameters such as number ranges, usually remain unchanged in a running system and are therefore well suited for client caching. The same is true for business application data, which is primarily accessed by reading.

Client caching enables demand-controlled loading of the buffer contents. Even ABAP/4 application programs are dynamically loaded into the shared memory of the application servers and buffered there in this way. This results in great flexibility in the installation and configuration of R/3 client/server systems. It is not

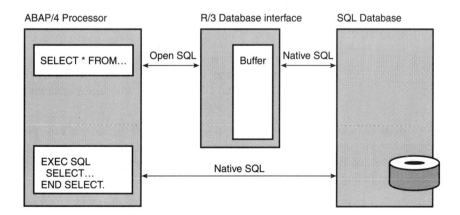

Figure 5.14 The R/3 database interface.

necessary to determine at the time of installation which application transactions will run on which application server. Rather, the downloading of the applicable module pool into the buffer of the application server does not occur until the call of a transaction. The buffered module pool is then available for common use by all of the work processes of this server.

The optimal use of buffer memories is ensured by a management mechanism that overwrites the longest-unused data when reloading the buffers. This mechanism is called the LRU (Least Recently Used) procedure. The management of the client cache is the task of the R/3 database services and is invisible to the business applications.

Applications use the buffer memory foremost in reading. But writing accesses, too, are possible, if the business requirements allow it. Local changes to the buffer contents are transmitted immediately to the database and are broadcast at short time intervals over the message handler to all other application servers.

5.6.3 SAP database administration

When it comes to backup and restoration of databases, most database suppliers refer to the basic services of the operating system, for example to the UNIX command cpio. What remains unaddressed is the fact that these basic services are not prepared to handle special problems in data backup and restoration or to manage backup storage media. In order to offer the database administrator a comfortable work environment, SAP has therefore developed a family of integrated database administration tools (Figure 5.15):

- BRBACKUP: Online and offline backup of application data, control data, and redo logs

- BRRESTORE: Restoration of application data, control data, redo logs, and archived offline redo logs

- BRARCHIVE: Archiving of offline redo logs

- SAPDBA: Menu-driven work environment for all of the administration tasks affecting the database. Calls BRBACKUP, BRARCHIVE, and BRRESTORE. Interface to external backup applications (BACKINT).

SAP's database administration tools are independent applications that can run independent of the availability of the R/3 System. Regular execution of BRBACKUP and BRARCHIVE can be controlled with the job management of CCMS (Computing Center Management System, see Section 5.7.2).

The open backup interface BACKINT enables the integration of external backup applications. Among others, links to ADSM (IBM) and Omniback II (HP) have been released.

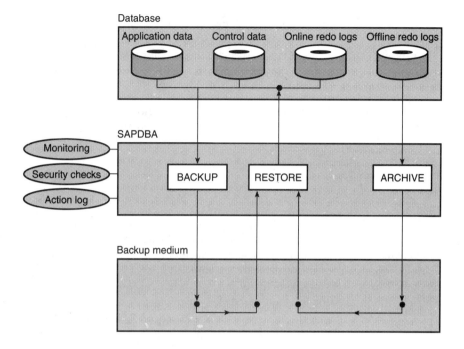

Figure 5.15 Integrated SAP tools for database administration.

5.7 System management

To ensure reliable and uninterrupted operation of SAP software in centralized and distributed environments, management tools are needed for:

- Software installation

- Release changes

- System control

- System monitoring

- System optimization

- Problem management.

The R/3 System includes all of the tools necessary to handle these tasks. The tools are, for the most part, concentrated in the Computing Center Management System (CCMS).

The Computing Center Management System is closely tied to the R/3 applications, as well as to the supported operating systems, database management systems, and network management systems. It offers the system administrator a graphic-oriented work environment that greatly reduces the control and monitoring effort for the entire system. This is especially important for small and mid-sized companies that do not have the opportunity to build an extensive, specialized base of system management knowledge.

The Computing Center Management System makes various functions available for reliable operation of the R/3 System. These can be classified as follows:

- System monitoring

- System control

- Management interfaces.

System monitoring collects relevant performance data for the R/3 installation and presents this data either alphanumerically or graphically. The system control components control the active management operations within R/3 installations. Open CCMS interfaces are available for attaching additional system management services. This is necessary particularly in large, heterogeneous environments, in which an R/3 installation is administered along with other systems. The functions of CCMS system monitoring also provide the basis for SAP's "Early Watch" concept, a service offered for future-oriented, proactive analysis of R/3 customer systems.

5.7.1 System monitoring and Early Watch

The system monitoring integrated in the Computing Center Management System offers the following functions:

- Performance monitors

- Alert monitors

- Performance database (history of performance figures).

Smooth operation of R/3 installations is ensured with the help of the CCMS monitoring environment. Detailed information about the behavior of applications and their interaction with the system software – operating system, database, network – is collected and displayed graphically (Figure 5.16). To do so, the CCMS system acquires performance-related data about the platforms from special data collectors, which have been defined in agreement with SAP's system partners. Problem situations, for example bottlenecks in certain system resources, can be recognized quickly and corrected.

Status and consumption data, for example memory utilization, network utilization, and CPU utilization or paging rates, are gathered system-wide, condensed, and displayed graphically. With optical warning signals, alert monitors point out the crossing of threshold values across system boundaries.

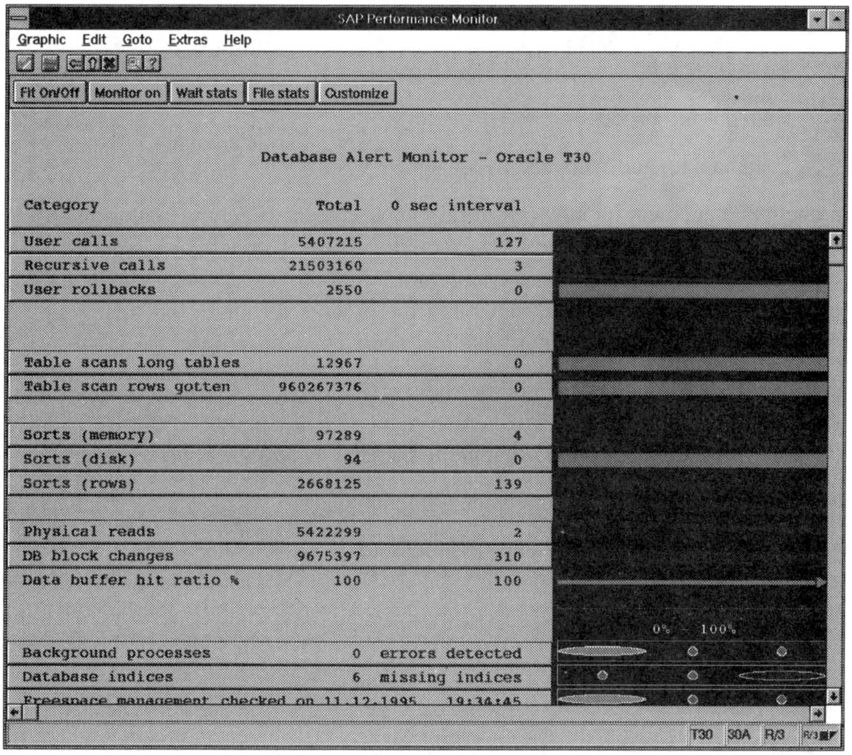

Figure 5.16 R/3 performance monitor.
© SAP AG

The history of all relevant performance data of an R/3 installation is stored in a performance database and can be used by the system administrator for predicting future system performance. For instance, it is possible to predict future bottlenecks of disk peripherals by observing the growth rate of application data. In addition, the performance databases of customer installations are used extensively by the Early Watch service. At regular intervals, Early Watch specialists analyze customer installations and provide notes in a written report on the optimal parametrization of the system, on performance improvement, and on bottlenecks that might appear in the future. A long-distance connection, for example over X.25, ISDN, or Frame Relay (US), is required for participation in the Early Watch service.

5.7.2 System control

In addition to containing monitoring tools, the Computing Center Management System contains control mechanisms that are needed for the operation of R/3 installations. The following areas are covered:

- System management

- Load distribution and load balancing

- Background processing

- Data backup and recovery.

System management includes all of the functions that affect the operation of R/3 installations, for example the start-up or shutdown of systems and processes or the reconfiguration of the entire installation. All of the servers belonging to an R/3 installation, along with their status and the processes running on them, can be displayed and manipulated in a graphical network model (Figure 5.17).

The R/3 System provides the ability to distribute loads, since different application services can be installed on different computers (see Section 5.5.5). To balance the application load on these computers, the CCMS provides two services:

- Load balancing for online work groups

- Load balancing for background processing.

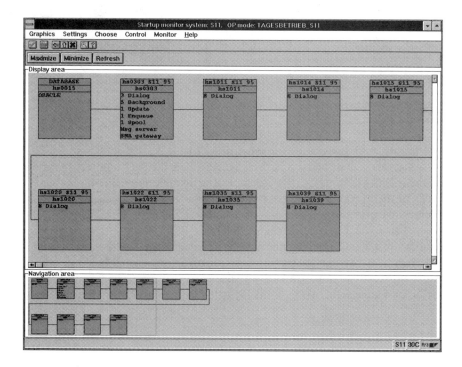

Figure 5.17 Configuration overview in CCMS.
© SAP AG

Load balancing for online work groups allocates separate application servers to the application groups. The online user indicates in a logon menu in which work area (for example, SD – order entry, SD – sales statistics, FI – vendors) he or she wants to log on. Each work area has one or more servers allocated to it in a server definition table. From the set of active, allocated servers, the CCMS system selects at logon the one that currently has the least load and is configured for the desired work area. The CCMS Alert Handler provides the information necessary to do so.

For background processing, automatic load distribution was implemented. It supports installations with several background servers as well as installations with several background work processes on one server. Unless otherwise specified, any background work process that becomes free carries out the next background job that is ready for processing in the entire system.

The load placed on an R/3 installation by online and background processing varies in the course of a 24-hour day. To offer optimal system support, different operation types can be defined in the CCMS system control. Examples are:

- **Online operation**: In this mode, the majority of work processes are defined as online processes. This is the standard operation type.

- **Night operation**: During night operation, most work processes run as background processes.

- **Maintenance operation**: In maintenance operation mode, only certain users have access to the system.

Switching between these modes is possible during regular operation; the affected systems do not need to be shut down.

CCMS supports background processing with functions for

- Job scheduling

- Flow control

- Job monitoring.

In the CCMS system, job scheduling is done with the graphical job scheduling monitor shown in Figure 5.18, which transfers SAP's experience in control station technology from the manufacturing industry to system administration.

Using CCMS, the user can schedule background jobs interactively as jobs. Each job is composed of one or more job steps, which are processed successively. Each job step in turn is characterized by the program to be called and by the input parameters that are to be given to it. Each job also gets an authorization assignment, which defines its access rights, and supplemental attributes (scheduling attributes) that control the job flow.

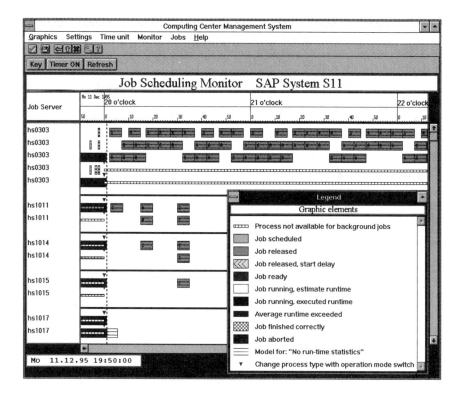

Figure 5.18 CCMS job scheduling monitor for background processing.
© SAP AG

The processing of a job should not generally follow immediately after its scheduling, but rather at a later point. Often it is necessary, for instance, to start a job at regular intervals, say daily or weekly. A scheduler is responsible for the automatic processing of jobs at a desired point in time. Using the scheduling attributes, it determines the start time and submits the job at the predetermined time to the dispatcher for processing.

Flow control ensures the correct, on-schedule execution of background jobs. The flow control functions provide the basis for operatorless operation, for example at night. Flow control services include:

- Differentiation of jobs according to certain classes

- Reaction to external events

- Start and control of external programs with RFC (Remote Function Call)

- Reservation of processing resources for jobs of highest priority.

To distinguish between jobs of higher and lower priority, background processing recognizes three job classes:

- Class A: high-priority jobs

- Class B: periodic jobs

- Class C: low-priority jobs.

As a supplement to general background job processing, the Computing Center Management System offers a separate environment for scheduling and monitoring data backup jobs (backup).

5.7.3 Open management interfaces

The use of additional system management services can sometimes become necessary, especially in large R/3 installations with different system platforms, multiple network services, and interfaces to foreign applications. For this purpose, the CCMS system offers open interfaces, which are, for example, already being used for integration with OpenView (HP) and Netview/6000 (IBM, Digital). These interfaces can be classified into

- Data collector interfaces

- Service interfaces

- Management interfaces.

The data collector interfaces describe the data collectors through which the CCMS system takes over performance-related data from the operating system, database system, and network. The data collector for the Ethernet, Token Ring, and FDDI (ATM planned) networks receives network information, for example the current segment load or the collision rate, from RMON-MIB (Remote Network Monitors Management Information Base, see Section 3.3.7), which is provided by certain network analyzers. RMON-MIB is an expansion of the standard network management protocol SNMP (Simple Network Management Protocol).

With service interfaces, the CCMS system can start and monitor foreign services, for instance the scheduling of jobs in mainframe environments or the execution of data backup jobs by external tools. With these open interfaces, various foreign products can be integrated. Conversely, external applications can transfer jobs to SAP job management and have them executed.

The interfaces for system monitoring, flow control, and alarm handling by external management tools are also based on the industry-standard SNMP. Foreign products can interactively query and process SAP System management data from a special SNMP MIB (Management Information Base), the Private Enterprise MIB 649. In R/3-specific exceptions, the SAP System also generates SNMP alarms (traps), which can start additional, fully automated processing steps, such as calling the system administrator with a pager.

Additional interfaces are planned between the CCMS system and external management tools. These include, for example, the integration of remote service tools from hardware suppliers with SAP's Early Watch concept.

5.7.4 Optimization of release changes

In order to do justice to the many different demands of customers, the functionality of the R/3 System is continually being further developed. SAP customers receive these expansions as new software releases. The changeover from one release to the next is called a release change. In addition to large software releases, small corrections are delivered that fix bugs in the current software version.

When a customer's old release is to be replaced by a new one, the R/3 System is not available for productive use for a certain period of time. In order to avoid unnecessary costs and business drawbacks for the customer, it is important to minimize this time period. With Release 3.0, therefore, SAP introduced the new Repository Switch Procedure for R/3 release changes.

The Repository Switch Procedure makes it possible to greatly reduce the downtimes of a productive system during a release change. The basis for this is the creation of a second, independent, and at first inactive shadow repository in the customer system. Into this shadow repository are loaded the development objects of the new R/3 release, as well as all customer modifications from the version database.

While the shadow repository is being created, the R/3 System with the old repository remains fully available for productive operation. Only after the creation phase is completed is productive operation interrupted and switched to the new repository by renaming the database files affected.

The following are the steps to be completed in the Repository Switch Procedure:

- Load the new release into the shadow repository. 2–3 hours

- Transfer customer modifications.   approx. 20 min./1000 objects

- Stop productive operation.

- Back up the old data set (recommended).

- Switch the active repository.   a few minutes

- Activate the customer dictionary objects.   approx. 20 min./1000 objects

- Import the control data (Customizing).   1–2 hours

- Convert the database.   2–4 hours

- Back up the new data set (recommended).

- Start up productive operation with the new release.

The Repository Switch Procedure is distinguished by the fact that a complete release change, including all preparations, can be carried out within a matter of days. Productive operation is only interrupted for a few hours during the process. Beginning with Release 3.0, only a few hours are needed to load correction versions.

5.8 Security and reliability

Special demands are placed on the security and reliability of enterprise-wide business application solutions. The following features must be guaranteed:

- **Availability** of data and applications

- **Security and integrity** of data and applications

- **Functionality** of applications.

Availability of data and applications means that, as often as possible, they are accessible at any point to the authorized user who wants to process or use them.

Security means that information is seen by authorized persons only. **Integrity** of data and applications means that all intentional and unintentional changes to data and applications are locked out if they distort data or allow applications to run incorrectly or incompletely or only appear to run correctly.

The guaranteed **functionality** of applications applies to the development process itself and demands that business applications fulfill their specified roles completely and exclusively.

The R/3 System is composed of different logical layers that must be taken into account when considering security and reliability:

- Desktop layer

- Application layer

- Database layer

- Operating system layer

- Network layer.

In these layers, R/3 proprietary security services, as well as services of the database management system, the operating system, and the network software, ensure reliable operation.

5.8.1 Availability

The availability of the system is the time that the system is entirely available for its intended purpose, measured in proportion to the total time of operation. In order to guarantee a high system availability, the length of downtimes must be minimized, and the average run time without downtime (MTBF, Mean Time Between Failures) must be maximized. A distinction is made between planned and unplanned downtimes. Unplanned downtimes are based on operating errors or quality defects in hardware or software and are not foreseeable. Planned down-times, on the other hand, are necessary to secure system operation in the long run and include tasks such as offline data backup, hardware and software upgrades, and so on.

As part of the "High Availability" project, SAP has combined all of the activities for optimizing availability of the R/3 System. It is important to note that the availability of the R/3 System is influenced by the R/3 software, as well as by the hardware, the operating system, the database management system, and the network.

Both planned and unplanned downtimes can be minimized by taking appropriate measures. For the R/3 System, for example, this means:

- Ensuring high software quality according to ISO 9001 in SAP's internal development process (see Section 7.1).

- System management with the Computing Center Management System:
  The Computing Center Management System supports the system adminis-trator in all monitoring and control tasks occurring in R/3 operations, at the application, database, operating system, and network levels. Graphical user interfaces reduce the training effort, enable a quick overview even in com-plex relationships, and ensure that critical situations are recognized early. For all problems, there are predefined procedures and check lists.

- Remote support concept:
  SAP offers a 24-hour support concept for R/3 installations. This includes a telephone hotline, an Online Software Service (OSS) as well as, at customer request, remote maintenance and proactive system management (Early Watch). All activities that SAP employees perform on customer systems as part of the Remote Support concept are logged, and the information is passed on to the customer.

- Automatic software distribution onto application servers and presentation servers (see Section 5.6.2).

- Proactive analysis of customer systems by the Early Watch service (see Section 5.7.1).

- Release changes using the Repository Switch Procedure (see Section 5.7.4).

- Backup during online operation:
  Delivered with the R/3 System are database service programs for the execution of database backups (BRBACKUP), restoration of the database (BRRESTORE), backup of archived redo logs (BRARCHIVE), and administration of the database (SAPDBA). These tools are described in Section 5.6.3.

- Archiving during online operation:
  R/3 data that is no longer current, but that must be stored long-term, can be erased in the R/3 database and stored in archive files. As of R/3 Release 3.0, this process can run parallel to online operation.

- Switchover technology for database downtimes:
  Database computer downtime can be tackled using twin computer configurations with common data disks. When the central database computer goes down, the monitoring software from the hardware manufacturer automatically activates the replacement server (switchover). Database accesses by the linked application servers are also automatically rerouted to the new database server.

5.8.2 Security and integrity

Security and integrity mean that only authorized persons have access to business data and applications. In R/3 Systems, these requirements are met by the measures described below. Of particular importance is the R/3 authorization concept, which is described in Section 5.8.3.

- **SAP Views for direct database access**: Owing to the transparent storage of SAP data in the relational database, it is possible to access this data directly with SQL. Access authorizations for this must be assigned by the database administrator. To support the administrator in his or her work and thereby avoid the unauthorized reading or changing of data, SAP offers predefined Views for access to the database. Interested users can then request access authorization for these Views from the database administrator.

- **RFC for database access through function modules**: Remote Function Call (RFC) allows SAP and non-SAP applications to call R/3 function modules across computer boundaries. R/3 function modules ensure that application data can only be read and changed in a consistent fashion. Since RFC calls are subject to the R/3 authorization concept (see Section 5.8.3), this concept offers the maximum amount of security and integrity for application data.

- **Activity logs**: All of the activities running in the R/3 System are listed in the system logs according to transaction and user. Also recorded are all parameter changes to the R/3 start-up profile, the customizing parameters, the UNIX kernel parameters, and the database parameters.

- **Transport systems**: SAP's transport system is responsible for the transportation of applications and control data across system boundaries, for example from the development system to the production system. It is also needed for release changes. As a rule, development objects are transferred into the production system with the tools provided by the transport system. The transport system is subject to the R/3 authorization concept. Version control and transport logs ensure that it is possible to reconstruct at any time which version of the production system was active at which point in time. This is crucial for the auditability of the R/3 System.

- **System passwords**: R/3 users receive no user authorizations and passwords at the operating system or database level; instead they are subject to the R/3 authorization concept (see Section 5.8.3). Only the R/3 System administrator has a freely selectable and changeable operating system password. Likewise, the R/3 System uses a freely selectable and changeable password for access to the database.

- **Separate directory structures for the R/3 System**: In order to prevent unauthorized access attempts, the entire R/3 System, including user data, is stored in separate directory structures of the operating system with exclusive access authorizations.

- **Encryption of network data**: For encryption of Remote-SQL-based data traffic between application and database servers, the services of the database supplier are used. Network traffic between presentation and application servers is compressed by an SAP process.

- **Kerberos and SecuDE**: Kerberos is a procedure developed at MIT (Massachusetts Institute of Technology) for securing distributed systems (see Section 3.3.8). SecuDE, a product by GMD (Gesellschaft für Mathematik und Datenverarbeitung, Society for Mathematics and Data Processing), has the same goal. Both products are already elements of the SAP project "Secure Network Communication," for securing communication over LAN and WAN links, for uniform user checking (authentication), and for central user logon (single logon).

5.8.3 R/3 authorization concept

In the R/3 authorization procedure, users of the R/3 System must, as a rule, log on with their user name and a unique password. The R/3 authorization concept enables assignment of general user authorizations as well as assignment of very sophisticated user authorizations that can extend as far down as the transaction, field, and value level. User authorizations are managed centrally in the master records of the users.

Most user authorizations authorize the manipulation of certain data, for example master data of materials, assets, projects, and so on, or of data that belongs to a particular organizational entity such as a company code, a plant, or a cost center. Authorizations can, however, also refer to a particular operation. That is how use of a particular transaction or report is allowed.

Often, an operation requires more than one authorization. For example, to change a material master record, one needs authorizations for the "change" transaction, for access to the actual material, and for working in the applicable company code. The resulting links can become very extensive. In order nevertheless to be able to offer an easily manageable procedure, the R/3 authorization concept was implemented on the basis of authorization objects. Together, several system elements to be protected (for example user groups, transactions, and so on) comprise an authorization object. Examples of combinations that can be defined as an authorization object are:

- Maintenance of any materials with just one transaction in a single company code

- Maintenance of a particular group of materials with all of the transactions in one company code.

To keep the need for maintenance to a minimum, authorization objects can be combined into authorization profiles, which can be assigned to the appropriate users and no longer need to be maintained individually in the user master records. Changes to access authorizations apply at once to all users who have the corresponding profile entered in their master record.

Composite profiles are another level at which one can combine authorization profiles. They are defined for users who must work with more than one authorization profile at a time.

To simplify the set-up of profiles, the R/3 System includes an extensive array of standard profiles for all application areas. These can be copied and modified to meet the current requirements. Reports support the display and maintenance of the authorizations defined in a company.

Chapter 6

Application Development with the ABAP/4 Development Workbench

The ABAP/4 Development Workbench is SAP's programming environment for development of enterprise-wide client/server business solutions (see Section 3.10). It supports the entire software development cycle with tools for modeling, programming in the 4GL language ABAP/4, definition of data and table structures, and the design of graphical user interfaces. Extensive resources for software testing, tuning, and maintenance, as well as for the work of large development teams, are also available. As a supplement to the development tools, SAP delivers a library of ready-made business and general software components that can easily be incorporated into custom programs.

Figure 6.1 shows an overview of the individual elements of the ABAP/4 Development Workbench.

In the ABAP/4 Development Workbench, application development metadata, such as the definition of table and data structures, is created, managed, and actively incorporated into the program execution with the ABAP/4 Dictionary (see Section 6.4.4). The ABAP/4 Development Workbench stores ABAP/4 Dictionary data, along with all other development objects, for example ABAP/4 programs, screen descriptions, documentation, and help texts, in the central R/3 Repository (Figure 6.2). The Repository Information System (see Section 6.4.2) enables comfortable access to this information.

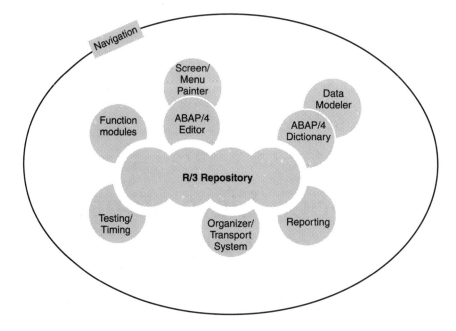

Figure 6.1 The ABAP/4 Development Workbench.

Using the tools of the ABAP/4 Development Workbench, entirely new developments are possible, as well as customization and expansion of the R/3 applications
delivered by SAP (see Sections 6.2.5 and 6.4.4). A fundamental part of this is the
fact that the developer does not have to worry about system-specific interfaces
or system-related communication and distribution aspects of the client/server
environment. Applications created with the ABAP/4 Development Workbench
can run without customization effort on all types of computers, database
management systems, and graphical user interfaces supported by SAP, and they
can do so in both centralized and distributed client/server configurations.

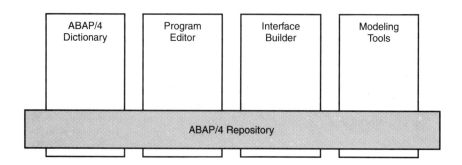

Figure 6.2 The R/3 Repository.

6.1 Dialog programming using the dynpro technique

Most R/3 online transactions include several dialog steps. Every dialog step begins with the preparation and subsequent transmission of the input screen to the user's screen. Receipt of the screen filled out by the user and the analysis and processing of the input data contained in the received screen follow. Deviations from this strict processing sequence, for example sending several screens before user input, are also possible. The two parts of dialog step processing are called PBO (Process Before Output) and PAI (Process After Input).

For each dialog step, the following attributes must be specified:

- **Screen layout**: Positioning of input windows, output windows, selection windows, control elements, and texts
- **Field attributes**: Definition of formats, value range checks, and display particulars (left aligned, right aligned, leading zeros, colors, and so on) for all screen fields
- **Flow logic**: Determination of which processing should take place at the time of PBO and PAI.

The determination of the screen layout, field attributes, and flow logic for a dialog step is referred to all together as a dynpro (dynamic program).

Dynpros support multilingual online processing. Documentation and help text, error messages, and screens can be managed and displayed according to language.

The dynpro concept is continually being further developed. The current emphasis is on runtime optimization through the shifting of graphical processing functions from the application server to the presentation server. An example of this is table display using the new table control (see Section 6.4.5). Functions such as "Sort Column" and "Expand Table" can now be executed purely locally, without accessing the application server.

6.1.1 Flow logic

The sections of the flow logic of a dynpro, PBO (Process Before Output) and PAI (Process After Input), each determine a single sequence of commands. These commands syntactically follow the constructs of the ABAP/4 language and control the following activities:

- Calling of ABAP/4 dialog modules
- Checking of field contents against a table or a fixed value range
- Checking of authorizations in the master record of the user.

ABAP/4 dialog modules called at the time of PBO prepare the screen in a context-sensitive manner, for example by setting field contents or by hiding fields not required in the screen layout. Dialog modules called at the time of PAI check the user's entries, carry out the necessary processing, and, if necessary, start additional steps, such as an update of the database by the posting software.

After the correction of input fields by the user, the dynpro processor does not usually run through all of the PAI commands again, but only those that could be affected by the input changes that were actually made.

6.1.2 Dynpro chains and module pools

The flow logic of a dynpro calls the ABAP/4 dialog modules that implement the business functions belonging to this dialog step (Figure 6.3). The dialog modules belonging to a dynpro are located in exactly one ABAP/4 dialog program. This dialog program is therefore also known as a module pool.

The dynpros belonging to an online transaction are numbered. For every dynpro there is a specific follow-on dynpro. The regular processing of an online transaction therefore usually follows a statically predefined dynpro chain. This chain ends as soon as a dynpro is encountered that has a zero entered as the number of its follow-on dynpro. Alternatively, dynpro chains can also be run through in cycles. In addition, it is possible for certain user entries or error situations to dynamically cause a deviation from the predefined sequence of the dynpros.

6.1.3 Automatic functions for screen fields

Normally, all screen fields reference fields of tables defined in the ABAP/4 Dictionary. Equal naming of fields in the ABAP/4 Dictionary and fields in the dynpro establishes this relationship automatically. As a result, a large portion of the field attributes in the dynpro is taken over from the ABAP/4 Dictionary. The

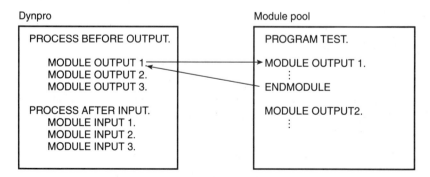

Figure 6.3 Communication between dynpro and module pool.

length and data type of the screen field are taken over from the dictionary, as well as the text that describes the business meaning of the field.

During input or output of field contents, conversion routines between internal and external display, which are stored in the dictionary, can be run. Amount and quantity fields can be displayed according to the reference fields in the dictionary in which the corresponding currency or quantity units are recorded. The dynpro processor also deals independently with online help, including glossary look-up. For every screen, field documentation is available to the user by pressing the F1 key. It contains the business description from the assigned data element and the technical field definition from the associated domain.

With the F4 key, the user can request a list of possible input values for certain fields and select the desired value with a simple mouse click. This help is available whenever a matchcode, check table, or constants have been defined for a field.

Screen entries are automatically checked for validity against the value range defined in the ABAP/4 Dictionary. Foreign key definitions, in particular, are considered in this process. The entered values are selected in the check table and only accepted if they are present there. As opposed to a later check during writing to the database, this procedure has the decided advantage that errors are recognized as early as possible and the user can immediately correct the input.

6.2 Application programming with ABAP/4

For the development of client/server business applications, the programming language ABAP/4 (Advanced Business Application Programming) was conceived in the 1980s and is still being further developed (Figure 6.4). This language is the basis for all R/3 applications.

Two different application types can be implemented with ABAP/4:

- Transaction applications
- Database analyses (reporting).

The essential attributes of the ABAP/4 programming language are:

- Portable 4GL language (see Section 3.10.1)
- Event-oriented program development
- Structured programming with all of the usual control structures
- Modularization of applications using subroutines and function modules
- Special language elements for business applications, for example for date calculation

- Open programming interfaces, for example on the basis of OLE Automation and Remote Function Call (see Section 3.3.6)

- Program development without specific consideration of the technical environment of the database management system, operating system, network, and client/server communication.

ABAP/4 language elements can be divided into four classes (see sample program, Figure 6.4):

- Declarative language elements describe the data that is to be processed in the program (for example, DATA, TYPES, TABLES).

- Operational language elements enable elementary data manipulation (for example, ADD, MOVE).

- Control language elements implement control structures like loops, branches, subroutines, and so on (for example, DO, IF, CASE, PERFORM).

- Event language elements link the execution of individual routines with certain events (for example, GET, TOP-OF-PAGE, AT USER-COMMAND).

ABAP/4 programs are not executed directly, but rather stored in an internal representation which can be optimally interpreted by the ABAP/4 processor. The link (binding) between an ABAP/4 program and the internal and external data structures used by it is established by the active ABAP/4 Dictionary. Changes to the data descriptions deposited in the ABAP/4 Dictionary do not require a redesign of the program, but simply cause an automatic regeneration of the runtime object.

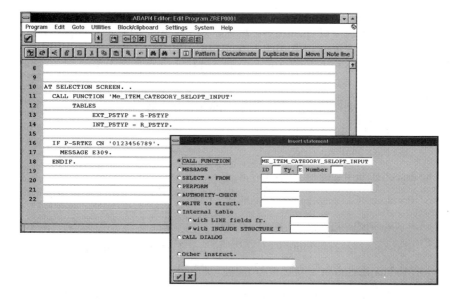

Figure 6.4 Sample ABAP/4 program.
© SAP AG

ABAP/4 makes program development supported by prototyping possible. The software developer first prepares a preliminary version of the program, or just the user interface, then adds missing functionality bit by bit. The interpretative nature of the language makes it easier to prepare temporary versions that can actually be run. These can then be evaluated and tested with the end user and incorporated in the final version (no "throw away" prototyping).

6.2.1 Data types and operations

Every data object that is defined locally in an ABAP/4 program or globally in the ABAP/4 Dictionary is an instance of a data type. As a standard, ABAP/4 supports the elementary data types shown in Table 6.1.

Building on the elementary data types, it is possible to define in a program or globally in the ABAP/4 Dictionary any number of complex, nested data types.

The ABAP/4 programming language includes all of the required core operations for manipulating data objects, such as value assignment, comparison, reset to default value, submission as function parameter, or import/export of durable, persistent objects. These operations are executed in type-dependent (polymorphic) fashion for all elementary data types as well as for derived, complex data types.

In addition to classic arithmetic, ABAP/4 also performs special date calculations. There are separate data types for date and time entries. In mixed terms, numbers are interpreted by automatic conversion as lengths of time intervals. For example, addition of the number n to a date results in a date that is pushed out n calendar days; subtraction of two time values results in their difference in seconds.

ABAP/4 also offers extensive functions for processing textual data. Operations on character strings, or tables whose lines are character strings, are also part of the language. These include searching and replacing a specified character string, deleting superfluous blank spaces, combining and separating character strings, moving a character string, and checking whether characters of one character string appear in another.

Table: 6.1 Elementary ABAP/4 data types.

Data type	Standard length (bytes)	Initial value	Description
C	1	SPACE	Text (Character)
D	8	00000000	Date (YYYYMMDD)
F	8	0	Floating point
I	4	0	Integer
N	1	'0'	Numeric text
P	8	0	Packed
T	6	000000	Time (HHMMSS)
X	1	X'00'	Hexadecimal

6.2.2 Table processing and SQL

The table is the most important data structure in the R/3 System. ABAP/4 offers abundant functionality for handling tabular data. A distinction is drawn between tables in the database, which store long-lasting data, and short-term, program-internal tables, for which there are no database tables.

- **Database tables**:
  In ABAP/4, database tables can be addressed using Open SQL and Native SQL (see Section 5.6.1). The Open SQL language elements of ABAP/4 support read and update access to the tables defined in the ABAP/4 Dictionary. The relational join operation, not contained in Open SQL, can be implemented in the ABAP/4 Dictionary using view definitions (see Section 3.5.2). With Open SQL, both individual lines and sets of lines can be read and processed (array operations). In addition, explicit cursor processing, available starting with R/3 Release 3.0, offers a new, more flexible mechanism for accessing data sets.

  The R/3 database interface of the runtime system changes Open SQL instructions from the ABAP/4 programs into instructions for the respective relational database management system being used. ABAP/4 programs that exclusively use Open SQL for database access therefore do not need to consider either storage particularities or incompatibilities between different database management systems, such as differing lock logic or incompatible return codes. Additional advantages of the integration of Open SQL in the ABAP/4 language realm are the performance-enhancing buffer mechanisms in the R/3 database interface and the immediate syntax checking of Open SQL commands by the ABAP/4 program editor (see Section 6.4.7).

  For Native SQL commands, which are forwarded to the respective database management system without being interpreted, the advantages described for Open SQL do not apply. Programming errors in Native SQL instructions are not recognized until run time by the database management system. Native SQL has the additional disadvantage of not being completely portable between different database management systems. On the other hand, Native SQL offers the advantage that the application programmer has access with this interface to all database expansions and proprietary expansions of standard SQL.

- **Internal tables**:
  In ABAP/4 programs, the developer can define, as well as the database tables, additional, internal tables that exist for the duration of only one run and that are not stored in the database. ABAP/4 offers various operations for processing internal tables, such as searching, attaching, adding and deleting lines, running a table in a loop, and sorting according to any field contents.

The memory space occupied by an internal table is dynamically adjusted by the R/3 runtime environment to the extent of occupancy. The developer therefore does not need to know in advance what size his or her internal table will maximally reach. Generous reservation of memory space that is in most cases not needed is thereby avoided. This leads to economic memory use and helps optimize the runtime performance of the applications.

6.2.3 Modularization with subroutines

For the modularization of programs, ABAP/4 recognizes the definition and call of subroutines (forms). Subroutines can be located either in the calling program or in foreign programs.

Both the name of the subroutine to be called and the name of the program in which the subroutine resides can be defined dynamically in the call. Recursive and nested subroutine calls are possible.

Data objects of any type can be submitted as parameters in a subroutine call. A parameter is submitted either as a fixed value (call by value) or as a variable (call by reference). In addition, it is possible for calling and called programs to use common, global data.

6.2.4 Modularization with function modules

Function modules (functions) are a special class of ABAP/4 subroutines. They form the basis for SAP's component software concept. In the calling interface of a function module, import, export, and table parameters are defined. With table parameters, references to entire tables can be submitted. The syntax for calling function modules is reflected in Figure 5.5 (Section 5.3.2).

Function modules are characterized by the ability to reuse routines, by the management of a central library, and by consistent data encapsulation. Function modules differ from simple subroutines in the following ways:

- Function modules have a clearly defined calling interface. The data objects of the calling program and of the function module are located in separate work areas. Changes to the data objects of the function module are only possible via the calling interface.

- Exception situations (exceptions) that occur during the processing of function modules can be individually handled by the application programmer.

- Function modules are managed in a central function module library.

- A separate test environment is available for function modules, which also offers the possibility of performing regression tests.

- Function modules can be called across system boundaries (Remote Function Call).

- It is also possible to call function modules using OLE Automation.

Execution of a function module can only be started through its calling interface. In order to be able to test function modules on their own, without incorporating them into a superordinate control program, a special test environment is available in the ABAP/4 Development Workbench. One only has to predefine the import parameters, execute the module to be tested and finally read the export parameters and time needed. Test data can be stored and later reused automatically.

Various alternatives are available for handling exception situations that occur during the processing of a function module. The programmer can choose between

- Program termination

- Message to the user with continuation of dialog that possibly deviates from normal operation

- Processing of previously specified exception situations by the calling program.

For the management of function modules, the ABAP/4 Development Workbench has a separate library with special search functions at its disposal. In the standard R/3 System, this library already contains a series of function modules, some of which are explicitly released for use in customer applications. In particular, modules for application functions that are usable system-wide, such as number assignment or graphical data display, are offered. In addition, the function module library can be expanded by the application developer with individual function modules.

Remote Function Call

Calling function modules is also possible across computer boundaries. Function modules thus serve as the foundation for the development of distributed ABAP/4 applications. The call is done using a Remote Function Call (RFC).

With RFC, the principle of the Remote Procedure Call (RPC) has been incorporated in the 4GL ABAP/4 (see Section 3.3.6). Both RPC and RFC carry out the request for an external service through a subroutine call. The actual target computer of an RFC is determined with a register table, independent of the program in question.

The essential attributes of Remote Function Call are:

- RFC is available in TCP/IP and SNA LU6.2 networks.

- Syntax and behavior correspond to the call of a normal function module in the R/3 System.

- All ABAP/4 data types such as single fields, internal tables, or complex, user-defined data types can be used as call parameters.

- During the submission of tables as function parameters, the RFC delta management function reduces the effort needed for communication between the caller and the called program. After the first transport of an internal table to the target system, only table changes (delta information) are exchanged.

- With RFC, synchronous function calls, asynchronous function calls, and transaction-secured, asynchronous function calls are possible.

- The type of link and the communication partners are set by the RFC parameter "DESTINATION" and a system table. Logical target system names determined during installation of the R/3 System are used in the process.

- The call proceeds dynamically. Generation of static communication modules (stubs) is not necessary in pure ABAP/4 environments.

- An EXCEPTION mechanism is available for individual error handling by the calling program.

- RFC calls support debugging across system boundaries with "Remote Debugging."

- With the Call-Back function, a program called by RFC can itself start the execution of a function module in the calling system.

- In an RFC communication between ABAP/4 programs, it is possible to carry out user dialogs within the called function module, as well.

- The inclusion of non-ABAP/4 programs in the RFC communication is possible.

RFC calls can be deposited by an application program even if the target system is not active, or if completion of the called function module should not be waited for. These asynchronous calls are stored temporarily in a local queue and sent at a later time.

Controlled call sequence and transactional integrity are guaranteed in asynchronous calling, too. This means that:

- The execution of RFCs in the target system proceeds in the same sequence in which they are sent by the calling system.

- It is guaranteed that an RFC call is executed only once.

- The execution status of an RFC call can be requested at any time.

Both the calling and the called RFC communication partner can be a non-ABAP/4 program. For different operating system environments, an RFC library is available as an API (Application Programming Interface). In Windows environments, it is implemented as a Dynamic Link Library (DLL). That way, all applications and development tools can use those functions of the RFC library that can call Windows DLLs. This applies, for example, to Microsoft's Visual Basic, Visual C++, and Visual Basic for Applications.

For different programming languages, RFC communication calls can be automatically generated. In addition, it is possible to generate complete sample programs in ANSI-C or Visual Basic, to test the generated RFC calls directly. Both generation functions belong to the RFC Interface Generator of the ABAP/4 Development Workbench.

Additional functions for communication between Windows applications and ABAP/4 programs are offered by the Open Object Interface (see Section 6.2.4) and the Desktop SDK (Software Development Kit, see Section 7.5.2).

Open Object Interface

Standardized interfaces for linking external applications and services are an elementary part of open programming environments. Object-based technologies such as OMG's CORBA and Microsoft's OLE (see Section 3.9 ff.) are increasingly gaining importance. As of Release 3.0, ABAP/4 also has an Open Object Interface at its disposal, with whose help applications, services, and objects that are managed by an external Object Request Broker (ORB) can be accessed. This object interface is implemented using special ABAP/4 language elements, which allow the manipulation of objects, attributes, and methods.

In the first stage, the Open Object Interface supports communication with OLE Automation server applications, for example Microsoft's WinWord and Excel. An interface to OMG's CORBA is planned for the future.

6.2.5 Function expansion with customer exits

The ABAP/4 Development Workbench is used both for development of entirely new applications and for modification and expansion of standard R/3 applications.

When changing SAP programs, one must take into consideration that faulty modifications could jeopardize uninterrupted operation of the R/3 installation. Under certain circumstances, the SAP warranty could even be nullified. In addition, modifications to SAP development objects lead to additional costs during release changes. To avoid these problems, function expansions should be implemented as customer exits, and table expansions should be implemented as append structures (see Section 6.4.4).

Customer exits are calls of customer-specific application modules that have been anticipated by SAP in the development of standard R/3 applications. The expansion of functions using ready-made customer exits prevents direct access to the logic of standard R/3 applications.

Some examples of implemented customer exits are:

- Function exits (CALL CUSTOMER_FUNCTION)

- Menu expansions

- Dynpro expansions (CALL CUSTOMER_SUBSCREEN)

- Text expansions for data element documentation

- Customer changes of keyword texts and short texts for data elements.

The objective of the customer exit procedure is to be able to change the behavior and the functionality of the standard R/3 software easily and across release changes if individual functions of the applications cannot be adjusted to individual requirements with R/3 Customizing. Uncontrolled access to the standard software programs themselves is thus avoided. This minimizes the maintenance effort and the resulting costs of custom adjustments.

Customer exits offer the following advantages:

- Potential customer requirements that are not part of the standard solution are considered by SAP as predefined interfaces within the standard applications. These interfaces are usable as required for incorporation of customized logic.

- The procedure guarantees a distinct separation between SAP logic and customer logic.

- Customer exits remain inactive in the standard applications until they are explicitly activated.

- The programs, text, and so on belonging to a customer exit are allocated to the customer system. SAP guarantees that they will not be overwritten during corrections and release changes.

- Upward compatibility is guaranteed. Accordingly, customer exits and their calling interfaces remain intact in future release versions.

6.2.6 Transaction variants

Transaction screens occasionally contain input and output fields that are not required for a particular application or that fundamentally assume certain fixed values. In this situation, the R/3 System's user management offers the possibility of hiding individual fields on the screen using Point&Click, or filling individual fields with fixed values. Afterwards, the screen is automatically compressed to the size prescribed by the remaining fields. Figure 6.5 shows the definition of fixed values for the organization data with compression of the input screen.

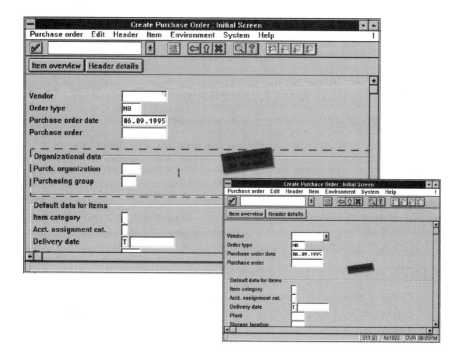

Figure 6.5 Definition of a transaction variant.
© SAP AG

The procedure for deriving variations from an existing transaction is an element of SAP's CTO (Configure to Order) concept for custom shaping of R/3 installations (see Section 8.2.4).

6.2.7 Development of multilingual applications

The R/3 System was conceived from the beginning for use in international markets. Multilingual texts, such as headings for report lists, can be assigned to ABAP/4 programs as text elements. These can still be changed later without accessing the program text. In the program text, text elements are addressed simply by their number. Output of texts takes place in the language in which the user has logged on to the system.

Of increasing importance for international standard business applications is support of pictographic languages with their extensive character sets, such as Japanese and Chinese. The R/3 System takes this into account by applying the two-byte code system (DBCS – Double Byte Character Set). The ABAP/4 Development Workbench has been expanded accordingly. For example, the data type W (Wide Character) and a series of additional functions for string handling have been provided so that double-byte characters in a character field can be processed together with normal one-byte characters.

6.3 Report development using ABAP/4

Reports are ABAP/4 programs that read and display part of the database to address certain information requests. They deliver a result in the form of a graphically displayed report list.

For access to the database, developers of ABAP/4 reports have two alternatives:

- Direct access with the help of SELECT instructions
- Comfortable access using logical databases.

The programming effort linked to report creation can be significantly reduced by using existing logical databases, since the database read need only be programmed once in the logical database (see Section 6.3.1).

The event-oriented character of ABAP/4 is especially clear in report development with logical databases. The programs are not processed sequentially in the order of the individual commands, but rather are dependent on the occurrence of defined events. Certain processing steps in the program correspond to every event. Possible events are, for example:

- Processing before the first table access (START-OF-SELECTION)
- Provision of the next table line by the logical database (GET table name)
- Pressing of a function key by the user (AT Pfnn)
- Selection of a report line by the user (AT LINE-SELECTION)
- End of the output page (END-OF-PAGE).

As well as the general processing of database contents, reports are also used for periodic updating of derived data sets (strategic indexes). These derived data sets can, for example, be the results of processing-intensive analyses whose values do not absolutely have to be up-to-the-minute current, such as a list of the 100 customers with the highest sales.

For the systematic management of report programs and report lists in a hierarchical structure, the ABAP/4 Development Workbench provides the reporting tree. This tree structure can be customized by the user according to his or her business requirements.

6.3.1 Logical databases

Logical databases are special ABAP/4 programs that read a hierarchically structured section of the database contents and prepare it for reports. In the process, they can combine the contents of several tables. Reports assign values to the information delivered by the logical database according to certain target provisions. The result of this analysis is a report list that can be viewed on screen, interactively processed, and printed.

The procedure introduced by logical databases, which separates database access from the ABAP/4 reports and implements it as special programs instead, has considerable advantages. Because a logical database serves several reports, similar access paths need be programmed only once. This affects not only the instructions for data access, but also the implementation of authorization checks and navigation in data sets with the help of foreign keys.

6.3.2 Calling reports

Before the execution of a report, the end user must delimit the data desired in the output list by entering selection criteria. In ABAP/4 reports, there is a special dynpro for this purpose, the selection screen, which is linked tightly to the report. Selection screens are automatically generated by the system and require no surface programming by the developer.

As selection parameters, both individual values and complex entries that contain intervals, comparisons, search texts, alternative conditions, and so on are valid. The user also has the ability to store large or recurring selection entries and to use these again when calling the report.

Reports can be called online as well as from within other ABAP/4 programs. The latter possibility is used especially in interactive reporting (see Section 6.3.3).

6.3.3 List display and interactive reporting

The data provided by an ABAP/4 report is temporarily stored in a report list. The display of a report list on the screen is accomplished with a special list processor. The user can interactively move the part of the list that is displayed with the help of a scroll bar or with commands in the command line.

ABAP/4 reports can insert input-ready fields in the report list. This allows the user to complete information before printout of the list. Additional processing can be defined, which the user can start during display of the list with function keys or entries in the command line. This is called interactive reporting.

In interactive reporting, for example, additional reports or transactions can be called. Reciprocal calling of reports provides the ability to branch from the display of a report list to another report and in the process take along data from the list as parameters for the new report.

In interactive reporting, a report can create several lists. For example, say a report first delivers a compressed basic list, from which the user selects the data records of interest. The same report subsequently delivers in another list more detailed information for the data records that were interactively selected. This process can be repeated step by step.

As part of the integration of PC applications, a special function module is available that enables R/3 applications to build list objects and export them to Microsoft Excel. This function module not only ensures that a list object is transferred to the user's presentation system, but, if desired, automatically starts the PC spreadsheet program Excel. Information can be added to the list object in the Excel application without the consistency of the object being destroyed. This way, it is possible to import changed list objects back into the R/3 System.

6.3.4 ABAP/4 Query

ABAP/4 Query offers the occasional user in a department the ability to define simple reports without programming (Figure 6.6). The user must simply determine which data is required and how the list should be laid out. The desired report is then generated automatically. This report can be modified and expanded, if required, with the tools of the ABAP/4 Development Workbench.

Users of ABAP/4 Query must first choose a subject area in which they want to work. Subject areas are collections of database fields that make sense in a business

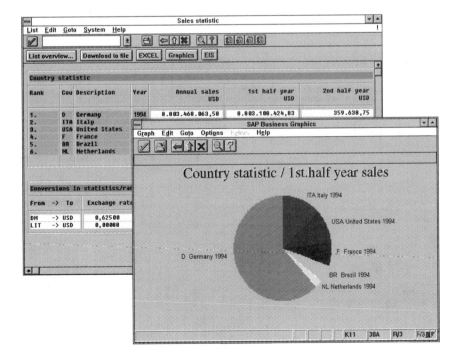

Figure 6.6 Database analysis with ABAP/4 Query.
© SAP AG

context, usually subsets of logical databases. The subject area determines which tables and fields the report should reference. The user then chooses the fields of the subject area desired for the list simply by marking them, and finally defines the desired list layout.

During execution of a report created with the help of ABAP/4 Query, a selection screen is automatically displayed for input of search criteria (database delimitation). This selection screen is determined by the logical database used. The database analysis can be output as a simple basic list (for example, a list of vendors), as statistics with average values, percentages, summations, and so on, or as ranking lists sorted according to business criteria. In addition, there are interfaces to SAP Presentation Graphics, to the management information system EIS (see Section 7.2.5), to MS Excel, and to file storage.

6.4 Tools of the ABAP/4 Development Workbench

The ABAP/4 Development Workbench contains all of the tools necessary for the creation and maintenance of ABAP/4 programs. With these, developers can create individual development objects using menu-driven work steps and combine them into complete applications (Figure 6.7).

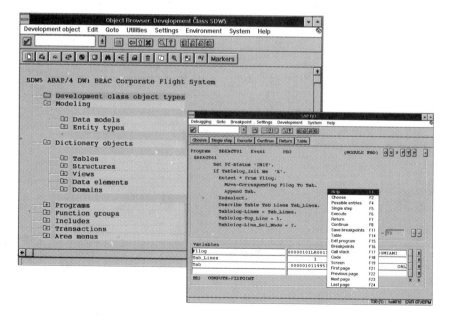

Figure 6.7 User interface of the development tools: Navigation, Editor, Debugger.
© SAP AG

To facilitate an overview of the components of an application, the ABAP/4 Development Workbench represents the development objects as a structured, hierarchical list. The developer uses a single tool to access this list, the Object Browser. The Object Browser manages object lists and offers general functions like display, create, copy, and so on.

By selecting an object with a double mouse click, a user automatically branches into the tool required for processing. This makes the Object Browser an essential element of the navigation concept realized in the ABAP/4 Development Workbench.

6.4.1 Navigation in the ABAP/4 Development Workbench

Quick navigation between tools and development objects can greatly improve productivity in the software development process. With this goal in mind, a comprehensive navigation concept was implemented in the ABAP/4 Development Workbench. The basic idea is to lead the developer to all of the necessary tools and development objects with intuitive mouse use.

The following navigation possibilities are available in the ABAP/4 Development Workbench:

- **Application hierarchy**: Hierarchical representation of the R/3 applications and their components down to the level of the Repository objects. The R/3 application hierarchy can be expanded to include custom applications, if necessary.

- **Repository Information System**: The Repository Information System offers display, search, and cross-reference functions for all of the development objects stored in the R/3 Repository.

- **Object Browser**: The Object Browser is the central tool for access to all of the development objects belonging to a program or project. Programs, dynpros, includes, models, CATT runs, and so on are depicted hierarchically as object lists. Double-clicking on an object starts processing with the corresponding tool.

- **Data Browser**: The Data Browser is the tool with which software developers display, create, and change data in newly stored tables. In addition, it is possible to navigate to the tables of the environment using foreign key relationships.

- **Navigation from the point of use to the definition point**: With a mouse click, it is possible to branch from any point of use of an object directly to the definition point. In this way, it is possible, for instance, to jump within the ABAP/4 Editor from a subroutine call to the subroutine definition, or from a table declaration to the table definition in the ABAP/4 Dictionary. It is equally possible to branch from the display of the flow logic of a dynpro in Screen Painter to the Program Editor, in order to process the corresponding ABAP/4 modules.

- **Navigation from the data model into the ABAP/4 Dictionary**: From the graphical display of entity-relationship data models, it is possible, using the mouse, to navigate down to the technical definitions in the ABAP/4 Dictionary and to the table contents.

- **Navigation from the status display into the current program code**: The status display of the R/3 System contains, among other things, information on the currently running transaction and on the current dynpro. By double-clicking on the status information, it is possible to jump directly into the corresponding program.

- **Navigation from the runtime analysis into the program code**: The ABAP/4 Development Workbench runtime analysis enables a detailed analysis of the required resources of the individual ABAP/4 modules of a program (see Section 6.4.9). From the list of ABAP/4 modules with their individual resource consumption, the developer can navigate directly into the program code, for example to carry out program optimizations.

It is possible to navigate in the ABAP/4 Development Workbench over several levels in a cascade fashion. Each starting position is stored in a push-down stack. This ensures that even in a multilevel navigation, it is always possible to return to the starting position.

6.4.2 R/3 Repository

All of the development objects of the ABAP/4 Development Workbench are collected in the R13 Repository. These development objects include:

- Models from data modeling and process modeling

- The entire ABAP/4 Dictionary

- ABAP/4 programs with all elements

- Function libraries

- Workbench Organizer objects

- Authorization administration objects

- Customer exits

- CATT runs.

Work in the R/3 Repository takes place with the help of the Repository Information System. The following functions can be used:

- Search

- Sort

- Whereused list.

Searching and sorting of repository objects is possible according to various criteria, for example according to certain object attributes, according to the date of the last change, and so on.

The Repository Information System's whereused list delivers all of the points of use for a specified object. In this way, it is possible to determine, for example, in which programs, dynpros, views, CATT runs, and so on a specified dictionary table is used, or at which point a certain function module is called.

The Repository Information System is fully integrated into the navigation of the ABAP/4 Development Workbench. Double-clicking on an object name activates the tool required for maintenance of this object.

The R/3 Repository is not only used by the tools of the ABAP/4 Development Workbench. It is also possible to access objects of the ABAP/4 Dictionary and of data modeling from external development environments, both read access and write access. Beginning with Release 3.0, the Open Repository Interface, implemented as an RFC interface, is available for this.

6.4.3 Data modeling

While the table definitions in the ABAP/4 Dictionary focus on technical development aspects, the SAP data model (Seubert et al., 1994) deals exclusively with business aspects.

The purpose of data models is to reflect the data required within the operational work environment in a formal fashion, in context across functions. In this sense, the SAP data model represents the operational information objects (entities) and their relationships from a business point of view. A structured entity relationship model (Figure 6.8) serves as the foundation. In this modeling procedure, data models for complex relationships can be constructed hierarchically from smaller submodels.

The SAP data model is divided into submodels for the R/3 applications Financial Accounting, Logistics, and Human Resources. In addition, information objects with a close business connection are modeled as "business objects." Examples of business objects are customer orders and general ledger accounts.

The ABAP/4 Development Workbench development tool for display and maintenance of data models is the Data Modeler. Using the Data Modeler, one can process SAP models and custom models. The Data Modeler supports the developer both in data modeling and in establishing links between the created models

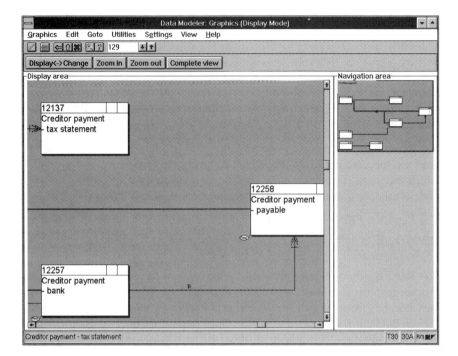

Figure 6.8 Data modeling with the Data Modeler.
© SAP AG

and the technical table definitions of the ABAP/4 Dictionary. The table fields correspond to the attributes of the entity types. The tight integration of the Data Modeler with the ABAP/4 Dictionary is a top-down design, with definition of the associated tables after the modeling phase being just as possible as a bottom-up approach with remodeling of existing table structures.

The SAP data model and the ABAP/4 Dictionary use the same, two-layer description concept for fields and attributes, the basis of which are domains and data elements (see Section 6.4.4). Having the same domains and data elements in the data model and in the ABAP/4 Dictionary reduces the development effort and automatically guarantees the consistency between the two levels.

Despite the tight logical connection between the SAP data model and the ABAP/4 Dictionary, it can sometimes be necessary for technical reasons to distribute entity types across several tables of the ABAP/4 Dictionary, or to combine several entity types in one table. In this case, database views are defined in the ABAP/4 Dictionary, which establish the link between the entity types of the data model and the tables of the ABAP/4 Dictionary. By selecting views, developers can display the instances of entity types and program with them in the same way as with other business objects.

6.4.4 The active ABAP/4 Dictionary

4GL development environments work with separately managed metadata, which describes the data structures used in the programs. Metadata includes table and field definitions, establishment of value ranges (domains), and the description of relationships between tables (see below).

All of the metadata of the R/3 applications is managed in the ABAP/4 Dictionary. In addition to the structure information, an unusual feature is technical settings such as the data type (master data, transaction data, organization data, and customizing data), the desired table buffering method, and the size category of tables. The R/3 runtime environment analyzes this information for optimization of internal operations.

The ABAP/4 Dictionary is part of the R13 Repository and is fully integrated into the navigation concept of the ABAP/4 Development Workbench (see Section 6.4.1). For example, table definitions from the ABAP/4 Dictionary can be displayed directly from within the ABAP/4 Editor.

The ABAP/4 Dictionary is an active dictionary. This means that changes in the ABAP/4 Dictionary have an automatic and immediate effect on all relevant application programs. The R/3 runtime environment ensures that the current definitions of the ABAP/4 Dictionary are always used. If, for example, a new value is entered in the value set of a domain, as a consequence, in all screens that contain a field with this domain, the help function F4 immediately displays this value in the list of possible values. In addition to this immediate activation, the ABAP/4 Dictionary also offers the developer the possibility of saving changes in an inactive version first. This way, for example, changes can be made to several interdependent objects that are subsequently to be activated together.

Active linking of the ABAP/4 Dictionary to the program flow is based on the interpretative mode of operation of the R/3 runtime environment. The ABAP/4 processor does not work with the original version of an ABAP/4 program, but rather interprets a runtime object (consisting of event tables, processing tables, and data tables) that is generated from the program text before the first execution. Runtime objects are automatically regenerated before their execution, if a comparison of time stamps determines an inconsistency with the ABAP/4 Dictionary. This combination of early binding and late binding ensures that active linking of the dictionary information does not come at the expense of efficiency.

Tables and fields

The central data structure in the ABAP/4 Dictionary is the table. Tables consist of fields. All of the attributes of fields in the generated database tables, in the dynpros and in the ABAP/4 programs are defined in the ABAP/4 Dictionary.

Table definitions in the ABAP/4 Dictionary give names to the table fields and specify attributes for each field, such as format, length, and so on. In addition, they determine the key fields of the tables and the relationships between the tables.

The attributes of individual table fields are described with the help of a two-level concept involving domains and data elements:

- Domains specify technical attributes like data type, length, value range, screen display, and so on.

- Data elements describe the business meaning and define key words, titles, documentation text, and a domain for each field. The documentation text is used by, among other things, the online help.

Since domains and data elements are independent objects in the ABAP/4 Dictionary, a domain can occur in any number of data elements. A data element can, in turn, be used repeatedly for fields in table definitions. Additional possibilities are offered by the embedding of entire data structures in tables. This is called an Include procedure. If a structure that is embedded in other tables is later changed, all affected tables are automatically adjusted. Taken all together, domains, data elements, and Include procedures result in a high degree of reuse and guarantee automatic retention of consistency of fields with the same meaning.

Structures from tables and fields stored in the database, as well as internal data structures of programs, can be described in the ABAP/4 Dictionary. Program-internal structure descriptions include, for example, the data type definition for fields that only appear in a dynpro, not in a database table, or the definition of tables that are stored only temporarily in an ABAP/4 program. Internal structures are used in the exchange of data between dynpros and ABAP/4 programs or in the definition of interfaces, such as in the submission of parameters to function modules. All automatic services in which the ABAP/4 Dictionary plays a role – online help, format checks, and so on – are also available for these internal structures.

With the inclusive description of internal and external data structures, the information contained in the ABAP/4 Dictionary goes way beyond that contained in the database catalog of the database system being used. To ensure consistency and ease of use, table and view definitions are generated automatically for all supported database systems from the information stored in the ABAP/4 Dictionary.

Generation of database definitions

The relational data model defined in the ABAP/4 Dictionary is independent of the database systems from individual manufacturers. To ensure a consistent link to the database system used, all catalog definitions and catalog changes for all of the database systems supported by the R/3 System are generated and performed automatically. In this process, the tables defined in the ABAP/4 Dictionary are copied onto the underlying database system.

From the ABAP/4 Dictionary, database tables, database indexes, and database views can be created, deleted, and modified. The developer requires no database-specific knowledge for this. Parameters for the storage of tables in the database can be derived from the database-independent characteristic values of the table. For the modification of existing tables, the R/3 System takes advantage of all of the possibilities offered by the respective database system for ALTER TABLE, for example INSERT FIELD, ADD FIELD, and so on. If an ALTER TABLE is not possible, programs are automatically generated that unload the data from the affected table and reload it in the new structure.

Foreign keys

Foreign keys are used to determine relationships between tables. A foreign key defines the allocation of fields of the dependent table to the key fields of another, referenced table.

The definition of foreign keys ensures that, for the fields of a dependent table, only those values are used that also appear as values for the key fields in the referenced table (Figure 6.9). Referenced tables are therefore also called check tables. The check takes place very early in the processing of screen input, not during writing to the database. This enables a high throughput to be reached in online processing.

To facilitate the definition of foreign keys, the ABAP/4 Dictionary contains the concept of value tables for domains. This allows the definition of dynamically changing value ranges as a supplement to value range definition by constants (for example, 1, 2, 3). The domain to be defined is allocated to a key field of the value table. The data of this table then determines the possible values of the domain.

Materials (Dependent table)

Material	Company code	Plant
1	01	01
2	02	01
7	02	03
3	03	04

Plant (Check table)

Company code	Plant
01	01
02	01
02	03
03	04

4	02	02	may not be inserted, because not part of the check table

Figure 6.9 Foreign key relationships.

Relational database systems can provide limited views of the data set oriented toward certain applications (see Section 3.5.2). This procedure is also available in the R/3 System. In the ABAP/4 Dictionary, views can be defined as virtual tables, which do not contain any of their own data, but solely provide an application-specific view of the tables recorded in the ABAP/4 Dictionary. A view consists of selected fields of a table or of several tables linked by foreign keys. By the definition of selection criteria, individual lines of the original table can be hidden in the view.

Matchcodes and indexes

Matchcodes are indexes (references), managed in the R/3 System, to application data stored in the database. They make interactive, targeted access to certain table entries possible. The implementation of matchcodes takes place either with the help of separate tables updated by triggers, or with database views. Extensive matchcodes should be supported by additional database indexes.

Matchcodes are used in the R/3 System because, unlike normal database indexes, they can also join fields from several original tables, while allowing individual, selected fields to be suppressed. In addition, limitation of the matchcode display to certain data sets is possible by defining certain selection criteria.

Table expansion with append structures

Standard R/3 application tables defined by SAP in the ABAP/4 Dictionary can be expanded by the customer to contain new fields without changing the affected tables themselves. With Release 3.0, the ABAP/4 Dictionary offers functions which whose help supplementary table fields can be created in independent append structures and logically linked to the original table. The separation between the original table and the append structure ensures that custom expansions of SAP application tables are not overwritten during release changes.

6.4.5 Screen Painter

The Screen Painter of the ABAP/4 Development Workbench is used to create, process, display, and delete dynpros. In addition, supplemental control information can be recorded for dynpros, such as the language used, the number of the follow-on dynpro, and the desired screen display (for example, dialog box, selection screen, and so on).

Oriented toward the three functions of dynpros, the Screen Painter supports the following development activities:

- Arrangement of field descriptions, screen fields, and control elements in the screens. The full-screen editor is available for this task.

- Description of field attributes for the screen fields created in the layout (for example, graphical display, display with leading zeros, and so on).

- Recording of flow logic.

For screen design, the Screen Painter has an alphanumeric editor and a graphical editor. In the graphical editor, the developer arranges the input and output fields and the accompanying field names on the screen. In addition, he or she can position control elements in the screen. All screen texts can be supplemented with or even replaced by graphical icons.

The following control elements are supported by the Screen Painter:

- **Scrolling input and output fields**: The length of input and output fields on the screen does not necessarily have to correspond to the actual field length. If necessary, scrolling within screen fields is possible.

- **Pushbuttons**: Pushbuttons represent keys on a dynpro. A mouse click on a pushbutton executes a defined function of the application. If necessary, this function can be displayed as a stylized icon on the pushbutton.

- **Radio buttons**: Radio buttons are selection fields that allow the selection of exactly one choice from a set of predefined alternatives.

- **Check boxes**: Check boxes make possible the selection of one or more choices from a set of predefined alternatives.

- **Borders**: Borders with an integrated title field visually combine logically related fields, for example a group of radio buttons. For list output of a variable number of input and output fields, the border size is adjusted automatically.

- **Table control**: Table control is a control element for the comfortable representation of large lists. The functions of table control include horizontal and vertical scrolling of the table, sorting according to selectable key columns, and selecting individual lines or columns.

In addition to the dialog in the primary dialog window, the Screen Painter makes secondary, modal dialog windows (subscreens) available. This type of window serves to simplify complex dialogs. For example, supplementary operations or error handling can run in secondary dialog windows.

6.4.6 Menu Painter

Graphical user interfaces allocate certain menus, function keys, and pushbuttons to the functions implemented by programs. In the ABAP/4 Development Workbench, the Menu Painter takes on this task. On a central work interface, which represents the structure of the menus and pushbuttons of an application, the developer can proceed with the corresponding definitions.

Menus can also be used across several screens. For rational program composition, overlapping menu definition is therefore desirable. The ABAP/4 Development Workbench fulfills this requirement in that menus created with the Menu Painter can be completely copied.

A main menu (action menu) can consist of up to three layers, and each layer can consist of up to 15 entries. Individual functions in the created menus can be activated and deactivated. When deactivated, although the function appears grayed-out in the menu, it cannot be selected. The maintenance language of a menu is determined during the creation of a program. It is also valid for the text elements, the Screen Painter, and the Menu Painter (see Section 6.2.7).

As well as the Menu Painter, in Windows 95 and Windows NT the Session Manager is available. It enables representation of the entire menu tree in a separate window with a PC-style display (see Section 5.4.4).

Guidelines according to the SAP Style Guide are available to the developer for the design of menus and pushbuttons (see Sections 3.7 and 5.4.1). Applying these guidelines enables consistent use of all interfaces created with the ABAP/4 Development Workbench. The guidelines can be taken over during interface design and modified or simply switched off in order to implement one's own requirements. For checking the defined entries, it is possible to create a checklist that shows the developer any errors or violations of the guidelines.

6.4.7 Program Editor

The Program Editor of the ABAP/4 Development Workbench has at its disposal all of the functions required for creating and processing ABAP/4 programs. In addition to the usual text operations like insert, search, replace, and so on, the following functions, especially, are of interest for program development:

- PC Editor functions like Cut&Paste, Lasso, Undo, Clipboard, and so on

- Starting and testing of programs

- Syntax checking of programs

- Display of information about syntax rules and valid key words

- Incorporation of ready-made routines (instruction patterns, templates), for example in loops, conditional instructions, call of function modules with import and export parameters, and in WRITE and SELECT instructions

- Structuring of the source code list with the Pretty Printer

- Comparison of two ABAP/4 programs with the help of the "Split Screen" editor.

The Program Editor is fully integrated in the navigation concept of the ABAP/4 Development Workbench (see Section 6.4.1).

6.4.8 Debugger

A separate debugger is available for debugging ABAP/4 programs and dynpros.

The debugger can be activated in various ways. It is generally possible to start programs explicitly in debugging mode. Alternatively, one can enter the debugger after program termination because of a runtime error or from process monitoring of the Computing Center Management System.

Programs that run in debugging mode can be interrupted either after every instruction (single step) or at certain points in the program. After every interrupt, the debugger provides information on the present status of processing. For example, the contents of previously selected variables, fields, work areas, and internal tables are displayed. These contents can be changed at will before processing continues.

Interrupts are either defined in the program or added and changed interactively in the debugger. Interrupts can be supplemented interactively by the specification of certain program lines or by the entry of stop conditions (for example, the value of the variable x is smaller than the value of the variable y). When Remote Function Calls are used, debugging across system boundaries is also possible (Remote Debugging).

6.4.9 Performance analysis and optimization of ABAP/4 programs

The tools for performance analysis of ABAP/4 programs determine the resource consumption of modular ABAP/4 elements like subroutines and function modules, of database accesses, and of operations with internal tables (Figure 6.10). Different levels of performance data can be provided as hit lists, sorted according to absolute or proportional consumption.

From these hit lists, it is possible to jump directly into the program code by double-clicking with the mouse.

6.4.10 Computer-Aided Test Tool (CATT)

For the description, combination, and automation of business processes that are required for program testing, the ABAP/4 Development Workbench includes CATT (Computer-Aided Test Tool). Tests are standardized and systematized by this tool and can be repeated as often as desired. Both individual functions and complex operations can be tested. The test flow and the accompanying parameter settings are logged by CATT. Input dialogs are either automatically simulated or manually entered step by step.

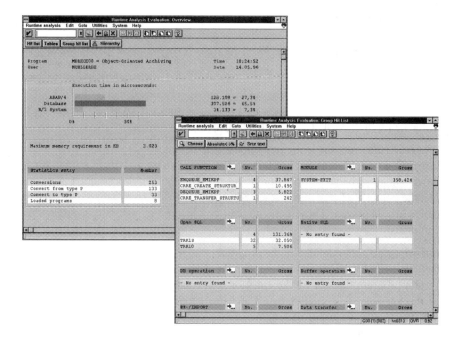

Figure 6.10 Performance analysis with the tools of the ABAP/4 Development Workbench.
© SAP AG

6.4.11 Organization of development projects

For the management of software development projects, the ABAP/4 Development Workbench provides the Workbench Organizer. It supports small and large development projects, as well as centralized and decentralized development projects.

With the help of the Workbench Organizer, development projects are divided into different tasks, on which individual developers or project groups collaborate. All changed development objects are recorded automatically in the tasks. They are then reserved for the exclusive use of these tasks. The development or maintenance of the development objects is blocked for use by other developers until the release of the task. The corresponding objects can only be displayed. This way, the tasks can be released independent of each other.

The developer responsible and a development class that identifies the subject area of the object are assigned to each development object. This ensures that contact persons can be found immediately for every object. The development class is also used as a structuring and training aid in the entire ABAP/4 Development Workbench.

The release of a task provides automatic version control for all objects, which allows comparisons as well as access to earlier versions. This way, the release conditions can be documented before and after a task or project and can even be restored.

For every task, the developers create structured documentation covering the project goals, the status, and any particularities. In addition, a log of all changed development objects is prepared automatically. Together with the documentation and version control, this log guarantees complete proof of changes for audits in single- or multi-system configurations.

Development projects are normally not carried out in the production system, but, depending on size, in one or more development or test systems. To guarantee the consistency of the objects, every object has a defined original location and release path in the linked systems, which can, however, be moved at any time. Changes can be made only to the original object, to avoid unintentional parallel development. When several development systems are used, the developers can develop and test their objects in isolation in their local development system after a Check-Out. To perform an integration test of objects from several local systems, the individual objects must be transported to a common integration system and tested there.

Closely linked to the Workbench Organizer is the Transport System, which carries out the transporting of development objects. Transports can be carried out according to the task, that is, the set of development objects to be transported results automatically after release.

For every transport, a transport log is automatically created. If, for example, a production system produces errors after an import from the test system, it is possible to ascertain immediately which objects were transported, who gave the transport order, and why the transport was carried out. To check the consistency of a transport in advance, it is possible to simulate the transport into the target system. The user can thereby get an early estimate of the possible consequences of his or her transport order on the target system.

With the tight link between the transport system and the Workbench Organizer, all pre-defined transport paths are automatically used, and unintentional over-writing of objects is prevented.

The Workbench Organizer ensures short downtimes during release changes (Repository Switch Procedure, see Section 5.7.4). Custom functions and data structures that diverge from the standard can be transferred easily, since they are completely recorded and both the SAP standard version and the customer version exist. Tools are available to perform the customization.

In addition to the Workbench Organizer and the Transport System, an information system is available for searching, displaying, processing, and analyzing tasks and transports. The following information can be displayed:

- Tasks and transports along with their respective development or transport history, sorted and selected according to developers or subject areas

- Tasks and transports that have not yet been released or transported

- Tasks and transports that affect certain development objects

- Development objects, selected and sorted according to subject areas, responsible developers, change date, and additional criteria.

Chapter 7

The Business Applications of the R/3 System

In this chapter, the fundamental properties of the business applications of the R/3 System (Figure 7.1) are described, as well as the basic functions available for all applications.

7.1 Principles of application development

Business application systems reach wide distribution only if they cover all of the business processes in companies. The functions must be constructed in such a way that as many industrial sectors and types of businesses as possible can implement the system in different countries.

The applications of the R/3 System have been designed according to the following principles:

- **Complete business processes with consistent quantity and value flows**: R/3 applications allow complete processing of business events. The quantities and values of a process are represented consistently and up to date in all business components at all times. They are available with up-to-the-second accuracy for control of business processes and for corporate planning. This complete approach is also known as "Enterprise Resource Planning" (ERP), which has evolved from the "MRP II Philosophy" (Manufacturing Resource Planning), with its expansive planning and control methods for logistics.

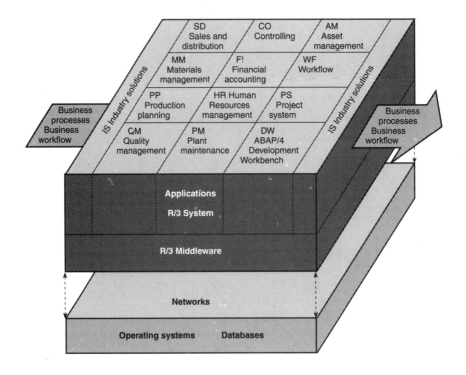

Figure 7.1 Architecture of the R/3 applications.

- **Data for a process is recorded only once**: Data for a process is recorded only once and is then available for all components involved in the processing. A process in which various business components of the R/3 System are involved, for example in the areas of Sales and Distribution, Production Logistics, and Accounting, is carried out in a general business process.

- **Configurable business processes through integrated customizing functions**: More than 800 business process chains with their associated functions are represented in the R/3 System. During implementation of the process chains, the different characteristics of the standard solutions needed for different branches of industry and company types, as well as multilingualism and national particularities, were taken into consideration. This diversity of functions, along with the customizability implemented in the system, is used to mold the system to the individual requirements of a customer installation. The users have the R/3 Customizing functions at their disposal for this. The basic advantage of this concept lies therein, that in every form, the system refers back to uniform data structures and process definitions. The system remains adaptable to changed business processes even after installation, while in productive operation.

- **Support for Business Process Re-Engineering**: "Business Process Re-Engineering" (BPR) could also be called "Business Process Optimizing." Businesses must continually check and improve their internal operations, particularly their cooperation with customers and business partners, to remain competitive. These activities should be supported by the application software implemented.

  For the R/3 System, these requirements result in fundamental standards for the architecture: scalability, portability, openness, and distributability, for example. Extensive provision of functions, integrated customizing functions, and business workflow support are also necessary for the system to be able to adapt to organizational changes and business process adjustments immediately. Changes in legal company structure, adjustment of profit center structures, or permanent, customer-oriented optimizing of logistical operations in procurement, production, warehousing, or sales and distribution are examples of possible changes in companies.

- **Independence of business solutions from system components**: The life cycle of business application software differs considerably from that of system components. Basic business operations naturally experience long-term, continuous development, which must not be dependent on short-term technological trends in hardware. R/3 middleware (see Section 5.1) ensures the independence of business solutions from system interfaces.

- **Internationalization of applications**: International implementation of R/3 applications is provided for at a fundamental level in the architecture of the R/3 System by language-dependent and country-specific functions.

  Language-dependent components in the R/3 System are designed in such a way that users who have logged on to the system with different language keys can work with the same business objects, such as material master records, customer data, and vendor data. This is relevant particularly for screens, system help, and online documentation, but also for master data, which is linked to language-dependent tables. At run time, the language entries are called up by the system according to the logon of the user.

  Currently, the R/3 System is available in over 20 languages (see Section 5.4.3). Additional languages are in preparation or will follow according to market demand. There is no technical limitation on the number of language versions in the R/3 System.

  Country-specific adjustments are part of the R/3 standard version. The system is usable internationally. Among other things, it takes into consideration the varying requirements of industrialized countries: multiple languages, flexible currency handling, and functions for taxes, reporting, and payment transactions that are customized for certain countries.

With the help of the dialog control of R/3 Customizing, country-specific business events are installed without altering the software of the R/3 System. For example, this applies to:

- Master data information
- Check rules
- Structure of the input fields on the screen
- Accounting rules
- Forms.

• **Quality assurance**: High quality demands are placed on the R/3 System. To meet these demands, SAP has introduced quality management in lieu of traditional quality control. Quality is no longer "checked" but produced. During software production, quality assurance is integrated into the processes, from design through development and release to maintenance of installed systems. The differences between quality control and quality management are presented in Table 7.1.

Table 7.1 Differences between quality control and quality management.

Quality control	Quality management
process-oriented	function in the entire company
product-oriented	process-oriented
at the end of a process	accompanying the process
separation of manufacturing and testing	manufacturer does the checking
effort lies in control, for error detection	effort lies in process improvement, for error prevention

ISO 9000 standards have prevailed as international guidelines for quality management. These guidelines describe the organizational structures and procedures necessary for quality assurance. The following parts of the ISO 9000 series are relevant for software producers:

- **ISO 9001** defines the requirements for quality management in the production process. This standard is valid for all branches of industry. It is also used in the software industry.

- **ISO 9000-3** is an additional guideline, which details the particularities for use of the ISO 9001 standard in the software industry.

- **ISO 9004-2** is a special standard for the service area.

To receive an ISO 9000 certificate, a company must show that its production process corresponds to the ISO quality requirements. Certificates are granted after testing by an independent, authorized company. SAP's development and consulting branches received ISO 9001 certificates at the end of 1994.

Additional quality requirements are contained in the GMP and GLP (Good Manufacturing and Laboratory Practices) standards published by the American federal agency FDA (Food and Drug Administration). These standards apply to companies that are active in medical technology and in food and drug production. Most industrialized nations have comparable standards, or standards that follow the American regulations. SAP is currently working on obtaining FDA certification for parts of the R/3 System.

7.2 Overview of applications

The standard business applications of the R/3 System include the following areas:

- Accounting
- Logistics
- Human Resources Management
- R/3 Industry Solutions
- Open Information Warehouse
- Office Functions.

The applications are based on business objects, their methods, and their relationships. In the world of business terminology, objects are materials, customer orders, production units, invoices, and so on, which are defined in terms of their relationships to each other and are linked together by processes.

7.2.1 Accounting

In the past few years, accounting has developed from the principle of "recording all business processes in accordance with bookkeeping principles" to an instrument for planning and control in an enterprise. Standard integrated software like the R/3 System meets these demands. It combines the record keeping of accounting with information from operational areas, creating a complete and always up-to-date view of the value-added chain in an enterprise.

R/3 accounting includes the areas of Financial Accounting, Asset Accounting, and Controlling.

Financial Accounting

The components of Financial Accounting meet the requirements of mid-sized companies as well as those of multinational corporations, whose reporting functions, for example, must take different currencies into account.

The following function areas are available in Financial Accounting:

- General ledger accounting with
  - Business accounting
  - Closing procedures
  - Balance sheet and profit planning
  - Reporting
  - Business area accounting
  - Expanded general ledger
- Accounts receivable with
  - Management of customers
  - Invoices and credit memos
  - Document and account processing
  - Dunning procedure
- Accounts payable with
  - Invoice receipt
  - Down payments and payments
  - Credits
  - Preliminary posting of invoices
  - Account displays
- Company consolidation with
  - Debt consolidation
  - Capital consolidation
  - Analyses and reporting
  - Closing during the fiscal year
  - Integration of internal and external company reporting
- Financial controlling with
  - Cash management
  - Electronic banking
  - Bank account clearing
  - Cash management position
  - Foreign exchange transactions
- Financial asset management with
  - Financial borrowing
  - Loans
  - Stocks
  - Currency exchange

- Funds management with

  - Planning and budgeting

  - Open item management

  - Expense account posting

  - Expense statements

  - Availability control

  - Fiscal accounting

- Financial Information System

The foundation of all posting processes in R/3 Financial Accounting is the data of the individual documents. Immediately after document posting, the affected account details, totals and balance lists, as well as balance sheet and profit/loss analyses, can be processed online. The basis for this is the principle of integrated processing of all document data, which ensures synchronous updating of accounting and controlling information.

The central integration element is the chart of accounts, which drives the update of all processes according to a uniform account structure. This applies to all financially relevant transactions of the R/3 System's application components. This guarantees the consistency of the quantity flow (logistics) and the value flow (accounting) within business processes.

With Release 3.0, new functions were introduced, such as:

- "Coexistence of distributed general ledgers," with which accounting data from different SAP Systems can be managed together in a centralized G/L accounting

- Investment management, which accompanies an investment from planning to accounting

- Workflow integration in Financial Accounting, for example in the accounting department.

Asset Management

The components of Asset Management control the entire life cycle of fixed assets. Even in the functions of Asset Management, there is integration with Financial Accounting and Logistics. This enables support of operations from investment planning, through procurement, to account processing. The value development of an asset can be represented consistently with the help of reporting.

The main components of R/3 Asset Management are:

- Investment controlling with
  - Investment planning
  - Efficiency calculation
  - Budgeting
  - Investment control
  - Order and project management
  - Depreciation simulation
- Asset accounting with
  - Value assignment procedures
  - Depreciation calculations
  - Depreciation simulation
  - Currency handling
  - Asset movement
- Technical asset management with
  - Connection to the Plant Maintenance System
  - Plant maintenance planning
  - Order processing
  - Plant maintenance controlling
  - Accounting

Controlling

Controlling enables the continuous, up-to-date control and monitoring of costs, revenues, resources, and deadlines. This complex task is handled with the help of the relationships between business objects described in the R/3 System. In the defined business processes, the respective controlling aspects are also taken into consideration.

Controlling components available in the R/3 System include:

- Cost center accounting, such as
  - Cost element accounting
  - Planning
  - Budget management
  - Accounting
  - Variance processing
  - Reporting

- Profit center accounting, such as
  - Total cost accounting
  - Planning and reporting
  - Transfer prices
  - Analyses

- Profitability and market segment analysis with
  - Revenue calculation
  - Sales and profit planning
  - Contribution margin accounting
  - Cost-of-sales accounting
  - Customer order calculation
  - Profitability analysis

- Order and project cost accounting with
  - Order types
  - Order planning
  - Open item management
  - Order accounting
  - Order report

- Product cost accounting with
  - Product costing
  - Job-order costing
  - Cost object controlling
  - Costing analyses

- Performance analysis with
  - Activity types
  - Cost rates
  - Charging of variances
  - Processes and services

In the R/3 System's Cost Accounting, profitability analyses are possible for products, for different market segments, or for different company areas (profit centers).

With activity-based costing, Release 3.0 includes a controlling instrument that takes the business process orientation of the R/3 System into account in the area of cost accounting, as well. The job of activity-based costing is to record and analyze the costs and performance of business processes and cost objects. Shared costs are assigned to business processes according to their resource consumption. Cost objects are debited from the business processes in proportion to their individual usage.

7.2.2 Logistics

The business-process-oriented application architecture of the R/3 System becomes particularly clear in the logistical functions, which cover the areas of marketing, sales and distribution, production planning and control, materials management, and procurement (Zencke, 1994).

Main components of Logistics

Logistical operations require a high degree of integration of the Sales & Distribution, Production, and Procurement function areas. During order processing, for example, current information, such as material stock or production planning data, is immediately available.

R/3 Logistics includes the following main components:

- Sales & Distribution with
    - Operative sales support
    - Request for quotation, quotation, orders
    - Contracts, scheduling agreements
    - Shipping, invoicing
    - Sales Information System

- Production Planning with
    - Sales planning, production planning
    - Material requirements planning, MRP II planning/simulation
    - Capacity planning
    - Production activity control, control station technology
    - Plant data collection
    - Costing, project management
    - Production Information System

- Materials Management with
    - Requirements planning
    - Vendor evaluation
    - Purchasing, Purchasing Information System
    - Goods movements, inventory management
    - Invoice verification
    - Definition of warehouse structures
    - Warehouse management, processing of stock movements
    - Cross-application classification

Additional R/3 Logistics components such as Quality Management, Plant Maintenance, and Project and Service Management are described in the sections that follow.

The Logistics components of the R/3 System can be used for different types of production, including make-to-order production, repetitive manufacturing, manufacturing of products with variants, and batch-oriented process manufacturing. Next to the classic procedures for requirements control, such as reorder point planning, forecast-based planning, and net requirements planning, impulse-controlled material replenishment according to Kanban and "Just-in-Time" principles is also possible.

For the chemical and pharmaceuticals industries and for the food and beverage industry, with their specific requirements for process planning and control, special solutions have been developed, such as

- Resource management

- Recipe management

- Process planning

- Process coordination

- Process documentation

- Links to process control and laboratory information systems.

For basic comprehension of the logistical operations in the R/3 System, the following two primary process chains are presented as examples:

- **Logistical Planning Process**: Data from Sales & Distribution, such as the analysis of customer needs, can flow directly into the planning operations of the R/3 System's MRP II planning functions. This process chain consists of business planning, which generates the input for sales planning. From sales planning, production program planning is derived, whose results, in turn, flow into master production scheduling and into material requirements planning and materials procurement. The actual control of production is thus based on a complete planning process, which obtains its basic data from the Sales and Distribution system.

- **Materials Procurement**: Within Materials Management, the following process chains can be described for materials procurement:
  The Purchasing Information System delivers information about materials and vendors for the procurement process, which is started with a purchase requisition. The subsequent purchasing process is supported by the system with functions for order processing. These include, for example, management of outline agreements and scheduling agreements. In warehousing, after the goods receipt, inventory must be managed on a value basis and handled according to its physical requirements. The procurement process chain ends with invoice verification and updating of the value and/or price

of the material. At this level of the process, there is again a tight link to the processes of Financial Accounting

Quality Management

With Quality Management, operations for checking and ensuring quality are planned and implemented within the logistics chain. The incorporation of quality assurance into the entire logistical system is an important contribution to the optimal design of business processes. The Purchasing Information System, for instance, receives quality scores for the evaluation of vendors and quality-related data for requests for quotation and purchase orders. For goods receipt, control data is generated, for example for inspection. This control data determines, among other things, which material is inspected according to which procedure and when. In the release of production orders, information relevant to inspection can be automatically assigned to individual operations. Sales and Distribution and Customer Service have access to current quality data for planning customer service activities. R/3 Quality Management components are:

- Quality planning, quality control, inspection

- Quality documentation

- Quality Information System.

Plant Maintenance

As an internal service function, Plant Maintenance makes a fundamental contribution to the success of a company by guaranteeing all technical functions for production and for implementation of services. In addition, abundant standards have been formulated with regard to the law for planning, processing, and verification of plant maintenance measures. In companies with a high degree of automation in production engineering, with complex equipment such as that used in the chemical industry, or a large number of instruments to be maintained, such as in airports, the plant maintenance area of a company and its tasks are unusually broad.

The R/3 Plant Maintenance system is structured to meet the described requirements. In this case, too, operations are closely connected to other company areas like Logistics, Financial Accounting, and Human Resources Management. Plant maintenance processes also use other functions available in the R/3 System, such as those of procurement, asset accounting, controlling, and human resources management. R/3 Plant Maintenance includes the following function areas:

- Maintenance planning and inspection planning

- Handling of maintenance orders

- Management of completion confirmations

- Asset history management

- Plant Maintenance Information System.

Project Management

Project management is a typical cross-section function that must support the interdisciplinary cooperation of different areas. The R/3 Project System contains all of the components necessary for project management, such as

- Work breakdown structuring

- Network plans

- Time scheduling

- Cost input

- Budget management

- Project analysis

- Interface to external project management systems.

The process chains that can be implemented in the Project System combine all of the activities for the planning and execution of projects across areas and applications. At any time, project employees can access all of the project-relevant data from Cost Accounting, Financial Accounting, Materials Management, Production, and Sales and Distribution. Conversely, the data created by the Project System is provided to other R/3 applications.

Service Management

Functionality, quality, and price of products from different suppliers are often almost identical. In that case, companies can only make purchasing decisions or longer-term customer relationships on the basis of service. Customer service is then the actual product of these companies. The R/3 System follows up on this situation with the Service Management component. All of the aspects of service management are implemented in this component, such as:

- Customer and device management

- Warranty management

- Handling of service activities

- Consideration of cooperation with partner companies

- Cost monitoring and accounting.

7.2.3 Human Resources Management

Traditionally, human resources management has been considered a relatively isolated area in many companies, a fact that is also reflected in the architecture and functions of most human resources management systems. These systems are not directly linked with logistics and accounting processes.

Designing optimal business processes, however, requires integration of human resource management tasks. These include, for example, flexible organization customizing and reconciliation of manpower plans, work schedules, and service plans with logistics and accounting processes. Therefore, the R/3 System's functions for human resources management are tightly linked to the components of Financial Accounting, Controlling, and Production Planning. These functions include:

- Master data management

- Payroll accounting

- Travel expense management

- Country-specific versions of payroll accounting for numerous countries

- Time management

- Applicant administration and applicant selection

- Personnel development

- Organizational planning

- Workforce planning and manpower requirements planning

- Information System (for example, for legal information), analyses, and statistical procedures.

SAP's Human Resources Management offers companies and management integrated processing of all personnel-related tasks. Country-specific versions are already available for Austria, Belgium, France, Germany, Great Britain, Japan, the Netherlands, Spain, Switzerland, and the USA.

A central element of the R/3 Human Resources Management system is the R/3 Organization Model (Figure 7.2). Its purpose is the representation of

- Organizational plans

- Organizational units such as planned positions, work groups, cost centers, and departments

- Work center description

- Staffing schedules

- Tasks and their assignment to people and work groups.

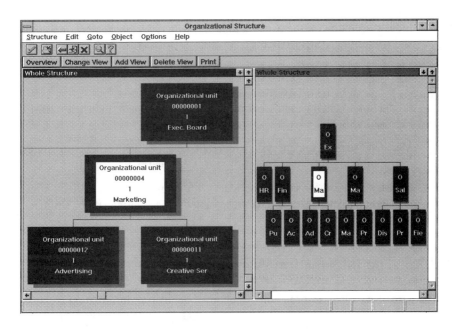

Figure 7.2 Graphical depiction of organizational plans in the R/3 System.
© SAP AG

With the assignment of tasks to organizational units and people, the R/3 Organization Model serves as the basis for workflow control of the R/3 System (see Section 7.4.1).

7.2.4 Industry solutions

On the basis of the standard R/3 applications, SAP has developed industry solutions for certain business sectors. These special versions of the R/3 System offer companies of a particular branch of industry all the advantages of a standard system.

The following industry solutions (IS) are available or are currently being developed:

- Budget management and financial planning for public administration (IS-PS, Public Sector)

- Hospital management with patient administration and patient accounting, as well as hospital controlling (IS-H, Hospital)

- Subscription and advertising management and sales system for newspaper and magazine publishers (IS-P, Publishing)

- Management of securities and loans for insurance companies and financial service companies (IS-IS, Insurance)

- Industry solution for the banking industry, with risk management, reporting, and controlling (IS-B, Banking)

- Industry solution for the oil industry, for exploration, transport, and distribution (IS-Oil)

- Production planning and control for process-oriented industries (IS-PI, Process Industry)

- Merchandise management system for retail industries, with product structures, distribution logistics, and "point-of-sale" systems (IS-RT, Retail)

- Industry solution for utility providers with equipment management, house installation, meter reading data processing and accounting (IS-U, Utilities).

7.2.5 The Information Warehouse

The term "SAP Open Information Warehouse" denotes an information architecture that provides an overview of all of the data in an enterprise. Data from department-specific, component information systems of the decentralized operative systems are gathered in an Information Warehouse (Figure 7.3). Different aggregations and views of the detailed data and the characteristic values derived from them serve as the basis for department-specific or strategic analyses and decision making (see Section 3.5.6).

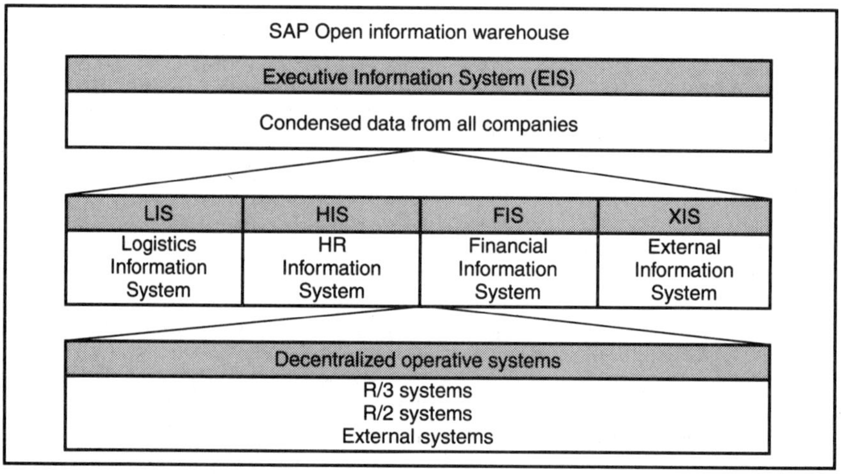

SAP Open information warehouse

Executive Information System (EIS)			
Condensed data from all companies			

LIS	HIS	FIS	XIS
Logistics Information System	HR Information System	Financial Information System	External Information System

Decentralized operative systems			
R/3 systems R/2 systems External systems			

Figure 7.3 SAP's Open Information Warehouse.

All connected systems automatically supply the SAP Open Information Warehouse with data. The data display can be tailored to the individual information needs of a company. This applies, for example, to descriptions such as sales organizations and customers, to characteristic values such as total sales and order entry, and to period selection.

In order to guarantee the consistency of business access keys, all of the keys used in the SAP Open Information Warehouse are unique and defined in accordance with the R/3 Repository. The term "sales" exemplifies the problem of defining business terms. Usually, sales means the receivables created due to invoicing. But sales can also mean order entry. When defining this access key, one must also decide, for example, if returns and cancellations should be included.

SAP's Open Information Warehouse consists of three information layers (Figure 7.3):

- **Business Events Layer**
  This layer describes business events and their relationships to one another. Concrete examples are purchase orders, production orders, projects, and customer orders. The business events are not only described from the point of view of an application (for example, goods receipt in Materials Management), but also for additional relevant applications (for example, goods receipt with account assignment for Financial Accounting). Simultaneous updating of business events in all applications involved and references to earlier processes are implemented in the operative business events layer. For example, a good receipt references a previous purchase order.

- **Component Information Systems Layer**
  For individual business function areas such as Logistics, Accounting, and Human Resources Management, component information systems are provided. On the basis of the business events, these information systems condense the business data according to time and subject area into area-oriented, higher-level views (product group and customer group, periods, and so on). In each of these component information systems, area-specific characteristic values can be generated (for example, level of service per customer, turnover per product group, cost considerations, and so on).

- **Executive Information System Layer**
  The Executive Information System (EIS) consolidates the component views of the business areas into a company-wide view. High-level reporting structures and analyses for strategic enterprise planning and management are provided in the EIS.

  Conversion of data from the operative areas for high-level reporting is also possible. This is necessary, for example, when you want to observe a strategically important market segment that is not defined in the operative systems in the form required for analysis.

7.2.6 Office functions

In the R/3 System, office functions are handled by the SAPoffice component. Its main functions are:

- Mail and filing functions
- Address management
- Integrated inbox
- Integrated word processing
- Office functions such as reminders, proxies, automatic answering, and so on
- Link to calendar
- Integration of PC documentation
- Application integration
- Workflow communication
- Optical archiving
- External communication.

With the SAPoffice mail and filing system, users can manage, send, and receive all kinds of documents, such as worksheets from a spreadsheet, word processing documents, or PC graphics. Every R/3 user has his or her own, hierarchical folder in SAPoffice. In addition, there are public folders that are accessible to user groups.

For immediate creation of short notes in the mail system, SAPscript, the internal word processor of the R/3 System, is available. It is integrated in the applications and is used to create forms such as purchase orders, invoices, and so on, and to create material descriptions, vendor descriptions, and other short texts.

The integrated inbox is a central online function that works like an inbox on a desk. With column selection, sorting criteria, and filters, it can be customized for every user. Electronic messages, which can contain attachments of any kind of object types and work items, are transferred to the user here for processing. Owing to the technical integration of SAPoffice with the R/3 System's business applications and with PC applications, processing transactions can be called up directly from within the inbox or the folder.

SAPoffice provides the following interfaces and integration functions for external communication:

- POP3 (Post Office Protocol, Version 3) is used for the exchange of mail documents between mail servers (Post Office) and mail clients (for example, PC Mailbox). In this environment, SAPoffice is a POP3 server that any mail system conforming to POP3 can access. This makes it possible to load mail documents on a laptop and process them independently.

- The "SAPoffice MAPI Service Providers" such as "Message Store," "Address Book," and "Transport" can be implemented in a PC mail system as Dynamic Link Libraries (see Section 7.5.2). They communicate directly with SAPoffice as mail servers, using RFCs (Remote Function Calls). This allows every mail system conforming to MAPI to be used with SAPoffice.

- X.400 for electronic exchange of messages and files (ISO 10021).

- SMTP – Simple Mail Transfer Protocol (UNIX Mail).

- Internet "MIME" (Multi-Purpose Internet Mail Extension) standard.

- Link to X.500 Directories (ISO 9594 standard) for management of X.400, Internet, and SAP addresses, as well as management of fax numbers.

- Fax link and connection of telephone equipment for initiating outgoing conversations.

7.2.7 Connection of optical storage systems

Optical storage media allow secure storage and archiving of mass data (see Section 3.2.2), which can exist as NCI (Non Coded Information) documents or CI (Coded Information) documents.

Most optical archiving systems work with the following disk sizes:

- 5.25-inch disks with a capacity of 1.3 Gbytes. This is the equivalent of about 400 000 pages of CI documents or 20 000 pages of NCI documents.

- 12-inch disks with a capacity of 6.5 Gbytes. This is the equivalent of about 2 000 000 pages of CI documents or 100 000 pages of NCI documents.

NCI documents are originals that have been captured with scanners and stored in uncoded format. For example, ordinary mail can be opened, scanned and delivered to the electronic inbox of the designated employee through workflow control (see Section 7.4). CI documents are stored in coded form (for example, outgoing documents, print lists, and so on) and can be processed by application programs.

The "SAP ArchiveLink" interface links optical storage systems to the applications of the R/3 System. For example, after a posted invoice is called up with the "display original" function, the original document appears in a second window.

The connection of optical storage systems is used by various applications in the R/3 System. Some examples of R/3 documents stored on optical storage media are:

- **SAPoffice**: Faxes, texts, graphics, images, and so on

- **Document management**: Mechanical drawings, texts, lists, graphics, images, programs for manufacturing machines, and so on

- **Financial Accounting**: Incoming invoices, detailed credit memos

- **Sales and Distribution**: Complaints, contracts, contract changes, scheduling agreements, requests for quotation, and purchase orders, as well as quotations, order confirmations, delivery notes, invoices, rebate credit memos, scheduling agreements, and correspondence

- **Human Resources Management**: Personnel files, accounting forms, payroll accounts

- **Materials Management**: Outline agreements, purchase orders, requests for quotation, schedule lines

- **Production Planning**: Manufacturing orders.

7.3 General application functions

7.3.1 Clients and company codes

A client is an autonomous unit in the R/3 System with regard to commercial law, organization, and data. It has a separate data environment and accordingly separate application and transaction data, associated user master data and chart of accounts, specific customizing parameters, and a separate organization of background processing.

The client technique allows different companies to be run independently of each other in an R/3 installation. Generally, different clients are used for test environments, simulation environments, and productive environments. But even in service computer centers, the client concept can be implemented to allow customers to use R/3 applications without having to install separate hardware or software.

For technical and organizational reasons, the following clients are usually defined in addition to productive clients:

- Test clients for testing the productive environment

- Training clients for education of employees

- Customizing client for parallel preparation of additional application components or for testing custom variants

- R/3 standard client with the system as delivered by SAP.

Business- and data-independent clients can be individually configured with the customizing functions, because, with a few exceptions, the customizing parameters are client-dependent.

Users of different clients coexist with their data independently and isolated in the same R/3 System. A user can see or process data in a certain client only if he or she is authorized to do so. This isolation rule is contained in the basic design of R/3 tables, both application tables and customizing tables. In addition, a client-specific selection parameter ensures that only data from one's own client can be accessed. This applies equally to read and write accesses. Client 000 is defined as the SAP standard or SAP presentation client, and its contents may not be changed. It also helps with the incorporation of new and pre-installed customizing tables during updates or release changes. This structure greatly eases the burden of maintaining the R/3 System.

To support the client structure, the R/3 System contains tools for setting up, copying, transporting, resetting, deleting, and comparing the clients defined in an installation.

For further subdivision of a company, the company code is provided, which represents an independent, legally accountable organizational unit. For internal accounting, which serves as the financial control instrument in a company, there is an additional level of subdivision, with allocation groups and planning groups for cost accounting, profitability analysis, and valuation. At this level, company departments are defined for differentiated financial accounting. All transaction figures and results (profit/loss calculation or balance sheet) can be stored, managed, and evaluated for every company department. With the help of internal allocation functions, it is possible within the company departments to subdivide any result level, like divisions or product lines, production units (plants), or sales organizations, according to additional, business-relevant criteria.

Logistical operations in sales and distribution, in production, and in procurement often require additional possibilities for structuring a company independent of financial requirements. To handle this, organizational units like plants, warehouses, and storage areas, as well as shipping points and loading points, are provided.

7.3.2 Calendar function

The holiday and factory calendar is a central calendar function in the R/3 System that all applications can access.

For integrated business process chains that span different business areas like Logistics and Financial Accounting, consistent definition of available man-days is a must. The factory calendar identifies a day of the year both by date and by continuous numbering of all work days and holidays. It is designed to convert back and forth between these two representations.

Regional particularities, for example different holidays, are taken into account with the help of different holiday calendars. The factory calendar calculates dates on the basis of the holiday calendar chosen and special rules defined for particular situations, for example company holidays or special shifts. The man-days resulting from the generation of the factory calendar are numbered sequentially as factory dates for a certain period of validity.

Calendar data is required constantly in a business application. Accordingly, it is directly accessible through a calendar buffer in the main storage area.

7.3.3 Number ranges

Number ranges determine the intervals from which business objects receive unique numbers. Such numbers are, for example, order numbers, material master numbers, vendor numbers, and customer numbers. A number range can be defined externally. Assignment of numbers is then performed manually by the user. In internal assignment, the numbers are generated by the system on the basis of defined number ranges.

For efficient management of a large number of very different business objects, system-supported differentiation functions are necessary for number assignment. Number ranges are tied to rules that are needed for the assignment of numbers to business objects. The R/3 System checks for correct assignment to a number range when creating a business object. Examples: The assignment of a material number is dependent on the material type. Company codes determine the intervals for invoice numbers.

7.3.4 Change documents

With the help of change documents, changes in master records, tables, business documents, and so on are automatically recorded in the system. Generation of a change document can be called from any application, if this is necessary for business or technical reasons. Change documents are an important basis for auditability of business applications.

Change documents also support the administration of development and corrections carried out with the ABAP/4 Development Workbench. It is possible to define in the ABAP/4 Dictionary, down to field level, that changes to contents automatically create a change document. For every change of an object, both the old value and the new value are recorded in the change document.

7.3.5 Global time management

Companies operating in the international arena, with branches in different time zones, have special requirements for processing date- and time-related information. Take, for instance, the case of an employee in an American company, who works from Japan with a database server installed in California, using a WAN connection. The following requirements must be met:

- The default dates automatically generated by the system during order creation or document creation must correspond to the local date.

- Analyses of the central database must also be possible using local time criteria, for example "which contracts were entered today worldwide?"

- Optimization of business processes must be supported by global use of resources. For example, a company in the electronics industry can satisfy a need that exists in Germany on 14 December 1995 at 6:00 p.m. from its plant in Japan as well as from its plant in California. With a transport time of 24 hours, in Japan the goods must be ready for delivery on 13 December 1995 at 10:00 p.m., whereas in California they need not be ready until 14 December 1995 at 3:00 am.

The solution to the problem of global time management is to give every event a time stamp that is unique worldwide and that contains the date and time in UTC (Universal Time Coordinated, Greenwich Mean Time), as well as a corresponding conversion rule with which this global time can be converted into local time. SAP is currently working on an appropriate solution.

7.4 Business workflow

Adjustment of business processes to continually changing market requirements is often not extensive enough or fast enough. In many companies, a less than flexible information infrastructure hampers the required changes. Operations are often cemented in information systems developed in-house. These systems implicitly prescribe to employees how to structure their work. They promote a tailored, function-oriented mode of operation instead of customer orientation, initiative, and team thinking across departments.

Flexible company structures with few hierarchy levels, and with transparent organization structures and operations that are always adaptable to market realities, are future-oriented. This is where the workflow concept comes in. Cooperation between employees and teams in the company, optimal cooperation between vendors, production, sales and distribution, and customers, as well as cooperation with partner companies, are all tasks that can be more effectively managed with workflow support.

The "Workflow Management Coalition (WFMC)," in which SAP is represented in addition to users, consulting companies, and several manufacturers of workflow systems, defines a workflow management system as follows:

> "A workflow management system provides procedures for automating business processes. It coordinates the sequence of work steps and the activities of the people involved, and it provides the software functions necessary for processing business processes" (Workflow Management Coalition, 1995).

A workflow management system must support the following tasks:

- **Control of business transactions across transaction boundaries**

- **Work list management** for active management of work lists that are assigned to employees or teams

- **Event management** for flexible, adjustable reactions to events such as status changes of material master data and customer orders or incoming messages from other systems, for example with EDI

- **Deadline management** for automatic starting of escalation procedures when certain events occur, for example missed deadlines or cost overruns

- **Optimization of business processes** with modeling and simulation.

Most workflow systems today are still oriented toward document management and relatively simple management operations, but not toward complete business processes. They lack technical integration with the operative business systems. Nevertheless, these workflow systems have contributed considerably to the streamlining of document processing and to more effective design of management operations. A typical example is operations in insurance companies, which were some of the first users of workflow technology. An "insurance request" document runs through different levels of processing by various employees, supported by the system, until the insurance contract is sent to the customer.

7.4.1 The SAP concept

The "SAP Business Workflow" concept is based on an application-spanning approach that goes beyond document-oriented workflow. It builds a layer over the business transactions of the R/3 System.

Essential workflow elements, such as technical integration of business processes, are already implemented in the applications of the R/3 System (Fritz and Lau, 1994). In addition to this integration, application-neutral workflow components have been developed that provide special functions for workflow management. These components enable flexible, cross-application design of business processes and integration of the business transactions and objects involved.

Operative "SAP Business Workflow Management" links information (for example, limiting values, service levels, time aspects, and so on) and business objects (customer order, production order, material, invoice, and so on) with the operational processes and places them at the disposal of the employees involved in a business process at the right time and in the required format.

The technical components of SAP Business Workflow are:

- **Definition tools** for workflow description with the help of the graphical Workflow Editor. A workflow description includes the task definition with a link to people and teams as well as the definition of business and desktop object types with methods, attributes, and events that are related to the defined tasks.

- The **runtime environment**, which controls the operation of the workflow along with the Workflow Manager and ensures the execution of individual work steps (work items), including the assignment of people and date monitoring with the help of the "Work Item Manager." The runtime environment operates a user's individual work list through his or her electronic inbox. With "Event Management," it controls the adjustable reactions to events, such as status changes of material master data and customer orders or incoming messages from other systems, for example with EDI.

- **The Information System**, which enables tracing of individual workflows.

Technically, the workflow functions are implemented as ABAP/4 function modules (see Section 6.2.4), which are available to all R/3 application programs through the function library. Because of the open APIs (Application Programming Interfaces) of the R/3 System, systems from other manufacturers can also be integrated into the workflow. This applies particularly to APIs for:

- Creating and processing workflows with external "workflow managers"

- Using an external inbox (Work List Client) outside the R/3 System

- Creating and processing work items by non-SAP systems linked to the R/3 System

- Creating events and communicating events such as "invoice received" across system boundaries.

SAP Business Workflow is based on a workflow architecture model (Figure 7.4) with an organization model, process model, and object model.

- **Organization model**
  In the organization model, all of the organizational elements of a company, such as the people, teams, departments, production areas, and so on, are defined, along with their assignments to each other and their specific tasks. Tasks represent the linking elements between the organization of the company and the processes depicted in the workflow. The organization model is edited using the functions of the R/3 Human Resources Management system.

- **Process model**
  The "workflow steps" of a business process are described in the process model. They reference the tasks from the tasks catalog of the organization model. Workflow steps are usually methods of the business objects, which are defined in the "Business Object Repository," for example:

  - **Activities** that have a reference to the organization model. They start concrete processing, in which a work item of the work list is allocated to a responsible person.

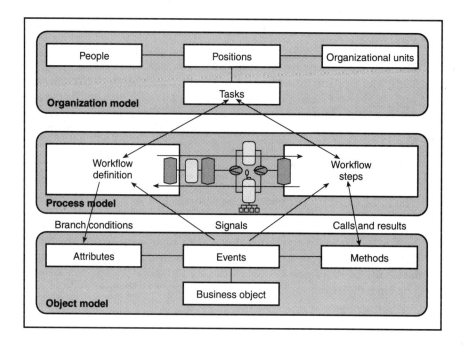

Figure 7.4 The SAP Business Workflow architecture model.

- **Conditions** and multiple conditions, which enable branching within a workflow.

- **Event creators**, which generate status changes (events) to which a workflow reacts (for example, invoice received, material stock depleted, and so on).

- **Control commands** for flow control.

- **User decisions**, with the presentation of alternatives.

- **Wait steps** for waiting for the occurrence of an event during the run time of a workflow. The event "receipt of payment," for example, ends the process "payment monitoring," which was in the corresponding wait step.

Individual "workflow steps" and the tasks linked to them are combined into a workflow in the graphical Workflow Editor, with its control flow and data flow. Here, the principle of event-controlled process chains (see Section 8.2.1) is used. Blocks containing a sequence of workflow steps and operations serve as structural elements for workflow definition.

- **Object model**
  Business objects are the central business objects in the R/3 System. They encapsulate application data and application functions with uniquely defined interfaces to the outside world. Their general structure is determined in the R/3 object model.

Examples of business objects are:

- Account
- Chart of accounts
- Business partner
- Work center
- Customer inquiry
- Purchase order.

Management of business objects takes place with the R/3 Business Object Repository. The first R/3 application to use the business objects is SAP Business Workflow.

Every business object is assigned a data model, which describes the inner structure of the object from the data point of view. Beyond that, the R/3 object model defines the following components of a business object:

- Object ID: unique identification
- Object name: unique semantic designation
- Component: component relation of the object (relation type "is part of")
- Subtypes: specialization of the object (relation type "is a")
- Constraints: object-internal consistency requirements (for example, purchase order date before delivery date)
- Business rules: cross-object consistency requirements (for example, delivery amount no greater than warehouse stock)
- Methods: functions that can be used on the object
- Attributes: object properties (status)
- Input events: external events that are relevant to the object
- Output events: events that the object creates depending on its status.

Applications do not directly access the business objects stored in the Business Object Repository, but instead use the services of the R/3 Business Object Broker to do so. In addition to internal R/3 access, the R/3 Business Object Broker also supports communication with non-SAP applications, for example with OLE 2 or CORBA (see Section 3.9).

Examples

The R/3 System contains predefined workflows (workflow templates) that implement recurring business operations. These can be modified with the help of R/3 Customizing (see Section 8.2) or can be used immediately, without any specific modifications. Examples of predefined workflows are:

- Handling of customer inquiries and orders across different company areas

- Release of invoice payments, budgets, purchase orders, and so on

- Control of product changes (Engineering Change Management, see the example described below)

- Processing of leave requests and business trip accounting with corresponding authorization procedures

- Document management (for example, release procedure for engineering drawings)

- Project handling

- Escalation procedures upon occurrence of certain conditions (service level falls below a certain value, payment period expires, and so on).

For the development of company-specific workflows that are not predefined or not completely predefined in the R/3 System, workflow definition tools and the "ABAP/4 Development Workbench" are available.

Workflow example: "Engineering Change Management"
The workflow predefined in the R/3 System for control of product changes (Engineering Change Management) highlights the integration of the business applications with the workflow functions.

Owing to events like a customer complaint or a new market demand, a product change becomes necessary. All affected business objects such as material master data, bills of materials, mechanical drawings, production schedules, cost centers, and so on, must be modified by the employees involved in a timely manner.

In the workflow defined for this, the entry of a change order (Engineering Change Request) serves as the catalytic event that starts a release procedure (workflow) at several levels. The release is the next event. It starts operations in different areas of the company (engineering, purchasing, production, and so on). These component operations are likewise described with the help of workflows and can be linked to one another.

The employees affected are called at the required point in time to process the business objects. In their electronic inboxes, they receive individual lists of their work items. For example, the system promptly informs the buyer of an affected material of the beginning of a procurement action.

All of the work items of a workflow for controlling product changes are steered by defined parameters (for example, material availability, costs, dates, and so on). Additional workflows, such as re-engineering, budget release, purchase order release, and marketing actions, can be linked to the product change.

Status controls using the Workflow Information System enable a complete overview at any time of all of the work items. However, it is not necessary to check the status of each work item individually. Escalation mechanisms in the workflow control automatically start operations (for example, notification of all employees involved by electronic mail) when the limit values of parameters such as costs or dates are exceeded.

Workflow functions guarantee the system-supported documentation of processes. This is needed in certain industrial sectors, for example when the described workflow controls the changing of a safety-relevant product. In addition, the description of process flows and their system-supported control is a basis for ISO 9000 certification of company departments.

7.5 Application interfaces

Standard software cannot generally fulfill all of the requirements in an enterprise. Special applications (technical subsystems, PC applications, and so on) must be integrated with the standard business system. The R/3 System meets this requirement with open application interfaces.

Direct access to R/3 data is possible using other manufacturers' tools. PC applications sometimes need to read application data directly from the database of the R/3 System. Access can take place over the Structured Query Language (Native SQL) of the database manufacturer in question or, if supported by the database, via Open Database Connectivity (ODBC).

At application level, various interfaces are implemented for communication with non-SAP systems. These include:

- The open RFC programming interface (see Section 6.2.4)

- The interface for file transfer between R/3 and PC applications (see Section 7.5.1)

- The integration of PC applications with the help of RFC and OLE (see Section 7.5.2)

- Functions for offline transfer of mass data (see Section 7.5.3)

- Interfaces for integration of technical subsystems (see Section 7.5.4)

- Electronic mail for exchange of messages between end users (see chapter 7.2.6)

- The EDI interface for exchange of business documents (see Section 7.5.5)

- Interfaces for electronic commerce functions (see Section 7.5.6)

- The ALE interface for application integration (see Section 7.5.7).

7.5.1 Interfaces for file transfer

R/3 applications are capable of exchanging data with external *databases*. This file transfer service of the System R/3 is based on ABAP/4 DATASET-instructions for binary and ASCII *databases*. For data exchange with applications such as word processing or spreadsheets additional functionality is available. The spool-*database* of the System R/3 can also be used to transfer data to external systems.

Examples of their use are:

- Transfer of R/3 data to a spreadsheet program on the PC
- Transfer of texts from the R/3 word processor in RTF (Rich Text Format) format to a PC word processing program, and transfer of texts back into the R/3 System
- Exchange of project plans from R/3 Project Planning and Tracking with MS Project.

7.5.2 Integration of PC applications with RFC and OLE

The implementation of Remote Function Call (RFC) and the use of Object Linking and Embedding (OLE) for external accesses ensures a controlled exchange of data between PC programs and the R/3 System (see Sections 6.2.4 and 3.9.2).

All of the services and interfaces that are required for the RFC and OLE integration of Windows applications with the R/3 System have been combined by SAP in the Desktop SDK (Desktop Software Development Kit) for Windows (see Figure 7.5).

The Desktop SDK includes:

- The RFC library
- The OLE Automation Server
- The Visual RFC Service Provider
- Documentation on the following topics:
  - RFC communication with external systems
  - OLE Automation communication with the R/3 System
  - RFC Generator
  - Session management with the Visual RFC Service Provider.

RFC communication between ABAP/4 applications and external programs is based on the **RFC Library**, which is available for different operating system environments such as UNIX and Windows.

The **Visual RFC Service Provider** gives external applications a standardized logon dialog for the R/3 System.

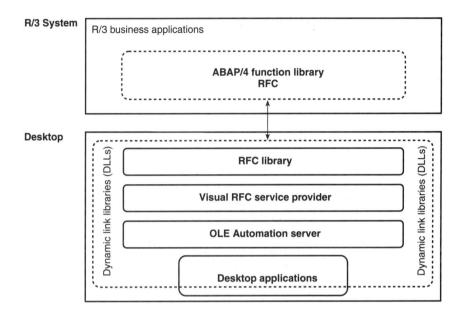

Figure 7.5 Components of the Desktop SDK for Windows.

Windows applications that do not support OLE call the RFC Library directly from the **Dynamic Link Library (DLL)**. This way, its functions are available to all applications and development tools that can call Windows DLLs. This applies, for example, to Microsoft Visual Basic and Visual Basic for Applications.

The **OLE Automation Server** translates OLE calls into RFC calls. This way, an external application can take advantage of the R/3 System's services as an OLE client.

Beginning with Release 3.0, the R/3 System supports both OLE Automation functions (see Section 3.3.6):

* **R/3 System as OLE Automation server**
  Applications like MS Word or MS Excel can access R/3 function modules directly with OLE Automation.

* **R/3 System as OLE Automation client**
  As an OLE Automation client, the R/3 System can use the functions of a PC, as long as the PC system sets itself up as an OLE Automation server. With the help of this technology, it is possible, for example, to call a PC word processor or spreadsheet program directly from the R/3 System.

Reusable software components are increasingly being implemented by SAP as OCX (OLE Custom Controls, see Section 3.9.2). This enables, for instance, the processing and display of large R/3 tables (for example, financial analyses). OLE Custom Controls provided by SAP can be called by any OLE clients (for example, PC applications).

Examples of integrated PC applications

The R/3 component "XXL" ("eXtended EXceL") uses MS Excel from Microsoft as a comfortable list viewer (Figure 7.6). On the one hand, the goal is to offer the Excel functionality that can be used in R/3 lists in the R/3 environment. On the other hand, the transferred data should also be recognized within the list viewer as linked SAP objects and accordingly be protected against consistency breaches. Two technical procedures are available for linking to Excel. Excel Version 4 is linked with a DDL, while Excel Version 5, which is OLE compatible, communicates using the OLE Automation client.

A user who works with the XXL list viewer can export the data contained in the list object to the standard Excel environment at any time for individual use; that is, he or she can remove the SAP-specific XXL configuration and re-admit all Excel operations. The data is then no longer under the control of the R/3 System. A special mode is the "Active Excel Link," which is used in the financial area for consolidation. In this mode, the values are automatically updated by the R/3 System when an existing spreadsheet calculation is called.

Another area where integration of PC applications with the R/3 System is implemented is mobile applications. What is meant by this is applications on mobile computers that usually operate without a link to the R/3 System, but which are capable of exchanging data with the R/3 System as soon as a network link is established. Such an application can be used, for example, by a sales employee

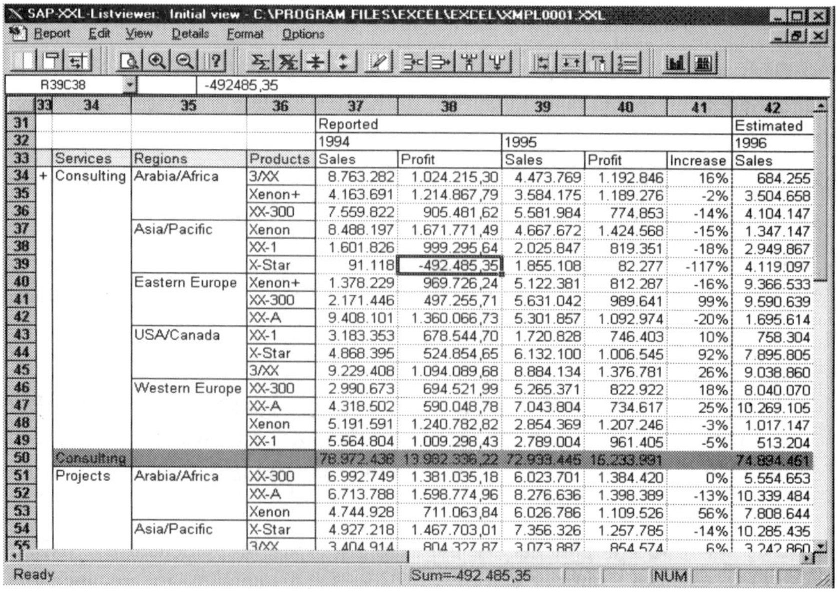

Figure 7.6 R/3 lists in the XXL List Viewer.
© SAP AG

on a portable PC, to record site visit report data. At certain times, the employee links his or her PC – for example over a modem – with the R/3 System and submits the recorded data to the R/3 applications. Over the same link, the employee loads current data such as master data, catalog information, prices, and so on, onto his or her computer.

The following examples are typical of the use of mobile applications:

- **Human Resources Management**: Mobile pre-entry of travel expenses on notebook computers.

- **Project Planning and Tracking**: The goal here is the exchange of project plans between the R/3 System and decentralized or mobile PC applications. Changes to the plans and recording of project progress can be carried out with the PC application.

- **Production Control**: Mobile entry of production data at production sites.

- **Sales and Distribution**: Mobile sales support.

7.5.3 Offline data transfer

The R/3 System has a standard function, BDC (Batch Data Communication), for offline transfer of mass data from non-SAP systems. Typical situations are the importation of existing data sets during original installation of the R/3 System and transfer of large data sets during regular operation.

The R/3 applications take over data in a transaction-oriented fashion. In order not to jeopardize the consistency of the R/3 database, the same checks must be carried out during offline transfer of data as in an online situation. It is therefore natural to use the same screen transactions and ABAP/4 programs in both cases. The BDC procedure works according to this principle.

The batch input session simulates a user dialog in background processing, but instead of expecting input from a terminal, it automatically places data from a prepared set (BDC file) into the screen fields. A special BDC log file records all errors that are reported during a batch input session.

Before the input data can be transferred, it must be placed in a format that meets the requirements of the business transactions. For the preparation of data, a special conversion program is necessary. This can be, for example, an ABAP/4 program or a C program. The data declarations required in the C program can be generated from the R/3 Repository.

An alternative to creating a BDC file is to call R/3 transactions directly and supply them with data using the ABAP/4 command "CALL TRANSACTION USING." This procedure is often used for synchronous transfer of smaller data sets. This is also true of the use of the ABAP/4 command "CALL DIALOG," which supplies data to a complete dialog that consists of a sequence of transactions.

7.5.4   Communication with technical subsystems

R/3 components such as Production Control, Time Management, Plant Maintenance, and Warehouse Management are elements of the production management level in the production plant. The process management level, with control and monitoring components close to the processes, must be linked to the production management level. Examples of components of the process management level are:

- Plant and machine data collection systems

- Quality data collection systems

- Process monitoring and controls

- NC (Numeric Controlled) controlled production facilities.

Communication between the R/3 System and technical subsystems in the production area takes place over specially defined communication channels (Figure 7.7). The interface software implemented for this has two components:

- The communication component of the R/3 System

- The linking software (Transceiver) on the technical subsystem.

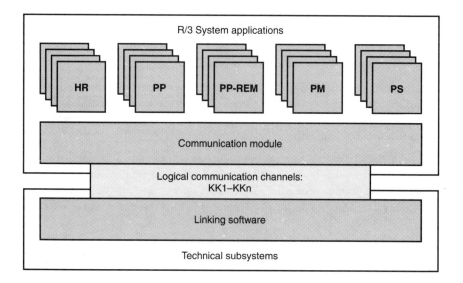

Figure 7.7 R/3 interface software for technical subsystems.

Data is exchanged with the technical subsystems using the logical communication channels (KK1–KKn), which are implemented with function modules (see Section 6.2.4). In addition to the communication channel provided for specific customer developments, the following standard channels exist:

- KK1: Transfer of payroll data for R/3 Time Management (HR)

- KK2: Exchange of production data with the R/3 Production Planning system (PP)

- KK3: Transfer of plant maintenance data to R/3 Plant Maintenance (PM)

- KK4: Exchange of project data with the R/3 Project System (PS)

- KK5: Reporting of production data from mass production to the R/3 module PP-REM (Repetitive Manufacturing, that is, production planning for mass production).

Data exchange between the R/3 System's communication components and the technical subsystems is carried out with files in which the data is stored as IDOC (Intermediate Documents) structures (see Section 7.5.7). This way, standardized business data structures are available to the subsystems.

- **Data flow from the R/3 System to a subsystem**
  Data transfer from R/3 applications to the subsystem proceeds by starting an ABAP/4 program in the R/3 communication component. This program first starts its partner program in the subsystem, called the Transceiver. Subsequently, the data is read from the R/3 database and submitted to the communication partner as an IDOC using RFC.

  The Transceiver takes over the data and stores it in the interface file. After that, the receiving module informs the application running on the subsystem that new R/3 application data has been sent and is ready to be picked up. The R/3 System ensures that the affected data from the R/3 database is written without error and in its entirety into the interface files.

- **Data flow from a subsystem to the R/3 System**
  In a data transfer from a subsystem to the R/3 application, the Transceiver hands over the data to a special function module in the R/3 System. Here, the data is prepared in an IDOC and distributed to the respective R/3 application using ALE distribution functions (see Section 7.5.7).

7.5.5 Electronic Data Interchange (EDI)

EDI enables automated exchange of business data, independent of the hardware and software setup of the companies involved. With the help of EDI messages, normal business documents such as purchase orders and invoices can be transmitted. The formats of EDI messages do not conform to the standards of the R/3 applications, but are oriented instead toward internationally recognized standards like EDIFACT (Electronic Data Interchange for Administration, Commerce, and Transport) or ANSI X12 (National US Standard).

The EDI solution of the R/3 System is implemented on three levels. The first level contains the applications capable of EDI, which communicate with the EDI interface through function modules. Conversely, the EDI interface can call function modules of the applications directly for automatic processing of EDI messages or forward the message for manual processing.

The second level consists of the EDI interface. It allows rules to be defined for the receipt and sending of business documents. The documents are exchanged over this interface in a general format as Intermediate Documents (IDOCs), which follow the standard EDI formats EDIFACT and ANSI X12. The EDI interface structure of the R/3 System is a system-independent API (Application Programming Interface). Different versions of a message type can be used in parallel. This is of importance, for example, when the release versions are different in the systems involved. In addition, specialized EDI subsystems from very different manufacturers can be used with the help of this open EDI interface.

As the third level, EDI subsystems can be connected to the R/3 System with the EDI interface. They take over the conversion and archiving of EDI messages, the management of partner profiles, and the exchange of messages with other systems. EDI generally uses widespread communications technology and standards like X.400, X.435, FTAM, and so on. This ensures that the processing of the contents of EDI messages remains fundamentally separate from the technical communication between different systems.

7.5.6 Electronic commerce

The term "electronic commerce" (EC) refers to electronically handled business transactions between private parties and/or companies. Next to the existing possibilities for electronic exchange of commercial documents (for example, with EDI), the World Wide Web (WWW, see Section 3.3.9), especially, has recently gained importance as a new "commercial center" for money, goods, and services. The foundation for this is a global computer network with a high transmission rate and network applications with simple, graphical user interfaces.

Electronic commerce enables business transactions to be conducted from any suitably networked computer. Typical examples of electronic commerce transactions are:

- Handling of bank transactions (electronic banking)
- Processing of work orders and purchase orders (electronic ordering)
- Sales of publishing products (electronic publishing, publishing on demand)
- Software purchase and distribution (electronic software delivery).

Electronic commerce creates the conditions for short response times to customer requests and saves money with fully automated business operations. For this reason, electronic commerce is of great importance to SAP itself as well as to SAP customers. Interested parties can already use the WWW to register with SAP for seminars, order CD-ROMs, or print documents. Order data is passed on directly to SAP's R/3 System, where it starts an SAP Business Workflow that automatically starts all of the activities necessary for processing the order.

SAP customers can use various R/3 interfaces to expand their R/3 applications with electronic commerce solutions. End users only need a WWW browser linked to a WWW server. The following alternatives are available for communication between the WWW server and the R/3 System:

- Direct access to the R/3 database using database technology. R/3 application logic is not executed in this case.

- Asynchronous communication with R/3 applications using IDOCs (see Section 7.5.7).

- Synchronous communication with R/3 applications using a common application interface or special application interfaces.

- Communication at presentation level over the SAP Automation interface of the Intelligent Terminal (see Section 5.4.4).

7.5.7 Application Link Enabling

Owing to technical, organizational, and economic needs, there is an increasing desire to decouple application systems, in order to install and run them in a decentralized and technically independent fashion (Kagermann, 1993).

Typical examples of distribution scenarios desired by industry are:

- Centralized financial system coupled with decentralized logistics systems.

- Decentralized processing of customer orders (purchase orders) and centralized shipping functions.

- Decentralized cost determination for aggregation of planned or current quantities and values for profitability analysis in the central system.

- Centralized sales planning and production planning with decentralized material requirements planning and delivery planning. Exchange of production planning data between the decentralized production planning and control systems.

- Centralized management of vendor contracts in purchasing, so that procurement can be processed in decentralized systems based on them.

- Linking of independent, decentralized warehouse management systems with centralized logistics.

- Decentralized plant maintenance systems for processing maintenance orders and the corresponding materials management, linked to the centralized financial system.

- Decentralized project management functions and a centralized financial system.

- Centralized bank functions and funds management with decentralized accounting.

Despite the desire for distributed solutions, the integration of the business processes must be retained across system boundaries. Since in distributed installations no centralized database is available for integration of data, other synchronization mechanisms are needed. For this, SAP developed the ALE (Application Link Enabling) concept.

The goal of the ALE concept is to loosely link business applications (Figure 7.8) on standalone systems. In addition to R/3-to-R/3 communication, the ALE architecture also supports the connection of R/2 mainframe applications and non-SAP systems to the R/3 System.

The distribution of business processes and their business integration take place as part of ALE with the help of message exchanges controlled by business mechanisms. ALE provides all of the mechanisms and APIs (Application Programming Interfaces) required for this. Essential advantages of the ALE solution are:

- Support for technically standalone systems with temporarily isolated operation. With message exchange, the business applications are largely independent of the availability of the systems involved.

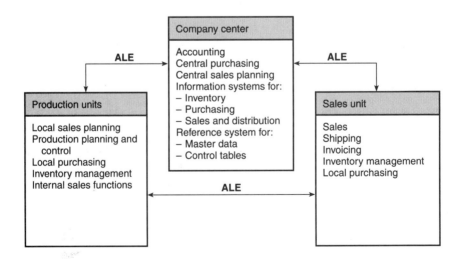

Figure 7.8 Example of applications linked with ALE.

- Release independence of the individual applications.

- Support for connection of non-SAP applications.

- Use of standardized procedures for message exchange between applications on standalone systems.

- Business process integration across application boundaries.

The ALE services are implemented in three layers:

- **Application services**
  The applications create ALE messages with specific attributes, like information for the determination of recipients defined in the distribution model, the type of transmission, and the type of receipt processing. They support the workflow in the processing of incoming messages. Business metadata is provided, such as the master data structure, for, among other things, configuration and synchronization of the messages. Events at data level, such as inventory changes, generate automatic messages for other systems in the linked systems.

- **Distribution services**
  This layer contains specific functions that are necessary for the loose coupling of business applications. These include:
  - Definitions of messages and attributes, independent of the release version of the systems
  - Description and control of the dependencies of linked systems and the resulting messages
  - Determination of the recipients of messages on the basis of the distribution model (see below)
  - Filtering and conversion of messages
  - Storage, transmission, and comparison of "reduced master data," that is, the subset of the master data needed in the linked systems, which are also called specific views
  - Compression of messages to reduce the amount of messages.

- **Communication services**
  The ALE communication services are responsible for the exchange of messages between the business applications involved. One function in the transference of the ALE messages to the transport system is the security of communication in the event of one communication partner being uncontactable.

  ALE messages are exchanged either by the asynchronous RFC or EDI. For information retrieval functions the synchronous RFC is also used. The EDI communication takes place with the help of external EDI subsystems, which are connected to the R/3 System EDI interface.

Data exchange over ALE is based on IDOCs (Intermediate Documents) that have a data structure that is independent of concrete application data.

The IDOC data structure is comparable to that of EDI documents. An IDOC type is defined for every business object exchangeable in the linked applications (for example, invoice, order, purchase order, and so on). ALE uses the EDI interfaces or the asynchronous RFC of the R/3 System for message interchange (see Section 7.5.5). Accordingly, the business applications see no difference between communication using EDI and communication using ALE. The communication path is determined in the respective exit processing of an application. In contrast to ALE, which supports the processing of entire business processes, EDI is just a standard exchange procedure for business documents.

Non-SAP systems can also use the IDOC format published by SAP (Figure 7.9).

IDOCs can transport various types of data. These data types can be classified as follows:

- **Control data** is for organization of the systems. The data in question is Customizing data, that is, user profiles and business organization data such as definitions of company codes, plants, purchasing organizations, languages, and so on.

- **Master data** is generally not distributed in the linked systems in its entirety, but as views. This way, the quantity of data to be distributed is considerably reduced. The data in question is sales and distribution views, production views, and procurement views of the master data. R/3 Release 3.0 can distribute master data for materials, customers, vendors, cost centers, activity types, general ledger accounts, and classification data.

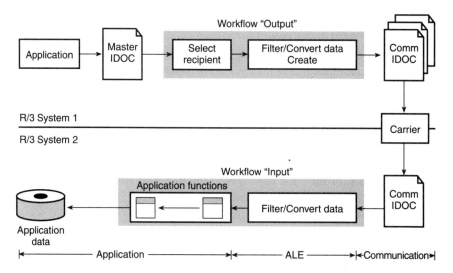

Figure 7.9 Principle of application linking based on messages.

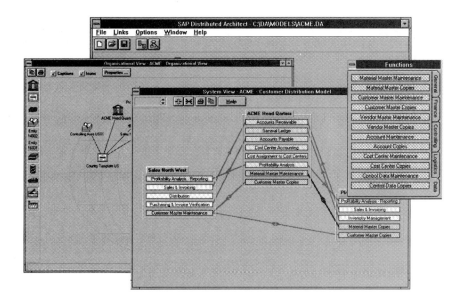

Figure 7.10 Graphical display of the Distribution Reference Model.
© SAP AG

- **Transaction data** includes, for example, customer orders, purchase orders, shipping notifications, and invoices. The distribution scenarios for transaction data are defined and stored in the distribution reference model.

Usually, IDOC communication is asynchronous, which means that the sending application does not require an answer from the receiving application. ALE functions ensure secure message exchange even in the case of occasionally interrupted links.

If information is required immediately for an application in the linked systems, synchronous read access is possible with the help of Remote Function Calls (RFC).

The standardized distribution model belonging to ALE describes distributed function types that belong together content-wise, such as inventory management or inventory controlling and the respective data exchange. With this model, distribution scenarios can be explored and planned. A customer's actual scenario is defined as a customer distribution model with the help of graphical tools (Figure 7.10). The customer model is used to describe the customer-specific linked systems and is distributed across all of the systems involved. It controls data distribution between the systems on the basis of the data flows described in the model.

The following distribution scenarios are supported, beginning with Release 3.0 of the R/3 System:

- Separation of accounting and logistics
- System-spanning sales and distribution, inventory, and purchasing information system
- Decentralized sales and centralized shipping
- Decentralized and centralized profitability analysis
- Decentralized and centralized sales planning and production planning
- Distribution of contracts from centralized to decentralized purchasing departments
- Connection of decentralized warehouse management and control systems.

Chapter 8

Implementation of the R/3 System in a Company

8.1 Standard software or custom software?

With the availability of standard software, task emphasis has shifted to the implementation of software solutions. Technical DP tasks are no longer in the foreground of projects; instead, the design of business operations is. In the development and implementation of custom applications, up to 75% of the costs are spent on function specifications, as well as development, documentation, and tests of the software. These are costs that are carried by all clients proportionately with the use of standard software. The acquisition and maintenance costs of standard software are accordingly generally lower than for custom software. Drastic differences can emerge here.

As an example, take a project for the planned company-wide financial accounting system of a multinational company. After a project duration of over four years, the first components of the custom solution were introduced in some branches. At the time, they did not yet meet all of the requirements. After about five years, the project had cost approximately US$ 24 million. In parallel, another project was started to explore the possibility of using standard software. It was decided that the standard software could not meet all of the specific requirements of the company. The company decided to go this route anyway and discontinued development of the custom solution. The standard software, in this case the mainframe solution R/2, was expanded to include company-specific functions with the help of the SAP development tools. The total cost for the standard software, including the necessary expansions and the new functions, totaled about US$ 5 million.

8.2 Implementation environment

The R/3 implementation environment (Business Engineering Workbench) contains all of the functions and information for process-oriented support of implementation projects, follow-up projects, and release-change projects (Figure 8.1). The R/3 implementation environment embodies project experiences from a large number of implementation projects.

As preparation for R/3 installation, the R/3 Analyzer (see Section 8.2.3), developed for PCs, can be used. After installation of the R/3 System on the customer's computer, the implementation environment integrated in the R/3 System is available for all project phases, with the following components:

- **R/3 Reference Model**, for business modeling of the R/3 System

- **R/3 Business Navigator**, for navigating within the implementation environment

- **Functions for custom configuration** of the R/3 System

- **Procedure Model**, for graphical description of the project steps

- **Implementation Guide**, with detailed descriptions of the implementation activities

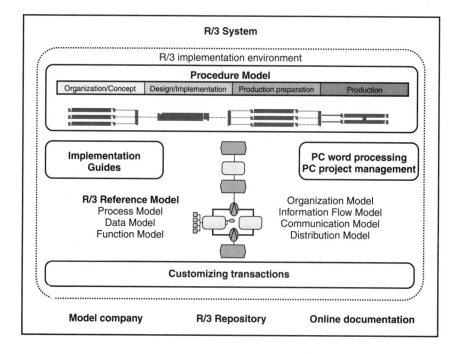

Figure 8.1   Components of the R/3 implementation environment.

- **Model company IDES** (International Demo and Education System)

- **R/3 documentation**

- **Project management and documentation tools**

- **Functions for release management**.

The R/3 implementation environment is used in three task areas:

- **Initial implementation**
  The R/3 implementation environment contains information and tools that enable customized system setting for customers (see Section 8.2.4). The standard project description with the Procedure Model (see Section 8.2.4) and the Implementation Guide contain all of the system implementation activities.

- **Follow-up projects**
  Follow-up projects are adaptations of the R/3 System to changing business processes or to the introduction of additional software components.

- **Release changes**
  Release changes can be planned and executed systematically with the help of the tools provided for this (see Section 5.7.4). Their implementation is described in the Procedure Model and in the Implementation Guide.

8.2.1 Reference Model

Complete business modeling of the R/3 System resulted in a reference model, with whose help the operational requirements could be compared to the processes realized in the system. The R/3 Reference Model is stored in the R/3 Repository and is a part of every R/3 installation. It consists of the following components:

- **Function Model**
  The function model shows the main business functions of the R/3 System with their subfunctions in a hierarchical structure. The configuration is oriented toward the business functions of a company, such as Financial Accounting, Controlling, Materials Management, Sales and Distribution, and so on.

- **Process Model**
  In the Process Model, dynamic aspects of the operational information system are represented. The goal of this representation is to describe the functions' chronological dependencies. The trigger mechanism for functions is called an event. Events determine the flow logic of event-controlled process chains (EPCs, see Keller et al. (1992)). In addition to the representation of the chronological sequence of functions, the input and output functions and the organizational units entrusted with function execution can be described.

- **Information Flow Model**

  The correct execution of functions generally requires information. During their execution, functions also generate information that is processed at other points. The Information Flow Model describes the information relationships between sender and recipient within the business application solution.

- **Communication Model**

  In contrast to the Information Flow Model, which is oriented toward the DP application solutions, the Communication Model reflects the communication relationships between the actual existing operational organizational units. The goal is to represent the communication between operational organizational units such as Purchasing and Accounting during the handling of business processes.

- **Organization Model**

  Organization Models describe the organizational structure of companies and allocate certain business tasks to organizational units.

- **Distribution Model**

  The Distribution Model supports the planning and implementation of the business integration of distributed applications as part of ALE (see Section 7.5.7). It describes the distribution scenarios supported by the R/3 System.

- **Data Model**

  The goal of establishing data models is to represent the data required within the operational service render in a formal fashion, in a cross-function relationship. SAP's Data Model represents the information objects relevant to a company and their relationships to each other from a business point of view, in the form of an Entity Relationship Model. The entities are representations of objects from the real world that have a business meaning and an equivalent in the R/3 System.

  The SAP Data Model contains different levels of detail. Every level of detail is consistently represented, from the introductory model, which organizes the most important entities and graphically displays them consistently in cluster structures, all the way to the fully expanded model, in which all of the entities present in the R/3 System are given attributes.

8.2.2 Business Navigator

With the R/3 Business Navigator, users can access the R/3 Reference Model directly from any R/3 workstation. Starting from the higher-level process and component view, it is possible to navigate to application transactions, to documentation, and to the Data Models.

With the function view and the process view (Figures 8.2 and 8.3), the R/3 Business Navigator offers two access paths to the R/3 Reference Model. The function view

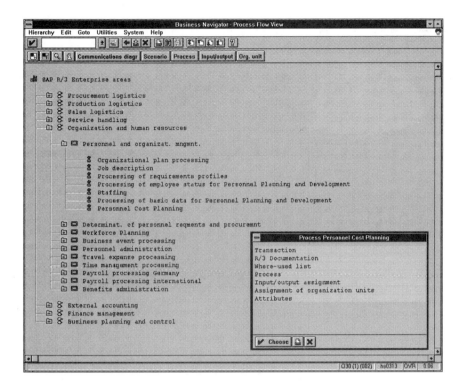

Figure 8.2 Process view in the R/3 Business Navigator.
© SAP AG

is divided into business areas such as Materials Management, Sales & Distribution, Accounting, and so on. From this view, it is possible to branch directly:

- into processes and functions
- to the business objects
- into the Organization Model
- into the Information Flow Model
- into the process selection matrix.

From the process view, the typical operations of a business area, such as material procurement in Purchasing, or customer order processing in Sales & Distribution, can be selected and displayed in detail. The collection and shaping of standard processes into industry scenarios such as the customer order processing of a particular branch are an additional form of representation of the process view.

For the exchange of model information with external modeling tools, the Open Repository Interface is available (see Section 6.4.2). With this, it is also possible to store custom models that were created with external modeling tools in the R/3 Repository and call them with the R/3 Business Navigator.

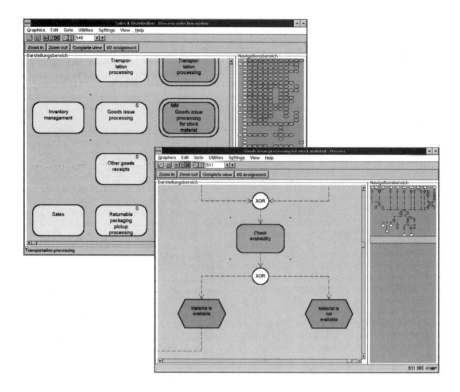

Figure 8.3 Process view in the R/3 Business Navigator.
© SAP AG

8.2.3 R/3 Analyzer

The R/3 Analyzer is a PC tool that helps with requirements analysis and the selection of the business solutions of the R/3 System. It contains a copy of the R/3 Reference Model and functions for project handling.

The R/3 Analyzer provides a consistent procedure for preparing for an R/3 installation. The data resulting from the requirements analysis is available for later phases of implementation, like customizing, user training, and integration testing.

Beyond testing the general implementation possibilities of the software, at the beginning of an implementation project one is faced with the task of familiarizing oneself with and selecting the appropriate components and functions for efficient reflection of the business processes. The R/3 Analyzer, with the R/3 Reference Model and its process selection matrices, has been specially developed as a knowledge base for this task.

During the analysis and concept phase of a project, the R/3 Analyzer offers the following support functions:

- **Information**

  Information about the functions and processes of the R/3 System is available on a PC at an early stage of the project.

- **Presentation and analysis tools**

  Tools for the description of the current company situation and the target concept to be derived from it are helpful in the systematic discussion and documentation of solution alternatives for the optimization of business processes. This leads to a direct comparison with the applications of the R/3 System.

- **Preparation for customizing**

  Preparations with the R/3 Analyzer support later customizing activities. After the concept has been prepared, the results can be used as a template for the custom configuration and customizing (see Section 8.2.4) of the system. In this process, a preselection of business processes and the customizing activities described in the Implementation Guides take place.

8.2.4 Custom system configuration

As far as the individual requirements of a company are concerned, the R/3 System has, as an industry-neutral standard system, a superset of processes and functions. The advantage of business process integration across all company areas is countered by the effort required to select and customize the individually required processes.

Experience with the different profiles of several thousand delivered systems shows that, as a rule, the entire range of processes and functions available in the R/3 System must be offered for customer selection. In smaller companies, multinational companies, or in different branches of industries, a high percentage of the same functions and processes is needed. The subset of processes, functions, and configurations implemented in each individual case, however, is very different. For this reason, SAP attempts to deliver the complete system to every customer and to configure the customer system according to need with the help of configuration technology.

The functions for custom configuration (Configure to Order) of the R/3 System are:

- Hiding of unnecessary
  - Application modules
  - Processes
  - Functions
  - Menus
  - Individual fields in dialogs
  - Documentation

- Generation of custom Implementation Guides

- Compiling of project-related customizing activities

- Reconfiguration upon later introduction of new components.

The company-neutral R/3 System delivered by SAP is adjusted to the specific business requirements of a company with the customizing functions. This applies to the business organization setup with the help of the Implementation Guides and to the transfer of settings from a test environment into a production environment. The integrated Procedure Model describes the project phases of system implementation. It is based on actual project experiences and is used as a planning foundation as well as to control the implementation project. The work steps of the Procedure Model are described in detail in the Implementation Guides.

Project control and documentation functions are elements of the R/3 customizing applications. PC tools such as Microsoft Project and word processors can be used in project work. The exchange of data is handled by the desktop integration functions of the R/3 System (see Section 7.5.2).

Upon installation of the system, Client 000 provides a complete system that is entirely set up with standard defaults. Client 000 represents the industry-neutral R/3 delivery system with:

- A simple organizational structure

- Consistently set parameters for all applications

- Country-specific charts of accounts

- Standard settings for account assignment

- Configurations for control of standard processes

- Standard settings for processes like "dunning and payment," "planning and forecasting," "pricing," and for printing and form layout, authorization concept, and so on.

Client 001 is a copy of Client 000. It is intended for customizing activities.

Procedure Model

The Procedure Model provides the foundation for every R/3 implementation. As a phase model, it graphically depicts the project flow. It describes the processing sequence of the project activities in every phase. The detailed description of the activities takes place in the Implementation Guides. They can be addressed from within the Procedure Model. The customizing transactions can be called directly from the activity catalog with a mouse click.

The project flow is structured as follows:

- Phase 1: **Organization and Concept**
  - Requirements analysis
  - Project organization
  - Set up test environment
  - Train project team
  - Determine processes and functions
  - Describe interfaces and system expansions
  - Quality check of the target concept

- Phase 2: **Detailing and Implementation**
  - Perform global system settings
  - Map company organization
  - Determine master data
  - Represent processes and functions
  - Implement interfaces and system expansions
  - Determine reporting
  - Determine archive management
  - Arrange authorization management
  - Execute final program test
  - Quality check of the implemented target concept

- Phase 3: **Preparation for going live**
  - Prepare for start of live operation
  - Create custom documentation for users
  - Set up live environment
  - Train users
  - Organize system administration
  - Data transfer
  - Quality check of the live system

- Phase 4: **Live operation**
  - Support for live operation
  - Optimize system operation

In addition to the four phases of an implementation project, the Procedure Model also supports other activities, such as:

- Project planning, project administration, and project controlling

- Maintenance, release changes, and system modifications.

Implementation Guides

The work steps of the Procedure Model are described in detail in the Implementation Guides, which are divided into application areas such as Accounting, Materials Management, Sales & Distribution, and so on. The following topics are dealt with in the Implementation Guides:

- Business concept information

- Dependencies of processes and functions

- Standard settings and recommendations

- Project activities

- Project status management and documentation.

The R/3 System offers several thousand custom setting possibilities (customizing activities). Selection functions enable the Implementation Guides to be prepared in a project-oriented fashion.

The following customizations are possible:

- Company-specific guides that are automatically generated by the selection of the implemented application areas and country

- Guides oriented toward subprojects such as the implementation of Materials Management or Controlling

- Sorting of customizing activities according to:

  - Required activities for every implementation

  - Optional activities that need to be carried out only if the standard settings are insufficient for the customer system

  - Critical activities which, for example, can no longer be changed in the productive system

  - Non-critical activities in which later modifications are possible

- Individual views of the Guides for project teams or individual employees.

The transactions for setting business parameters can be called directly from the Implementation Guides. No knowledge of table names, table connections, or transaction codes is required. Leading the user to the right place is done on the basis of business questions and objects.

Individual bits of information can be stored in the Implementation Guides for date monitoring, resource management, and project status management. Project-specific documentation can be assigned to every customizing activity.

8.2.5 Model Company

The model company IDES (International Demo and Education System) is part of the R/3 System. It represents an internationally operating model company and its national branches in all business aspects. The model company is used for demonstration of the capabilities of the software, for the training of users, and for standardized system tests. Maintenance of the model company is handled by SAP. The current version of the model company is delivered with every R/3 System.

8.3 Implementing custom expansions

8.3.1 Expansions without changes to application logic

The expansion of standard functions of the R/3 System with the help of custom versions of prefabricated Customer Exits is a procedure that prevents direct access to the logic provided (see Section 6.2.5).

The objective of this procedure is to change the behavior and the functionality of the standard software easily and robustly, if individual application functions cannot be adapted for certain business processes using the customizing functions. Uncontrolled and uncoordinated access to the standard software is avoided. This simplifies software maintenance and helps to keep down the costs of customizing the standard applications.

Two other procedures for customizing standard R/3 applications without changing the application logic are

- Transaction variants

- Append structures.

With the help of transaction variants, R/3 transaction screens can be individually limited (see Section 6.2.6). Append structures allow the expansion of standard R/3 tables without changing these tables in the ABAP/4 Dictionary (see Section 6.4.4).

8.3.2 Expansions with changes to application logic

Access to the logic of the standard software using the maintenance transactions of the ABAP/4 Development Workbench may become necessary to undertake custom function modifications. There are three areas where this is done:

- Standard solutions are supplemented with additional customer logic.

- Preliminary corrections and priority developments.

- Standard logic is replaced by customer logic.

Direct changes of the application logic are not recommended, because maintenance of the standard software, for example during release changes, can become very costly. Such expansions are better candidates for future Customer Exits.

8.3.3 Development of custom components

For custom development projects, the ABAP/4 Development Workbench is available, which offers the following advantages (see Chapter 6):

- Custom components can be integrated with standard components.

- The programming language ABAP/4 has been optimized for the development of business applications. An extensive library of ready-made and tested function modules relieves developers of routine tasks.

- Communication and distribution aspects in the client/server environment are solved transparently for the applications developer. Custom developments run on all operating systems, databases, and presentation managers supported by the R/3 System.

- The ABAP/4 Development Workbench contains all of the development tools used by SAP itself for prototyping, testing, optimizing, and debugging as well as for maintaining software.

8.4 Services

Companies depend on reliable operation of their business software. This requires services from the software manufacturer, such as:

- Support in removing problems caused by software bugs, usage errors, setup errors, and so on

- Provision of all of the information needed for implementation, user training, and operation of the software.

For the R/3 System, which is in operation 24 hours a day in many companies, these services must be available at any time. Administratively, this task is handled by the SAP Service Network, with support centers in Germany, the USA, and Asia. This network automatically passes customer inquiries on to the active support center. There, software specialists can in most cases provide immediate help (First Level Support) with error correction and reference databases. More serious errors or problems that the First Level Support cannot entirely handle are passed on to the responsible development groups (Second Level Support).

The following services are available from the SAP Service Network:

- **Online Service System (OSS)**
  This service enables recording of error messages, access to the reference database, registration for training, and communication with SAP employees using electronic mail.

- **Early Watch Service**
  Software specialists at SAP can analyze R/3 installations in operation with the help of the "Early Watch" functions (see Section 5.7.1).

- **Error Correction**
  Support center employees can dial directly into the customer system for error correction with the SAP Service Network.

- **Remote Consulting**
  Remote Consulting offers consulting support with the SAP Support Network.

- **Upgrade Support**
  Release changes and downloading of software corrections usually take place on weekends. Software specialists are available at any time with the SAP Service Network to handle any problems that may arise.

8.5 Practical experience

The companies presented below are among the most successful in their industries and are distinguished by the following features:

- Their company culture promotes change and openness to early adoption of new technologies.

- Business re-engineering and technology re-engineering are closely linked in these companies.

The reports contain examples of their project experiences.

8.5.1 Autodesk, Inc.

Autodesk is one of the leading manufacturers of CAD/CAM (Computer-Aided Design/Computer-Aided Manufacturing) software products. With sales of 400 million US dollars in 1994 and an average annual growth rate of 20%, Autodesk is a fast-growing software enterprise. The company's headquarters are in San Rafael, California. Autodesk has 1900 employees in five development centers in the USA and Switzerland, as well as in 20 subsidiaries in Europe and Asia.

Before the introduction of the R/3 System, Autodesk was in the typical situation of a quickly growing, internationally expanding company, whose business processes and business application systems no longer corresponded to the requirements of a multinational operation. Autodesk needed radical re-engineering. The project set up to do this, "System 2000," focused on fundamental objectives such as:

- Globalization of business application software
  - Business processes should not be hampered by system boundaries or national borders.
  - Real-time information should be provided for all aspects of international business, for example:
    - Market information
    - Information about customers
    - Order processing
    - Product availabilit
    - Pricing
    - Profit
    - Product costs.

- The new application system should be able to support all languages and country-specific operations, such as different tax calculation procedures.

- Lead time for all business processes should be reduced. This means, for example:
  - Guaranteed delivery of all products within 24 hours
  - Processing of customer orders within a few minutes.

- Precise inventory management. Autodesk must produce from stock.

- As a manufacturer of software products for UNIX, DOS, and Windows NT, Autodesk insisted on an open client/server system for the business applications.

Autodesk's software selection team was comprised of employees from operational data processing, accounting, order processing, development, and production. The R/3 System proved to be the system that could best fulfill Autodesk's requirements. The R/3 components Financial Accounting, Controlling, Materials

Management, and Sales & Distribution were implemented in all American company locations in just six months.

The goal of the first stage of the System 2000 project was to achieve initial success as quickly as possible and not invest time, money, and project team energy in a total solution. Therefore, the pilot project concentrated on re-engineering 25 core processes with 240 subprocesses, and creating a pilot company ("Mini Autodesk") in which the new business processes could be tested and improved. The pilot project serves as a basis for worldwide installation of the R/3 System as part of the System 2000 project.

An example of the reorganization of core processes at Autodesk with the R/3 System is customer order processing:

- During a telephone inquiry by a customer, a quotation can be processed in a few minutes, directly online, with customer-specific pricing that includes discounts, taxes, and costs for shipping and handling.

- Product variants are automatically managed by the R/3 System in order processing. This eliminates the extensive effort formerly needed to process the 12000 possible order variations, each with their own code for release, configuration, platform, distribution path, and so on.

To date, Autodesk has achieved the following results with the System 2000 project:

- Real-time information about sales and costs

- Direct measurement of business success when new products are introduced

- Order processing time in the minute range

- Reduction of delivery times from 2 weeks to 24 hours on average

- Price calculation integrated with cost accounting and profitability analysis

- Reduction of the number of order codes from 12000 to 1500

- Inventory precision close to 100%

- Quarterly results within a week

- 500 users currently on the system in the USA.

The R/3 System is serving as the technical basis for additional re-engineering projects at Autodesk:

- Flexible adjustment of business processes to new market demands, expansion of business activities, and unforeseeable changes within the company

- Improved proximity to customers and readiness to provide service through the use of "electronic commerce" technology (see Section 7.5.6). Customers, sales partners, and sales employees will be able to communicate with the R/3 System directly, for example to place an order electronically or to inquire about a product or the status of a delivery. Delivery of software products over international networks is planned as the next step.

8.5.2 KAESER Compressors, Ltd

The company KAESER Compressors, Ltd, with about 1600 employees and sales of 300 million DM, is among the leading manufacturers of air compression products. In addition to the German parent company with its headquarters in Coburg, it includes two additional production centers in Gera and Lyon, as well as sales and service companies in Europe, North America, Australia, and Asia.

The company's situation before its decision to use the R/3 System was marked by:

- insufficient support for business processes across departments;

- insufficient expansion possibilities for the existing mainframe solution;

- a heterogeneous system world in terms of hardware and application software;

- absence of integration of PC applications with information processing on the mainframe;

- isolated solutions and interface problems.

The goal of the completely new concept of company information management was the formation of a powerful and flexible infrastructure for information processing in the entire corporation. The following specifications were stipulated:

- Support for company objectives oriented toward the customer

- Optimization of operations within the individual companies and between the companies of the corporation with the support of general business processes

- Uniform system concept for all work areas and locations, on the basis of the client/server concept

- Standard products that can be used in any country

- Custom development of company-specific solutions only as a supplement to the standard solution, with the help of an integrated development environment

- Company-wide usage of a consistent user interface

- Integration of business applications, technical applications, and PC programs.

Introduction of the R/3 System was process-oriented. After the current status was recorded in the form of a rough analysis, the business processes were redesigned in workshops:

- The representation of processes as process chains (see Section 8.2.1) was reality-based and easily understood by the department employees. Deficiencies in the previous operations were uncovered quickly and comprehensively.

- The description of the new processes and the decision of the teams to use the optimal process in each case were accelerated considerably and were immediately converted during customizing of the R/3 System and in employee training.

- With the described implementation method, the users could be included in the system installation in an early phase of the project.

The implementation plan of the KAESER corporation (Figure 8.4) is an example of the business process orientation during the implementation of the R/3 System. The installation proceeded on the basis of the technical infrastructure sketched out in Figure 8.5.

Implementation plan for the business processes of the KAESER Corporation		
Impl.	Supported process	R/3 components
1/93	Business cross-section processes	FI – AM – CO
8/93	Warehouse – Material Requirements Planning – Purchasing	MM
1/94	Quotation Processing – Customer Order Processing – Warehouse – Shipping	SD – MM
1/94	Cross-section processes Human Resources Management	HR
7/94	Quality Assurance	QM
1/95	Production Plan Generation – Material Requirements Planning	PP – MM
1/95	Capacity Planning – Production Processing – Warehouse	PP – MM – SD
6/96	After Sales Service	PP – MM – SD

Locations of the KAESER Corporation working with the R/3 System		
Since	Company	R/3 components
93/95	Headquarters in Coburg, Germany, and all German plants	FI – AM – CO – HR – MM – SD – PP – QM
94/95	Gera Compressor Plant, Ltd, in Gera, Germany	FI – AM – CO – HR – MM – SD – PP
94/95	KAESER Austria, Linz	FI – CO – MM – SD
94/95	KAESER Switzerland, Zurich	FI – CO – MM – SD
95	KAESER USA, Fredericksburg	FI – CO – MM – SD

Figure 8.4 Implementation plan of the KAESER Corporation.

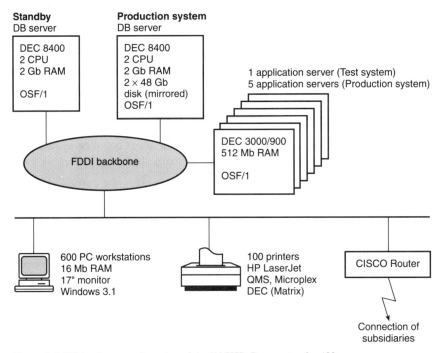

Figure 8.5 R/3 hardware configuration of the KAESER Corporation for 600 users.

The challenge for the project was to master the complete changeover with parallel reorganization of the hardware and system software, application systems, and the organization itself. Not only did a new infrastructure have to be constructed for information processing, but there was also continual adjustment of its capabilities to the increasing load imposed by additional users and new application modules. Critical situations arose during this phase due to the varying availability of the required features of the application software, database, and hardware components.

After the application software became operational at the headquarters in Coburg, the project experience could be put to direct use in the follow-on projects within the corporation. The complete conversion of operational information processing in the KAESER corporation, with implementation periods of only a few months in individual companies of the corporation and a total period of barely two years for the entire corporation, was a relatively ambitious goal. The project objectives listed in the report were, however, all accomplished.

8.5.3 KAPP Machine Tool Factory, Ltd

A family enterprise founded in 1953, KAPP is a worldwide leading manufacturer of grinding machines and grinding tools for special processing (superfine processing) of gears and profiles. As a system supplier, KAPP offers, in addition to the machine tools, a complete solution with technology consulting and service. At two locations in Coburg, Germany, and subsidiaries in the USA, Japan, and Brazil, the company employs a total of 500 employees with yearly sales of approximately 100 million DM. Purchasers of KAPP products are mainly the automobile and airline industry and general mechanical engineering.

As a technologically innovative company, KAPP implemented extensive technical data processing early on, with a large number of CAD (Computer-Aided Design) workstations, NC (Numeric Control) programming for the control of machine tools, and desktop publishing for documentation. Their related experiences in the UNIX environment were a deciding factor in the selection of UNIX-based application software in the re-orientation of business information processing.

In 1992 the KAPP company was one of the first 10 users of the R/3 System. The main reasons for implementing the latest information technology in business information processing were:

*   Support for business operations and information flow across all department boundaries

*   Integration of technical and business information processing with databases, operating systems, and hardware platforms that were as uniform as possible

*   Rescue from the maintenance-intensive custom solution by using standard applications

*   Escape from the central mainframe system.

In addition to the specialized requirements imposed by extremely customer-order-centered production, the technological requirements for the application solution were also very future-oriented. The project team worked on the order catalog in the knowledge that this was the basis of a decision that would influence the company for the next 10 to 15 years. The extensive conceptual work, which began in 1990, was the foundation for the relatively short implementation of the system (Figure 8.6), which began in mid-1992. The implementation project for the KAPP company clearly demonstrates that very short implementation periods are possible for the R/3 System if there is a complete business concept that is approved by all of the departments involved.

In addition to support for business operations, the following characteristics were part of the requirements catalog:

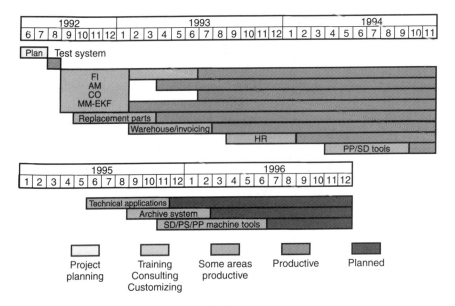

Figure 8.6 Course of the project at the KAPP Company.

- Integrated system for all business applications

- UNIX as the operating system

- Use of relational databases

- Graphical user interfaces

- System that can be adapted to the specific operations of the company

- Open interfaces

- Scalability within a client/server architecture

- Support for the latest hardware technology.

The live system, which was originally installed centrally with database and application services on a single computer, was converted to a distributed architecture
after the introduction of Sales & Distribution (SD) and Production Planning (PP),
because of the higher performance requirements (Figure 8.7), in only four hours.
This demonstrates the usefulness of a scalable application system (see Section
2.3). Complete installation of the R/3 System's business applications in the grinding
tools branch and the integration of technical applications has already led to the
attainment of the following goals:

- Quick access to current information

- Cross-departmental information flow in all core processes

- Shortening of lead times.

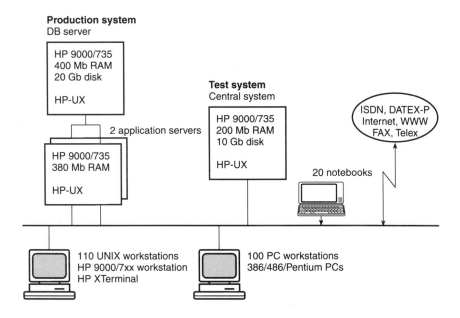

Figure 8.7 R/3 hardware configuration of the KAPP Company for 230 users.

The implementation project currently under way in the machine tool branch includes the following components:

* Linking of the technical applications with the help of the ABAP/4 Development Workbench

* Implementation of Business Workflow and an archive system

* Implementation of the Project System (PS) and Production Planning and Control (PP).

8.5.4 The Seattle Times Company

The *Seattle Times* is the largest daily newspaper of the Northwestern US state of Washington. In addition to the newspaper business, the Seattle Times Company has subsidiaries for general information services (where, for example, 500 000 inquiries per month are processed), a printing facility, and a sales and distribution service for mailed subscriptions and home delivery of newspapers. Annual sales for the enterprise currently total about 300 million US dollars.

Before the company made the decision to go with SAP's Financial Accounting, an outdated mainframe system was in use, which delivered reports only once a month, at the end of the month, in the form of lists.

Deciding factors in favor of the R/3 System were:

- Integration of the applications

- Processing of all business events online

- Immediate availability of all information, prepared, for example, as online reports, from which it is possible to navigate directly to any piece of detail information

- Graphical user interfaces with intuitive navigation between functions and data

- A fast software implementation procedure.

The introduction of the R/3 System at the *Seattle Times* was offered as a package by those supplying the technical infrastructure, the data conversion from the old system, and the implementation consulting and training. The business reference model of the R/3 System was directly converted during business process structuring. Experience from such projects has contributed to the continued development of the R/3 System's integrated implementation environment (Business Engineering Workbench, see Section 8.2).

A prerequisite for the short time (less than three months) needed to implement the Financial Accounting, Cost Accounting, and Asset Accounting components was that a team of employees from the departments should be completely available for the project. This allowed decisions to be made unusually quickly when business questions arose. Integrated in the team were consultants experienced in this implementation procedure.

Once the R/3 System became productive, the quality and effectiveness of the business processes in the financial area could be greatly improved:

- Synchronous updating of information in Financial Accounting. Immediately after the posting of a document, the affected account displays, total and balance lists, balance sheet displays, and profit/loss analyses are available to all parties, online.

- Accounting reconciliation procedures are performed much more quickly online.

- Up-to-date cost center reports are available at any time.

- Interactive analysis procedures, with direct access to all detailed information, have led to considerably better use of the data available in the SAP System. From the complete display of a cost center, it is possible to navigate directly on screen to an invoice.

- The graphical R/3 user interface, which follows the "Windows Style Guide," supported speedy training. The users can navigate intuitively in the system, without having to know transaction names. Calling up data is greatly simplified. The application systems that were replaced could deliver data on an asset only if the asset number was known. In the R/3 System, this data can be called up in various ways, for example by name, description, department, or asset number.

The following problems arose during the project:

- Specific American tax accounting requirements were not yet entirely available in Release 2.1.

- Practical implementation of the authorization concept still appeared troublesome in Release 2.1.

- Later performance requirements required a new hardware configuration.

The advantages of the R/3 System's application integration are currently useful to the *Seattle Times* only in the area of accounting. Implementation of the R/3 Purchasing functions and of R/3 Materials Management is being explored.

8.5.5 Voest Alpine

The Austrian company Voest-Alpine, Long Products Division, manufactures technically high-grade steel products like rails, seamless pipes, barbed wire, and pure steel products. With 4000 employees and approximately US$ 630 million external sales, the company is among the leaders in this branch of industry.

To emphasize their consistent customer orientation, for some of their products the company offers Just-in-Time shipments that include complete logistics all the way up to the construction site at which the products are needed. This requires high-performance information processing. High quality, currentness, and flexibility in providing information to the departments were central requirements of the project. Substitution of the central mainframe with client/server computing was accompanied by the integration of the DP team into the departments, so that the talk in the company is now of "competence and computer power on location."

Table 8.1 compares the current and target situations for the commercial EDP system at Voest-Alpine.

At the moment, the hardware and network configurations at Voest-Alpine are designed for Financial Accounting, Asset Management, Cost Accounting, and Materials Management, with 100 users altogether (Figure 8.8). Implementation of R/3 Plant Maintenance is planned. Because of the scalability of the R/3 System, the network and hardware performance can be expanded according to need, without the R/3 applications that are running being affected.

Table 8.1 Comparison of the current and target situations at Voest-Alpine.

	Until the end of 1993	Beginning in 1994
Hardware	Central mainframe	Decentralized minicomputers in a client/server configuration
Software	Custom software with high modification and maintenance costs	Standard software with function reserves, maintenance by the supplier
Operation	System knowledge in the DP department	System knowledge in all departments
	Centralized system setting and flow control	Decentralized system setting, department-oriented flow control
	Centralized control of batch processing	Background processing during online operation with decentralized request
	Centralized data entry	Decentralized data entry

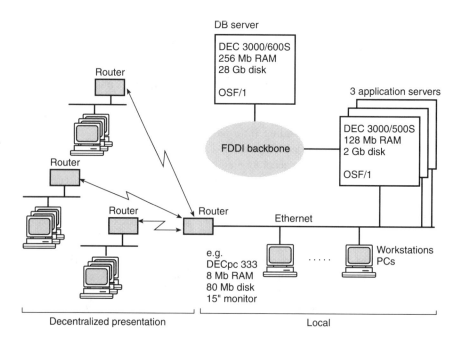

Figure 8.8 R/3 hardware configuration at Voest-Alpine for 100 users.

8.5.6 Adolf Würth & Co., Ltd KG

The Würth company is active in the area of assembly and connection technology. In the sales program, there are currently about 35 000 different items, such as screws, nuts, cable connectors, plugs, furniture fittings, and tools. With 14 300 employees, Würth targets over US$ 2 billion in sales. The company is represented in 36 countries and serves more than a million customers worldwide.

Because of its high performance requirements, the R/3 installation at Würth is an important test of productive use that provides essential knowledge for R/3 development.

The following performance figures in the daily profile were reached in 1994 with the configuration for 200 users presented in Figure 8.9 and extensive background processing with daily data upload from non-SAP systems:

- Processing of 25 000 documents per day

- 101 000 business transactions per day with a performance peak of four transactions per second

- Response time on average 0.5 seconds, 98% under one second.

The reports prepared for the Würth R/3 conference (Würth Akademie, 1994), describing practical experience with Financial Accounting and Human Resources Management, give an impression of the benefits of, but also the problems caused by, early usage of the R/3 software:

- Benefits:
    - Uniform accounting system and reporting in the entire company
    - Immediate current information in response to customer inquiries
    - No processing backlogs (formerly 3–6 weeks)
    - Monthly and annual financial statements can be produced more quickly.
    - Integration of personnel management with payroll accounting in R/3 Human Resources Management
    - The R/3 System was easily customizable in international implementation, as well.

- Problems:
    - Long background processing run times for the dunning procedure in Financial Accounting and for the payroll run in the Human Resources Management system
    - Some partially immature functions in the first releases
    - Frequent release changes.

Despite some start-up problems, the early entry into client/server computing with the R/3 System is considered to be the right choice at Würth. A quote by

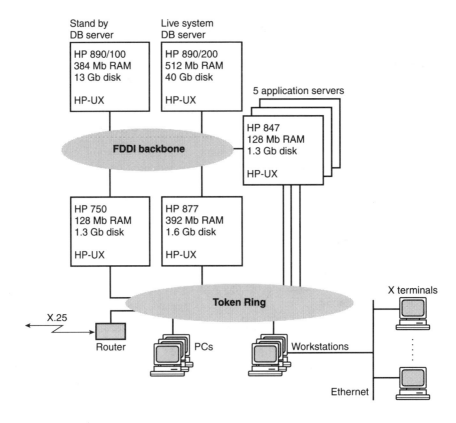

Figure 8.9 R/3 hardware configuration at the Würth Company.

Dr Harald Unkelbach, Manager for Business Integration, at the Würth R/3 conference in 1994: "Open systems based on a multilayer client/server architecture can also function in the commercial environment with large amounts of data."

8.5.7 Yamaha Motor Corporation

The Japanese Yamaha Motor Corporation, with sales of over US$ 19 billion, is one of Japan's largest enterprises. Motorcycles, outboard motors, boats, and automobiles are produced in Japan, Asia, and the USA. The company employs 8500 employees worldwide. Yamaha products are successful in the global market, but the cost situation in Japan forces the company to undertake radical organizational changes and changes in operations in order to continue to be successful in the international arena. Because of the high production costs in Japan, international division of labor and globalization of business application systems are increasingly important for Japanese companies.

In Japanese companies these days, software is still overwhelmingly developed in-house. This has resulted in extremely high costs. Further developments and adaptations to international requirements are very costly with custom software.

Because of this situation, Yamaha introduced company-wide business process re-engineering. The marked reduction of production costs was only one of the goals for which the implementation of standard software was explored. The following specifications had to be taken into consideration:

- The application software must support the Japanese language.

- Access to data and processes consistent worldwide should be possible at any time. The application software should provide current information time-wise (online) and location-wise (distributed worldwide).

- The application software should not hamper changes in the structures of the enterprise and in the operations.

- It should be possible to view and assign values to worldwide Materials Management, which includes the management of raw materials, product components, and finished goods, and Financial Accounting in an integrated manner.

The project began by unifying the different accounting systems in the corporation. As part of the project, the R/3 System was examined. In mid-1994, the decision was made to use this standard software in the area of financial accounting. The implementation project began in the fall of 1994. The R/3 System was implemented before the actual re-engineering process of the company areas involved took place. That way, the SAP System could be integrated directly into the reorganization of the business processes. Together with a very high identification of company management with the project, this method of action led to a relatively short implementation period of six months. In July 1995, Financial Accounting using the R/3 System went live. In this area alone, the system today manages a data volume of 20 gigabytes. That corresponds to approximately 4.2 million stored invoice documents.

Since going live with the R/3 System, Yamaha Motor Corporation has had the following experiences.

User-related:

- The R/3 System can be used immediately by management without intensive training.

- Profit/loss analyses, for example differentiated by product, are substantially clearer and are immediately available. The bases for making decisions are available now.

System-related:

- The implementation period for the R/3 applications was very short in comparison to the custom software used previously.

- Analyses, as well as search and display of individual invoices, proceed very quickly, even with very large data sets.

- The open architecture and high degree of portability of the R/3 System enable the use of powerful hardware and database technologies in a client/server environment. This is one of the prerequisites for "Technology Re-Engineering" (see Section 1.1) at Yamaha.

Integrated implementation of additional components of the R/3 System in the areas of Production, Sales and Distribution, and Human Resources Management is currently being explored.

Abbreviations

4GL	4th Generation Language
ABAP/4	Advanced Business Application Programming/4GL
ACID	Atomic, Consistent, Isolated, Durable
AFS	Andrew File System
ALE	Application Link Enabling
ANSI	American National Standards Institute
ASCII	American Standard Code for Information Interchange
API	Application Programming Interface
APPC	Advanced Program-to-Program Communication
APTM	Application to Transaction Manager Protocol
ARP	Address Resolution Protocol
ARPA	Advanced Research Projects Agency
ATM	Asynchronous Transfer Mode
BLOB	Binary Large Object
CAD	Computer-Aided Design
CASE	Computer-Aided Software Engineering

CATT	Computer-Aided Test Tool
CCITT	Comité Consultatif International Télégraphique et Téléphonique
CCMS	Computing Center Management System
CDDI	Copper Distributed Data Interface
CDE	Common Desktop Environment
CDIF	CASE Data Interchange Format
CD	Compact Disc
CD-ROM	Compact Disc Read-Only Memory
CI	Coded Information
CICS	Customer Information Control System (IBM)
CISC	Complex Instruction Set Computing
CMIP	Common Management Information Protocol
CMIS	Common Management Information Service
CMOS	Complementary Metal Oxide Semiconductor
COBOL	Common Business Oriented Language
COLD	Computer Output on Laser Disk
COM	Component Object Model
CORBA	Common Object Request Broker Architecture
COSE	Common Open Software Environment
CPI-C	Common Programming Interface – Communication (IBM, X/Open)
CPU	Central Processing Unit
CSMA/CD	Carrier Sense Multiple Access/Collision Detection
CUA	Common User Access
DBA	Database Administrator
DBCS	Double Byte Character Set
DBMS	Database Management System
DCE	Distributed Computing Environment
DDE	Direct Data Exchange
DIME	Distributed Integrated Media Environment

DME	Distributed Management Environment
DPAM	Demand Priority Access Method
DRAM	Dynamic Random Access Memory
DSOM	Distributed SOM
EBCDIC	Extended Binary-Coded Decimal Interchange Code
ECL	Emitter Coupled Logic
EDI	Electronic Data Interchange
EDIFACT	Electronic Data Interchange for Administration, Commerce, and Transport
EPC	Event-controlled process chains
FDDI	Fiber Distributed Data Interchange
FTAM	File Transfer, Access and Management
GUI	Graphical User Interface
HTML	Hypertext Extended Markup Language
HTTP	Hypertext Transport Protocol
ICMP	Internet Control Message Protocol
IDL	Interface Definition Language
IDOC	Intermediate Document
IEEE	Institute of Electrical and Electronics Engineers
IMAP	Internet Mail Access Protocol
IP	Internet Protocol
ISAM	Indexed Sequential Access Method
ISDN	Integrated Service Digital Network
ISO	International Standard Organization
LAN	Local Area Network
LAPI	License API
LLC	Logical Link Control
LU	Logical Unit (IBM)
LUW	Logical Unit of Work
MAC	Media Access Control
MAPI	Messaging API

MHS	Message Handling System
MIB	Management Information Base
MIME	Multi-Purpose Internet Mail Extension
MIPS	Million Instructions Per Second
MO	Magneto-Optic
MRP	Manufacturing Resource Planning
MTBF	Mean Time Between Failures
NCI	Non-Coded Information
NFS	Network File System
NMOS	N-Type Metal Oxide Semiconductor
OAG	Open Application Group
OCX	OLE Custom Control
ODBC	Open Database Connectivity
OLE	Object Linking and Embedding
OLAP	Online Analytical Processing
OLTP	Online Transaction Processing
OMA	Object Management Architecture
OMG	Object Management Group
OO	Object Orientation
OOA	OO Analysis
OOD	OO Design
ORB	Object Request Broker
OSF	Open Software Foundation
OSI	Open System Interconnect
PAI	Process After Input
PBO	Process Before Output
PC	Personal Computer
PDA	Personal Digital Assistant
POP3	Post Office Protocol, Version 3
POSIX	Portable Operating System for Computer Environments

PPP	Point-to-Point Protocol
Q-API	Queue Application Programming Interface (SAP)
RAD	Rapid Application Development
RAID	Redundant Array of Independent Disks
RDBMS	Relational Database Management System
RFC	Remote Function Call
RISC	Reduced Instruction Set Computing
RMON	Remote Monitoring
R/3	Realtime System Version 3 (SAP)
ROM	Read-Only Memory
SAA	System Application Architecture (IBM)
SAP	Systeme, Anwendungen und Programme in der Datenverarbeitung (Systems, Products, and Programs in Data Processing)
SDK	Software Development Kit
SLIP	Serial Line IP Protocol
SMP	Symmetric Multiprocessor
SMTP	Simple Mail Transfer Protocol
SNA	System Network Architecture (IBM)
SNMP	Simple Network Management Protocol
SOM	System Object Model
SQL	Structured Query Language
SRAM	Static Random Access Memory
TAPI	Telephony API
TCP/IP	Transmission Control Protocol/Internet Protocol
TLI	Transport Layer Interface
TP	Transaction Processing
TPC	Transaction Processing Council
UDP	User Datagram Protocol
URL	Uniform Resource Locator
WABI	Windows Applications Binary Interface

WAN	Wide Area Network
WORM	Write Once Read Multiple
WOSA	Windows Open Services Architecture
WWW	World Wide Web
XTI	Extended Transport Interface

Bibliography

Advanced Manufacturing Research, eds (1995). SAP builds a $5 billion empire:
    Who'll stop the reign? In *AMR Report*, August/September, Boston

Angell D. and Heslop B. (1995). *The Internet Business Companion*. Reading,
    MA: Addison-Wesley

Bluestein W. M. and Hill N. (1993). Defining Social Computing. Forrester
    Research, *Computing Strategy Report*, Vol. 10, No. 9, July 1

Brenner, W. and Keller G., eds (1995). *Business Reengineering mit Standard-
Software*. Frankfurt/Main: Campus Verlag

Brown D., Magrassi P., Rin A., Sinur J., West M. and Zbikowski E. (1994).
    Symposium '93 and ADM6: Highlights, Questions and Answers. *Gartner
    Group ADM Strategic Analysis Report R-200-121*, January 28

Brown D. and Rin A. (1994). The Degree of 4GL's Productivity Advantages over
    3GLs. *Gartner Group ADM Research Note SPA-500-1006*, April 25

Buck-Emden R. (1991). Unix-Systeme bilden künftig den Kern der DV-
    Vernetzung. *Computerwoche*, Nr. 25, Juni

Buck-Emden R. (1993a). Chancen für kommerzielle Lösungen in neuer Qualität.
    Computerwoche, Nr. 43, Oktober

Buck-Emden R. (1993b). Grundlagen für den Entwurf innovativer betrieb-
    swirtschaftlicher Anwendungs- und Informationssysteme. In *Client/Server
    Architektur* (W.-R. Hansen, ed.). Bonn: Addison-Wesley

Buck-Emden R. (1993c). Client/Server-Systeme: Schlüsseltechnologie für die
    betriebliche Datenverarbeitung der 90er Jahre. In *VDI-Forschungsbericht
    "Gestaltung verteilter Informationssysteme,"* Reihe 10, Nr. 251. VDI-Verlag

Buck-Emden R. (1993d). Client/server-computing. *UnixOpen*, No. 12, December

Buck-Emden R., Kagermann H. and Zencke P. (1993). Koexistenz von R/2 und R/3 – zwei leistungsstarke Standard-Anwendungssysteme im Verbund. *SAPinfo*, Nr. 38, März

Buck-Emden R. (1994). Integrierte Standard-Anwendungssoftware für DV-Lösungen nach dem Client/Server-Prinzip. *MM Maschinen Markt*, Nr. 9, Februar

Buck-Emden R. and Curran T. (1994). Entwicklung betriebswirtschaftlicher Client/Server-Anwendungen. *OUTPUT Sonderausgabe "Das System SAP R/3"*, Juli

Buck-Emden, R. and Galimow J. (1994). Grundlagen der R/3 Software-Architektur. *OUTPUT Sonderausgabe "Das System SAP R/3"*, Juli

Buck-Emden R (1995a). System R/3: Die führende Standard-Software für betriebswirtschaftliche Client/Server-Anwendungen. *unix/mail*, 13. Jahrgang, Heft 1

Buck-Emden R. (1995b). Tools für das Highend – Qualifikation für das Werkzeug. *Business Computing*, Heft 9, September

Burger J. (1995). *Multimedia for Decision Makers*. Reading, MA: Addison-Wesley

Butler Group, eds (1995). Technology Audit – ABAP/4 Development Workbench. In Butler Group Development Tool Series. Butler Group, Hull, England

Carr J. (1992). An array of protection for server data. *Data Communications*, May

Caspary R. (1994). SAPDBA: Werkzeuge zur Administration produktiver R/3 Systeme auf Oracle. In *Proc. 7. DOAG-Konferenz*, Fellbach, November

Codd E.F. (1970). A relational model of data for large shared data bases. *Communications of the ACM*, No. 13

Comport J. and Zbikowski E. (1994). Replacing Financial and Human Resource Applications. *Gartner Group SMS Research Note M-868-1448*, April 11

Conway B. (1994). Are AD Management Technologies Converging? *Gartner Group ADM Research Note T-420-977*, January 13

Davidow W. and Malone M. (1992). *The Virtual Corporation*. New York: HarperCollins

Davis J. R. (1995). Object-Relational Database Managers. In Patricia Seybold Group's *Distributed Computing Monitor*, Vol. 10, No. 2, February

Deitel H. M. (1990). *Operating Systems*. Reading, MA: Addison-Wesley

Donovan J. J. (1993). *Business Re-Engineering with Technology*. Cambridge: Cambridge Technology Group

Digital Equipment Corporation, eds (1991). *Digital's RISC Architecture Technical Handbook.*

Eberleh E. (1994). Industrielle Gestaltungsrichtlinien für graphische Benutzeroberflächen. In *Einführung in die Software-Ergonomie* (E. Eberleh, H. Oberquelle and R. Oppermann, eds), 2. Auflage. Berlin: Walter de Gruyter

Effelsberg W. and Fleischmann A. (1986). Das ISO-Referenzmodell für offene Systeme und seine sieben Schichten. *Informatik-Spektrum*, Band 9, Heft 5, Oktober

Färber G. (1991). 20 Jahre Mikroprozessoren. *Online*, Nr. 7, Juli

Flynn S. (1993). 1993/1994 Information Technology Budgets and Practices Survey. *Gartner Group Strategic Analysis Report R-962-121-1*, November 29

Fritz, F. J. and Lau H. (1994). Workflow requirements for enterprise applications. In *Digest of Papers of the Spring COMPCON'94*, IEEE Computer Society, San Francisco, March

Galimow J. (1992). Bürokommunikation und betriebswirtschaftliche Anwendungen – zwei Welten? In *VDI Bericht 991 "Bürokommunikation für Ingenieure"*. Düsseldorf:VDI-Verlag

Gimarc C. E. and Milutinovic V. M. (1987). A survey of RISC processors and computers of the mid-1980s. *IEEE Computer*, September

Groff J. R. and Weinberg P. N. (1994). *LAN TIMES Guide to SQL.* Berkeley: Osborne McGraw-Hill

Hammer M. and Champy J. (1993). *Reengineering the Corporation.* New York: HarperCollins

Hansen W.-R., ed. (1993). *Client-Server-Architektur.* Bonn: Addison-Wesley

Härder T. and Reuter A. (1983). Concepts for implementing a centralized database management system. In *Proc. International Computing Symposium 1983 on Application Systems Development*, Teubner, Stuttgart

Harding E. U. (1994). Middleware emerges as next battlefield. *Software Magazine*, April

Hart J. M. and Rosenberg B. (1995). *Client/Server Computing for Professionals.* Reading, MA: Addison-Wesley

Heinrich W., ed. (1993). *Client-Server-Strategien.* Bergheim: DATACOM-Verlag

Hennessy J. L. and Jouppi N. P. (1991), Computer technology and architecture: An evolving interaction. *IEEE Computer*, September

Hofmann M. and Simon L. (1995). *Problemlösung Hypertext.* München: Carl Hanser Verlag

Hurwitz Consulting Group, eds (1995). SAP's ABAP/4 Development Workbench. Hurwitz Consulting Group White Paper, Newton, Massachusetts, May

International Data Corporation, *Worldwide Client/Server Accounting and HR Software Markets and Trends*, May 1994

International Data Corporation, *Client/Server Applications: Forecast and Leading Vendors Final Estimate for 1994*, IDC, Framingham, Masachussets, June 1995

Janssen R. and Schott W. (1993). *SNMP: Konzepte, Verfahren, Plattformen.* Bergheim: DATACOM-Verlag

Johnson J., Roberts T. L., Verplank W., Smith D. C., Irby C., Beard M. and Mackey K. (1989). The Xerox Star: A retrospective. *IEEE Computer*, **22**(9), September

Jones O. (1991). *Introduction to the X Window System*. Englewood Cliffs, NJ: Prentice-Hall

Kagermann H. (1993). Verteilung integrierter Anwendungen. *Wirtschaftsinformatik*, Band 35, Heft 5

Kahlbrandt B. (1992). Evolution der Datenbank-Technologien. *Computer Zeitung*, Nr. 11, Mai

Keller G., Nüttgens M. and Scheer A.-W. (1992). Semantische Prozeßmodellierung auf der Grundlage "Ereignisgesteuerter Prozeßketten (EPK)". In *Veröffentlichungen des Instituts für Wirtschaftsinformatik* (A.-W. Scheer, ed.), Heft 89, Saarbrücken

Keller G. and Meinhardt S. (1994). DV-gestützte Beratung bei der SAP-Softwareeinführung. *Handbuch der modernen Datenverarbeitung – Theorie und Praxis in der Wirtschaftsinformatik*, Band 31, Heft 175

Keller G., Meinhardt S. and Zencke P. (1994). Business Process Reengineering im SAP-Umfeld. *Management und Computer*, Band 2, Heft 4

Kersten H., ed. (1993). *Sicherheit in der Informationstechnik: Internationale Sicherheitskriterien*. München: Oldenbourg-Verlag

Kyas O. (1993). *ATM-Netzwerke*. Bergheim: DATACOM-Verlag

Leger L. (1994). Multimedia. *Diebold Management Report*, Nr. 1

Lippert M. (1992). Sechs Befehle pro Taktzyklus. *Computer Zeitung*, Nr. 20, Oktober

Meyer H.-M. (1993). Softwarearchitekturen für verteilte Verarbeitung. In *Client-Server-Architektur* (W.-R. Hansen, ed.). Bonn: Addison-Wesley

Meyer H.-M. and Obermayr K. (1994). *Objekte integieren mit OLE2*. Berlin: Springer-Verlag

Meyer-Wegener K. (1988). *Transaktionssysteme*. Stuttgart: Teubner-Verlag

Orfali R., Harkey D. and Edwards J. (1996). *The Essential Distributed Objects Survival Guide*. New York: Wiley

Ovum Ltd, eds (1995). ABAP/4 Evaluation. In *Ovum Evaluates: 4GLs and Client/Server Tools*, Issue 5, May

Plattner H. (1991). Der Einfluß der Client/Server-Architektur auf kaufmännische Anwendungssysteme. In *Schriften zur Unternehmensführung*, Band 44. Gabler Verlag

Plattner B., Lamz G., Lubich L., Müller M. and Walter T. (1993). *X.400, elektronische Post und Datenkommunikation*. 3 Auflage. Bonn: Addison-Wesley

Plattner H. (1993). Client/Server-Architekturen. In *Handbuch Informationsmanagement* (A.-W. Scheer, ed.). Wiesbaden: Gabler-Verlag

PRISMSolutions, Inc., eds (1993). *What is a Data Warehouse?* Sunnyvale, California

Rymer J. R. (1994). Middleware road map. *Distributed Computing Monitor*, **9**(5), May

Schäfer S. (1994). *Objektorientierte Entwurfsmethoden*. Bonn: Addison-Wesley

Scheer A.-W. (1993). ARIS-Architektur integrierter Informationssysteme. In *Handbuch Informationsmanagement* (A.-W. Scheer, ed.). Wiesbaden: Gabler-Verlag

Schill A. (1993). *DCE: Das OSF Distributed Computing Environment*. Berlin: Springer-Verlag

Schulte R. (1994). Middleware: Panacea or Boondoggle? *Gartner Group SMS Strategic Analysis Report R-401-130*, July 5

Seubert M., Schäfer T., Schorr M. and Wagner J. (1994). Praxisorientierte Datenmodellierung mit der SAP-SERM-Methode. *EMISA-Forum, Gesellschaft für Informatik*, Heft 2

Sheldon T. (1994). *LAN TIMES Encyclopedia of Networking*. Berkeley, CA: Osborne McGraw-Hill

Stevens W. R. (1990). *UNIX Network Programming*. Englewood Cliffs, NJ: Prentice-Hall

Strange K. (1995). OLAP Council: Criticizing Relational DBMS Products. *Gartner Group SDM Research Note E-350-023*, February 15

Sun Microsystems Computer Corporation, eds (1992). *Multiprocessing Technology: A Primer*.

Sundt G. (1992). Starting the ATM Dialog. *Gartner Group, ETS Research Note T-123-297*, August 17

Tanenbaum A. (1989). *Computer Networks*. Englewood Cliffs, NJ: Prentice Hall

Tschira K. E. (1994). Konzepte der Personalwirtschaft: Vom Kostenfaktor zum kritischen Erfolgsfaktor. In *Computergestützte Personalarbeit – Extra*. DATAKONTEXT-Verlag, 2. Jahrgang

Vaskevitch D. (1994). Microsoft's vision for the transaction environment. *OTM SPECTRUM*, **8**(1), February

Wahl P. (1995). Verteilte Datenbanken in der Warteschleife. *Online*, Heft 1

Widerhold G. (1983). *Database Design*. McGraw-Hill

Will L., Hienger C., Straßenburg F. and Himmer R. (1995). *R/3-Administration*. Bonn: Addison-Wesley

Winkler S. (1994). SP2: Massive Parallel Unix From IBM. *Gartner Group SMS Research Note P-IBM-1456*, April 25

Workflow Management Coalition, eds (1995). The Workflow Reference Model. *Document Number TC00-1003*, Draft 1.1, Brussels

Würth Akademie, eds (1994). Tagungsunterlagen zum Würth R/3 Kongreß. Künzelsau-Gaisbach, 28. April

Zencke P. (1004). Softwareunterstützung im Business Process Reengineering. In *Schriften zur Unternehmensführung*, Nr. 53. Gabler-Verlag

Index